Heidinger/Hubalek/Pramberger

INTRODUCTION TO THE LAW AND LANGUAGE OF THE EUROPEAN UNION

INTRODUCTION TO THE LAW AND LANGUAGE OF THE EUROPEAN UNION

Einführung in das Recht und die englische Rechtssprache der Europäischen Union

für

Rechtsanwälte, Wirtschaftsjuristen, Wirtschaftstreuhänder und EU-Interessierte

von

MMag. Franz J. Heidinger

Andrea Hubalek

Michael Pramberger

Wien 1994

Verlag Orac

Die Deutsche Bibliothek — CIP-Einheitsaufnahme

Heidinger, Franz J.:
Introduction to the law and language of the European Union = Einführung in das Recht und die englische Rechtssprache der Europäischen Union für Rechtsanwälte, Wirtschaftsjuristen, Wirtschaftstreuhänder und EU-Interessierte / von Franz J. Heidinger ; Andrea Hubalek ; Michael Pramberger. – Wien : Orac, 1994
ISBN 3-7007-0584-0
NE: Hubalek, Andrea:; Pramberger, Michael:

Information an unsere Leser

Das vorliegende Buch wurde auf chlorfrei gebleichtem Umweltschutzpapier Bio Top 3 gedruckt.
Auch die Plastikfolie, in die unsere Bücher eingeschweißt sind, ist ein umweltfreundliches Produkt. Sie ist aus Polyäthylen chlor- und schwefelfrei hergestellt und verbrennt in Müllverbrennungsanlagen völlig ungiftig; sie zerfällt unter Lichteinfluß langsam, verhält sich auf Mülldeponien grundwasserneutral und ist voll recyclingfähig.

ISBN 3-7007-0584-0

Verlag Orac, Wien

Hersteller: Druckerei Robitschek & Co. Ges.m.b.H., Wien

PREFACE

This book is the first of its kind in introducing the non-native English speakers to European Community law using English. With this method, the reader actively learns what the European Union is all about, while expanding his/her use of the English language.

With Austria's accession to the European Union, the importance of understanding the laws and the legal framework constituting the European Union is taken to an even greater height. This book provides an overview of the European Community's regulatory framework and is an excellent source of information on the progressive build-up of a "legal area", which is truly unique, many aspects of which are relevant to international co-operation and regional integration.

In addition to understanding EC laws and the regulatory framework, it is essential to become familiar with the terminology associated therewith. This book provides the reader with the opportunity to learn those terms and also practising their use in the corresponding workbook.

The information provided in this book is easily understood, yet detailed enough to provide the reader with a good basis to understanding the laws and terminology of the European Union. I commend the authors on their fine work and hope the reader will enjoy as much as I did this venture in English into the law of the European Community.

Dr. Corrado Pirzio-Biroli
Head of Delegation of the European Union
Commission of the European Community in Austria

EINLEITUNG

Mit diesem Kurzlehrbuch haben wir den Versuch unternommen, eine Überblicksdarstellung des Rechts der Europäischen Union zu geben. Dabei wurde besonderes Schwergewicht auf die Einführung in die Geschichte der Europäischen Gemeinschaften bis herauf zur Europäischen Union, die Organisation und die Institutionen der Europäischen Union, die Rechtsquellen des EU-Rechts und die wichtigsten materiellen Rechtsgebiete gelegt, um den Lesern/-innen, Studenten/-innen und Rechtsanwendern/-innen die Möglichkeit zu geben, einen ersten informativen Einblick in die wichtigsten Grundlagen des Rechts der Europäischen Union und der damit in Zusammenhang stehenden spezifischen englischen Rechtssprache zu geben.

Dieses Buch verfolgt drei wesentliche Ziele: Einerseits soll der Leser/ die Leserin beim Studium eine grundlegende und zeitgemäße Einführung in die genannten Rechtsgebiete erhalten, andererseits lernt er/sie die englische Rechtssprache der Europäischen Union kennen. In einem eigenen Arbeitsteil werden die jeweiligen Kapitel sowohl inhaltlich wie auch sprachlich aufgearbeitet, um den Lesern/-innen, Studenten/-innen oder Rechtsanwendern/-innen auch die Möglichkeit zu geben, ihr Verständnis des Textes, ihre erworbene Fach- wie auch Sprachkenntnis zu vertiefen und zu überprüfen. Weiters wurde ein umfassendes Glossar angefertigt, welches die wichtigsten Fachausdrücke der deutschen und der englischen EU-Rechtssprache enthält und ein wertvolles Instrumentarium für die EU-Rechtsanwender/-innen darstellt. Schließlich ergänzt auch eine Zusammenstellung wichtiger Entscheidungen (Case summaries) das Lehrbuch in sinnvoller Weise, da der/die Leser/-in nicht nur mit einigen der wichtigsten Fälle, sondern auch mit dem Instrument der Fallstudien vertraut gemacht wird.

Aus unserer Erfahrung ist gerade für Juristen/-innen oder angehende Juristen/-innen die Auseinandersetzung mit der wohl wichtigsten Sprache der EU, nämlich der englischen Fachsprache, von großer Bedeutung, da die diesbezügliche Ausbildung nach wie vor überwiegend auf Deutsch geschieht und die Kommunikation mit nicht-deutschsprachigen Kollegen/-innen über EU-Rechtsangelegenheiten, aber auch das Rechtsquellenstudium neben dem Französischen insbesondere auch profunde Kenntnisse der englischen EU-Rechtssprache verlangt.

Wir sind uns bewußt, daß aufgrund des Umfanges des Buches die rechtliche Darstellung nur einen einführenden Überblick geben kann. Wir erheben daher weder Anspruch auf Vollständigkeit, noch darauf, daß die vorgeschlagenen Texte abschließend sind. Sie sollen vielmehr Anregung zur Auseinandersetzung sein.

Wir wünschen den Benützern dieses Buches viel Freude an der Arbeit mit dem Recht und der englischen Rechtssprache der Europäischen Union. Da dieses Buch in seiner Art ein erstmaliger Versuch ist, die englische Rechtssprache der Europäischen Union darzustellen und für die Leser/-innen, deren Muttersprache nicht Englisch ist, zugänglich zu machen, ist sowohl die inhaltliche wie auch die methodologische Annäherung neu und offen für Veränderungen. Wir sind daher für Hinweise und Verbesserungsvorschläge dankbar und würden uns freuen, von Ihnen diesbezüglich zu hören.

Die Verfassung dieses Buches wäre ohne die tatkräftige Unterstützung von Frau *Mag. Martina Leitner*, welche insbesondere in der Erstellung des Glossars intensiv tätig war, von Herrn *Dr. Peter Hubalek*, dessen Ausdauer uns über so manche Durststrecke half, sowie ohne Mithilfe von Frau *Cindy Lea Willheim*, welche die Korrekturen gelesen hat, nicht möglich gewesen. Ihnen gebührt der Dank für die Mithilfe an diesem Projekt. Für die Erstellung der Case Summaries danken wir Mr. *Tim Smith*, London und für die Gestaltung der Graphiken Herrn *Mag. Klaus Fister*, Wien. Gleichfalls Dank gebührt Frau *Marie-Christine Stepski* und insbesondere der Rechtsanwaltskanzlei *Dr. Alix Frank* für die tatkräftige Unterstützung unseres Projektes.

Wien, im September 1994 Die Autoren

TABLE OF CONTENTS

PART FOUR - SECONDARY SOURCES OF EC LAW

PART FIVE - SUBSTANTIVE LAW

SECTION A

TEXTBOOK

PART ONE - INTRODUCTION

CHAPTER 1: EARLY HISTORY

The desire to unite Europe reaches as far back as the *Roman Empire*. The first work of significant importance was written by *Pierre Dubois,* "De recuperatione terrae sanctae" (1306), in which he proposed to establish a confederation of European states. Its main purpose was to free the Holy Land from the Arabs (the fall of Akko 1291).

Other plans were mooted to set up a European federation in protection against the Turks.

On an institutional basis, *European conferences* were held through several centuries, at which European matters were discussed. The first big conferences were the Congress of Münster and the Congress of Osnabrück, peace conferences ending the Thirty Years War (1648). These two and other conferences created a European peace order which remained in effect until the French Revolution. This system of congresses determined all important European affairs, however, the ponderous proceedings were a big disadvantage.

Abbé de Saint-Pierre wanted to create a European Confederation, which he suggested at the Congress of Utrecht (1713), in order to ensure permanent peace. Treaties alone would not be sufficient, he thought. This confederation should also serve economic purposes like the abolition of trade obstacles and the standardization of measurement and weight units.

After Napoleon had been defeated at Waterloo in 1815, the *Holy Alliance* was created in order to protect Russia, Austria and Prussia and maintain peace.

Specific plans for a European integration were developed after World War I. Coudenhove-Kalergi's essay *"Paneuropa"*, in which he suggested to create the "United States of Europe" by taking the United States of America as a model, was of some significance. Some Paneuropean conferences were held in order to disseminate this idea. Following this concept, Aristide Briand, who was Foreign Minister of France at that time, and his German colleague, Gustav Stresemann, spoke up for a United Europe. But the growing powers of Mussolini in Italy and Hitler in Germany as well as the world economic crisis stopped this plan from becoming reality.

The *Hanseatic League*, in which brave businessmen joined forces to secure commercial routes, was of significance, too.

After World War II the idea of a united Europe intensified. Sir Winston Churchill was the first to express the idea of a united Europe by calling upon reconciliation between France and Germany in his speech in Zurich in 1946. One year later, on 14 March 1947, Belgium, Luxembourg and the Netherlands signed a treaty setting up the *"Benelux Economic Union"*. This was the first economic supranational organization in Western Europe. It became clear that plans for European integration would only extend to Western Europe, because the eastern part was controlled by the Soviet Union at that time. The destroyed continent was in bitter need of financial support, which was offered by the US through the Marshall Plan. This plan demanded an international organization to distribute and use the funds in an effective way: the Organization for European Economic Cooperation (OEEC) was established in Paris in 1948. This European Recovery Programme (ERP) was directed to the Eastern European countries, too, but they refused to accept, fearing exposure to American economic domination. [Having fulfilled its post-war purposes the OEEC changed into the Organization for Economic Cooperation and Development (OECD) in 1961. It proved to be an essential contribution towards the recovery of the European national economies.

The foundation stone of a European Community was laid by Robert Schuman, the French foreign minister, and Jean Monnet, a French businessman. "Europe cannot be built by mere cooperation", Schuman once said and together with Monnet developed a plan in 1950. This plan proposed the fusion of the coal and steel industries, especially those of France and Germany but also of other European countries. His basic idea was that by joining the French and German heavy industry, a further war between these two countries would become impossible. In 1951 their plan became reality and the Treaty of Paris was signed on 18 April by Belgium, the Federal Republic of Germany, France, Italy, Luxembourg and the Netherlands. The European Coal and Steel Community (ECSC) was created and came into force on 23 July 1952.

The objectives of this international organization were very broad: protection of peace, European integration and a common market for coal and steel. New institutions were established: the *Council* as the highest authority of the ECSC, the *High Authority* (now: the Commission) as executive body with an *Advisory Committee* at its side, the *European Parliament* and the Court of Justice. These institutions were independent of the six Member States and had the power to supervise the development of the coal and steel industries of the Member States. As a result, the legislative and administrative powers in this field were transferred to the institutions, and the first step towards integration was thus taken.

There were two different schools of thought as to what would be the best way to achieve a European community: the first preferred the federalist approach, wanting to set up a federal state, the United States of Europe, in one go; the other preferred the functional approach. Thereafter unification would be achieved as sector after sector became integrated, the so-called "sectoral integration". Progressive sectoral integration would gradually but inevitably lead to a federal state.

As regards the functional approach, the foreign ministers of the ECSC countries decided to take further steps towards economic integration at the Conference of Messina in June 1955. Under the chairmanship of the Belgian foreign minister, Paul Henri Spaak, an intergovernmental expert committee prepared two extensive treaties. They were signed on 25 March 1957 in Rome by the six Member States and created the European Economic Community (EEC) and the European Atomic Energy Community (Euratom). The two treaties came into effect on 1 January 1958. The ECSC and these two new international organizations were known as the European Communities.

The term "European Community" was often used. Legally this was not correct, but in 1977 the European Parliament decided to use the term "European Community" as a collective name. Now "Europe speaks with one voice".

Euratom was a result of different developments. First of all, it soon became clear that Europe might be exposed to an energy crisis (i.e. during the Suez conflict in 1956/57 crude oil could not be transported through the Suez Canal). Secondly, nuclear energy was considered the energy resource of the future. In consideration of these facts, the Euratom Treaty speaks of a peaceful use of nuclear energy and of nuclear energy as an essential source for development and stimulation of the economy.

The treaty contains a similar structure of bodies as the ECSC treaty European Parliament, Council, Commission and the Court of Justice. The Commission and the Council are supported by an Economic and Social Committee and several other subcommittees with advisory function. An agency under the supervision of the Commission was set up, which not only had a subscription right to all produced raw material in the Member States but also the exclusive right to conclude contracts with non-Community countries concerning these materials.

On 1 December 1975 Euratom entered into a treaty with the International Atomic Energy Agency (IAEA), in which Euratom took over IAEA's responsibility for its regional area.

The EEC is the most important of the three communities and its scope of activities is wider than that of the other two.

The task of the Community is "establishing a common market and progressively approximating the economic policies of the Member States to promote throughout the Community a harmonious development of economic activities, a continuous and balanced expansion, an increase in stability, an accelerated raising of the standard of living and closer relations between the states belonging to it" (Article 2 EEC Treaty).

Article 3 EEC Treaty lists the activities and objectives of the Community, such as the elimination of customs duties and quantitative restrictions on the import and export of goods, the establishment of a common customs tariff and of a common commercial policy towards third countries, the abolition of obstacles to freedom of movement for persons, services and capital, common policy in the sphere of agriculture and transport, the institution of a system ensuring that competition within the common market is not distorted and approximation of the laws of the Member States to the extent required for the proper functioning of the common market. Defence, diplomacy, education and culture were withheld from the Community, however, only to a certain extent because even these aspects of state sovereignty were sometimes subject to Community competence.

The EEC also comprises the four institutions: the European Parliament, the Council, the Commission and the Court of Justice. The Council and the Commission are assisted by an Economic and Social Committee (Article 4 EEC Treaty).

Although the three Communities remained separate, the idea of merging the institutions for the purpose of rationalizing their administration came up: the treaty dated 25 March 1957 for a joint European Parliament, a joint Court of Justice and a joint Economic and Social Committee; as well as the treaty dated 8 April 1965, which came into effect in 1967, regarding the fusion of the three Councils into one single Council and of the three Commissions into one single Commission.

It must be emphasized that these two merger treaties produced a fusion of the institutions but not a fusion of the three Communities. They remained separate.

Article 7 EEC Treaty sought to progressively establish the common market within a transitional period of twelve years divided into three stages of four years each. The following paragraphs determine an exact set of actions for each stage. All objectives were achieved; the internal customs duties and quotas were even abolished 18 months ahead of schedule.

Concerning defence issues the West Union was set up in March 1948 by Great Britain, France and the Benelux countries (Treaty of Brussels). The West Union developed into the Western European Union (WEU) by Germany's and Italy's joining in 1954. Its purpose was to protect Europe against the Soviet Union.

Truman's containment policy also showed great interest in protecting the free European countries against communism. On 4 April 1949, the North Atlantic Treaty Organization (NATO) was founded in Washington, D.C. There were also plans to set up a unified European Army within a European Defence Community (1952). A treaty was even signed but it was never ratified due to the fading French support and the growing importance of economic relations.

With the establishment of a common external duty towards third countries many of the other OEEC countries felt discriminated. On the initiative of the United Kingdom the European Free Trade Association (EFTA) was founded on 20 November 1959. The members were Austria, Denmark, Norway,

Portugal, Sweden, Switzerland and the United Kingdom. In 1970, Ireland joined the EFTA and in 1971 Finland signed an association treaty. The OEEC had divided itself into two rivalling economic communities. This conflict was only solved in 1972, when the United Kingdom, Ireland and Denmark joined the European Community (see Chapter 18: 'The European Economic Area).

The division of Europe after World War II into a Western and an Eastern part also reflected a different economic development. At the beginning of the Eastern European integration a number of bilateral and multilateral treaties were signed; it was only thereafter that the Socialist Commonwealth of Nations was set up, which is better known as the Council for Mutual Economic Assistance (COMECON), namely in 1949. The COMECON was a reaction to the successful realization of the Marshall Plan in Western Europe, the creation of the OEEC and of pursuing the wish to establish the Soviet planned economy in the Eastern and South-eastern European countries. These two big economic blocks faced each other until the late 1980s when most of the European COMECON countries started opening their economies towards Western Europe. Today the COMECON is of no importance although it has not yet been dissolved.

CHAPTER 2: EXPANSION, SINGLE MARKET AND SINGLE ACT

After the difficult times during the war the global economic situation slowly improved. The Community entered the prosperous times of the 1960s, which were characterized by low unemployment and substantial economic growth. Naturally trade between the six Member States increased, and many of them even preferred trading with each other than with their former partners. Within the Community the competitiveness improved and wealth increased. The common market was developing well and sometimes the partners were even able to achieve their treaty timetables much before the agreed deadlines.

The Community Members were enjoying their success while neighbouring countries were watching and envying the prosperity. Especially the United Kingdom showed division in its interest in joining the Community. On the one hand the UK was a leading member of the Commonwealth and thus had difficulties in committing itself to the Community. On the other hand it was still trying to cling to its position as one of the world's superpowers although its strong position had already started to diminish during World War II. At the beginning, the UK chose to remain outside of the Community and instead established the European Free Trade Association (EFTA) in 1960. The EFTA could not meet the economic expectations of the United Kingdom, which was by far its economically strongest member. In the early 1960s, the Conservative Party decided to take up negotiations to enter the Community. This was not an easy task. The first set of negotiations, conducted by a Labour Government, failed due to a French veto forced by General de Gaulle in 1963 and a second time in 1967. Later on, under the Conservative Government of Edward Heath a membership treaty was signed between the Community and the United Kingdom. Since 1973 the UK is a member of the European Community. In the same year Denmark and the Republic of Ireland joined the Community, making it consist of nine members. The three new Member States were granted a transitional period in which they had to align their economies to the requirements of the Community. This transitional period contained, for instance, the progressive reduction and elimination of tariff barriers and quota systems. In 1977, after the transitional periods had expired, the UK, Denmark and the Republic of Ireland were accepted as full members.

Norway also applied for membership but had to withdraw its application because of the negative outcome of a referendum on joining. The second enlargement took place in the 1980s when the Community was increased from nine to twelve Member States. This was a southward expansion with Greece joining in 1981 and Spain and Portugal entering the Community in 1986.

With the collapse of the Berlin Wall, followed by the unification of the German Democratic Republic and the Federal Republic of Germany, the Community grew in a spectacular way (1990).

According to all three Community Treaties, every European state can apply for membership to all three Communities. Accession to the EC is not unrestricted. Only European countries can file an application, which makes the organization a regional one. Secondly, the applying countries have no right to admission but are dependent on the political will of the members. Thus becoming a member is actually not a process of accession but one of admission.

Article 237 EEC used to state the accession proceedings of a state to the Community. At Maastricht, Article 237 EEC was repealed and replaced by Article 0 of the Treaty on European Union. However, the contents of both Articles are identical:

> Any European State may apply to become a Member of the Community (Union). It shall address its application to the Council, which shall act unanimously after consulting the Commission and after receiving the assent of the European Parliament, which shall act by an absolute majority of its component members.
>
> The conditions of admission and the adjustments to the Treaties on which the Community (Union) is founded which admission entails shall be the subject of an agreement between the Member States and the applicant state. This agreement shall be submitted for ratification by all the contracting states in accordance with their respective constitutional requirements.

In the European Parliament, the application will be considered by the appropriate committee. This committee may propose to the Parliament that the application may be discussed before negotiations with the applicant state start. By a simple majority, the Parliament can decide to request the attendance and participation of the Commission and the Council in the discussion. Once the negotiations are completed, the Parliamentary Committee will report to the Parliament, where a further debate and a vote on assent to the application will be held.

In principle, the Member States are free to determine the conditions under which the applicant may join the Community, but in practice, the principle of the "aquis communautaire" is followed. Accordingly, the acceding state must accept the Community in that way as it presents itself at the time of accession. This means not only taking over primary and secondary legislation but also the interpretations of the Community law by the Court of Justice.

The Community treaties do not mention any possibilities of withdrawing from the Community. Therefore a withdrawal can only result according to the reasons of international law, e.g. if one of the Community Members cannot fulfil the objectives anymore, if the membership of a country cannot reasonably be expected due to changed circumstances, or when one or more Members severely violate the Community law with regard to another Member.

Economic integration was developing at high pace. On the other hand, important political and diplomatic structures were developing rather slowly. For a long time the member countries of the Community had been consulting each other on a very informal basis to coordinate their foreign policy positions. This intergovernmental foreign policy forum was the so-called European Political Cooperation (EPC). The Single European Act gave it a more formal status.

Due to the two oil crises of 1973 and 1979 and a world-wide monetary instability the need for economic convergence and monetary union became apparent. In March 1979 the European Monetary System (EMS) was established with the purpose of closer cooperation in monetary policy. The Exchange Rate Mechanism (ERM) and a European Currency Unit (ECU) were created. The launch of the EMS helped to stabilize exchange rates and encourage Member States to pursue strict economic policies (see Chapters 28 and 29).

These enlargements of the Community made it necessary to develop structural programmes which would reduce the economic disparities between the twelve members. Additionally, with the world recession and internal wrangling on the Community's finances the pace of integration had slowed down by the early 1980s. Trying to overcome this period of "Europessimism", Commission President Jacques Delors presented the White Paper in 1985. The White Paper was a plan on how to complete the internal market by the end of 1992. It described a strategy to remove the existing trade barriers which stood in the way of putting the single market into reality. The trade barriers were of physical, technical and fiscal nature. Although customs duties and quotas had been removed earlier, these other barriers kept the national markets of the Member States protected. Physical barriers such as passport controls and checks at the Community's internal frontiers were real obstacles. Today systematic checks are only carried out at the Community's external borders. Technical barriers were, for example, differences in standards for electrical appliances and fittings or different national requirements for automobile type approvals. Restrictions on the supply of services across EC borders were also to be lifted. Now companies can bid for government contracts in another EC country without being discriminated against, as long as they are based in a Member State. Fiscal barriers such as the national systems on perceiving and collecting indirect taxes were to be restructured. This has shown to be very difficult. For instance, a harmonized VAT system was not agreed on in time for 1992, but the different rates will be brought closer. Altogether almost 300 measures needed to be adopted to create a single market.

Support for implementation of this plan was given by Paolo Cecchini, an Italian economist, who wrote an impressive report about the benefits of the Single Act. He enumerated the merits for the Member States if the barrier-free market would be established, which were very convincing: the common market would consist of over 340 million consumers, manufacturers would be able to cut their unit costs due to the increased production volume and cheaper raw materials, and consumers would have more choice. The single market would add 5% to economic growth rates and create 5 million new jobs. This report initiated a big debate throughout the Community and got approval from business, industry and - with some reservations - also from trade unions.

On 18 February 1986 the Single Act was signed and came into effect on 1 July 1987.

Article 7a EC Treaty speaks of adopting "measures with the aim of progressively establishing the internal market over a period expiring on 31 December 1992 [...] The internal market shall comprise an area without internal frontiers in which the free movement of goods, persons, services and capital is ensured in accordance with the provisions of this Treaty."

Many of the objectives would not have been achieved if - as had often been the case before - one dissenting member had vetoed the plan in the Council. The Single European Act introduced a formal change in Community decision-making procedures: instead of the required unanimity in Council Article 100a, "by way of derogation from Article 100", stated that a qualified majority vote of measures was needed to achieve the objectives set out in Article 7a EC. This change in decision-making procedures would make it easier to pass difficult decisions in the Council, even if one or more members objected to the decision. The majority vote therefore ensured the attainment of the internal market.

The Act also introduced new Community responsibilities, such as economic and social cohesion, research and technological development, and the environment. The European Monetary System (EMS) had been in operation since 1979 but had no formal reference. This was changed by the Single European Act.

The Parliament received increased influence in legislation: a second reading of legislation in the cooperation procedure was introduced; the Parliament might form an alliance with the Commission and at least one Member State (see Chapter 6).

The very important Article 7a EC Treaty, introduced by the Single European Act, very generally speaks of an internal market as "an area without internal frontiers in which the free movement of goods, persons, services and capital is ensured". In order to achieve this frontier-free market the Schengen Agreement was signed by Belgium, France, Germany, Luxembourg and the Netherlands on 14 June 1985. In this agreement these five countries committed themselves to the gradual abolition of checks at common borders and free passage for everyone crossing these borders. Five years later, on 19 June 1990, the same five countries signed a further agreement stating conditions and guarantees for implementation of the free-movement arrangements. Italy joined in 1990, Spain and Portugal in 1991.

According to the Schengen Agreement, the free movement applies to everybody, even to citizens of non-Member States residing in the Community. For Community nationals, this objective has been translated into reality through the respective arrangements for tourists, asylum seekers and legal immigrants from non-Member States.

Controls at internal borders are to be abolished and transferred to the external borders of the Member States. This plan claims a common policy of external borders. The policy of open borders has caused severe disagreement: especially the UK does not accept the complete abolition of physical checks at borders. Other problems such as drug-trafficking, terrorism, the flow of dangerous goods across internal frontiers, and the lack of common rules concerning asylum make it difficult to establish a complete border-free community. Common external policies and a coordination of internal administrative practices are needed.

The complete elimination of all barriers for free movement of persons between the Member States by the end of 1992 was not put into reality. By the end of September 1991 75% of all measures had already been adopted. The completion of the internal market varies sector by sector. Measures such as harmonization of taxation, liberalization of capital markets and financial services, liberalization of public procurement, and standardization of certification and testing have already been achieved. Sensitive issues such as the abolition of border checks, freedom of establishment, services and business cooperation are not that far yet.

CHAPTER 3: EUROPEAN UNION, FURTHER EXPANSION AND DEMOCRATIC REFORM

Even during the first year after the Single European Act had entered into force further steps towards a political and monetary union were taken by the European Council. A special Intergovernmental Conference (IGC) was set up to elaborate a new treaty on an economic and monetary union.

Although the power of the European Parliament had been increased by the Single Act, it was obvious that its role was a mostly consultative one. With Eastern Europe's interest to cooperate with the EEC, the unification of Germany, economic deepening and the transfer of more power from national governments and parliaments to the Community a political union was needed, too.

This became more and more obvious, above all due to the fact that numerous problems could not be solved by the countries on their own and the former ways of cooperation in the field of common foreign policy by the EPC had not been very efficient (e.g. the Yugoslavia crisis). Thus, in June 1990, a second IGC was established in order to prepare the political union. At the meeting of the European Council in Luxembourg in June 1991 a draft treaty was already being discussed. The negotiations were continued in Maastricht, where the European Council agreed on the contents of the treaty on 9 and 10 December 1991. The Treaty on European Union was signed in Maastricht by the Member States' ministers of foreign affairs and ministers of financial affairs on 7 February 1992.

The Treaty of Maastricht forms a framework for various stages of integration towards the creation of a European Union. It states objectives of the future union and institutional structures of the Community. The Treaty also contains a big reform of the founding treaties. The objectives are:

1) intensification of economic and monetary union and inclusion of new areas in the EC responsibility,
2) introduction of a common foreign and security policy with the development of close cooperation in legal and home affairs,
3) Union citizenship and
4) increased powers for the European Parliament.

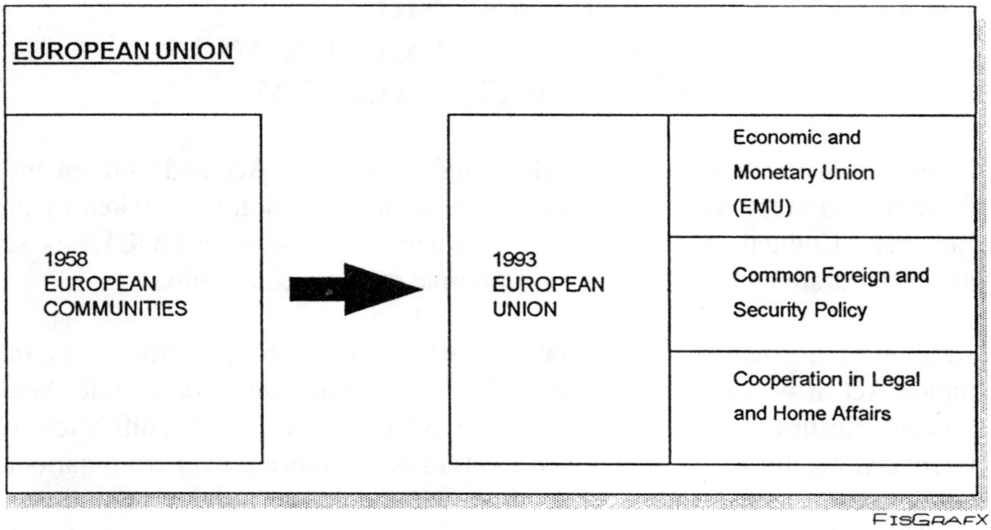

Economic and monetary union is the most ambitious goal of the Maastricht Treaty. According to Article 3a EC Treaty, it seeks "the irrevocable fixing of exchange rates leading to the introduction of a single currency, the ECU...". This objective shall be reached in three stages.

The first stage of the EMU began on 1 July 1990, preceding the Intergovernmental Conference. The remaining restrictions on capital movements were removed, coordination of individual economic policies was to be increased and more intensive cooperation between central banks was besought.

The second stage was due to commence at the beginning of 1994 and supposed to continue until 1997; however, if necessary, it may be extended for two more years. During this stage inflation rates must be reduced and excessive deficits in national budgets must be avoided. The economic performance of the Member States must be brought closer, which means that the poorer EC countries - Greece, Ireland, Portugal and Spain - must catch up with the wealthier ones. In order to do so a Cohesion Fund will be established to provide financial support. The European Monetary Institute (EMI), as prefiguration of the European Central Bank, will be established to prepare the third and final stage.

The third stage will not start before 1 January 1997, however, not later than 1 January 1999, depending on whether a majority of the Member States will have reached the expected key indicators for economic and monetary stability by then. The key indicators are a low inflation rate, a budget deficit below 3% of GDP, a public debt ratio of less than 60% of GDP, two years of currency stability within the exchange rate mechanism (ERM), and low long-term interest rates. (In 1992 only Luxembourg met these requirements.)

During this final stage the exchange rates will be irrevocably linked to each other and the European Central Bank (ECB) will control the money supply as well as the stability of the ECU.

The ECU will reduce the risk of exchange rate fluctuations and the costs of business transactions. The monetary union will also increase the competitiveness of companies and national economies and will also bring further growth and price stability. (A more detailed approach of the European economic and monetary union will be undertaken in Chapters 27, 28 and 29.)

With the creation of the common market and the abolishment of borders between the Member States many problems have emerged which cannot be solved by an individual state on its own. The Community countries will have to trust that people entering a Community country will be checked according to the requirements of all EC countries because further checks will not be carried out at the borders connecting the individual Member States. Many responsibilities will be transferred from the national level to the European Community.

One very important field of competence relates to visa policy. The Council has the power to decide whether nationals of non-Community countries must possess a visa to enter the EC. The Council is able to react fast to a sudden influx of people from one country by imposing a visa requirement for a limited period of time. An extension can then be decided unanimously. By 1996 the Council will also decide on a uniform design for visas.

Another new field of competence of the EC is education, vocational training and youth - a chapter introduced by the Maastricht Treaty. The mobility of students and teachers shall be improved b recognizing diplomas and periods of studies. To stop the high unemployment and to keep the European industry competitive on the world markets, vocational training and retraining will adapt workers and instructors to industrial changes (see Articles 126-127 EC treaty).

Article 129a EC Treaty states that "the Community shall contribute to the attainment of a high level of consumer protection..." With the large internal market and its dangers for the individual the consumer must be able to rely on a certain level of protection. Due to the Community's competition policy there is already a broad range of joint protection provisions, e.g. on the liability of manufacturers for the safety of their products, on door-to-door selling and on labelling of goods. The Union Treaty provides more guidelines to pursue effective consumer protection.

Maastricht also introduced the Union citizenship, stipulated in Article 8 EC Treaty. Union citizenship will not only mean rights but also duties for the Europeans. They will be able to vote and stand for election in municipal elections in whatever Member State they reside. Union citizens also have the right to petition the European Parliament and present their problems to an ombudsman. Until now the citizens of the European Community were only entitled to take part in the direct elections of the European Parliament. Since 1985, European passports have been issued by the Member States. Member State embassies outside the EC have the duty to protect Community citizens of other Member States that do not have a national diplomatic representation in that country. These are the results of integration noticeable for the individual. S/he will not only be able to drive from Berlin to Madrid without being checked at the borders but also to buy goods in Spain and bring them to another Member State without having to pay any import duty. Later on, the economic and monetary union will make it unnecessary to exchange currencies.

Additional new powers for the European Community are public health, industrial policy, culture, progress on social policy, an increase in research and development, the establishment of trans-European transport, telecommunications and energy networks and greater importance of environmental protection.

The introduction of a common foreign and security policy is a very important part of the Treaty on European Union. Cooperation in these matters shall be further developed so that, according to the new structure, the Community can act and react in a more effective way. All areas of foreign and security policy shall be covered, "including the eventual framing of a common defence policy, which might in time lead to a common defence".

Article J.1 lays down the objectives of the common foreign and security policy:

* to safeguard the common values, fundamental interests and independence of the Union
* to strengthen the security of the Union and its Member States in all ways
* to preserve world peace and strengthen international security in accordance with the principles of the United Nations Charters as well as the principles and objectives of the Conference on Security and Cooperation in Europe (CSCE).
* to promote international cooperation
* to develop and consolidate democracy and the rule of law, and respect for human rights and fundamental freedoms.

These policies will gradually develop and include the WEU, which will elaborate and implement decisions and actions of the Union (J.4 TEU).

The European Council defines the principles and general guidelines. The Council takes the decisions on the basis of general guidelines. Except for procedural questions, the Council acts unanimously. Some matters can be taken by a qualified majority in order to facilitate decisions on a common position. These matters must be defined by the Council (Article J.3.2 TEU). It can be referred to by any Member State or the Commission on any question concerning the common foreign and security policy. In urgent cases an extraordinary Council meeting shall be convened within 48 hours. A Political Committee consisting of Political Directors shall prepare and monitor the common foreign and security policy.

The European Parliament and the Commission play an active role in these fields as well. The Member States have agreed that the first areas for joint action are the CSCE process, the policy on disarmament and arms control in Europe, non-proliferation of nuclear weapons, and controls of exports of weapons. As mentioned earlier, the WEU will take a central position in the Community's security policy. In a special declaration the nine Community States, which are also members of the WEU, have agreed on developing the WEU to the defence component of the European Union. Cooperation with NATO will also be intensified.

Denmark, Greece and Ireland are not presently members of the WEU but have been invited to accede or to assume observer status. The non-Community European members of NATO, i.e. Turkey, Norway and Iceland, are planned to be brought closer to WEU through associate membership.

The Treaty by which WEU was established will expire in 1998. There are suggestions that WEU will then merge into a European Union with its own security policy. The Treaty on European Union seeks to enhance cooperation on legal matters and home affairs which shall later on develop into a Community policy. Such matters of common interest, as Article K.1 TEU states, are:

* asylum policy
* rules governing the crossing of the external borders of the Member States and exercise of controls thereon
* immigration policy and policy regarding nationals of third countries
* combating drug addiction
* combating fraud on an international scale
* judicial cooperation in civil law and criminal law matters
* customs and police cooperation

In these fields the Council acts unanimously. A very important aspect of these policies is to determine the rules for entry and movement of nationals of non-member countries within the territory of the Community and for residence there. For many countries it has been very difficult to monitor illegal immigration, illegal residence and illegal work even in the past. With the borders having disappeared between the Member States it will be an even more difficult task. The Community has already considered these problems in the Schengen Agreement.

The establishment of a central police office consisting of high-ranking officials is a big step further in this direction (Europol). Its duty will be to support the national criminal investigation and security authorities. Moreover, databases will be set up so that criminal investigation work can be evaluated centrally. Joint programmes will be established for training and research and criminal records departments.

The Protocol on Social Policy of 1989 was extended to an Agreement on Social Policy concluded between all Member States except for the United Kingdom at Maastricht. The objectives on promotion of employment, improved living and working conditions, proper social protection, dialogue between management and labour, the development of human resources with a view to lasting high employment and the combating of exclusion. The adopted provisions shall not prevent any Member State from maintaining or introducing more stringent preventive measures. According to Article 2 Social Agreement (also "Social Charter"), the provisions shall not apply to pay, the right of association, the right to strike, or the right to impose lock-outs. In Article 6 every Member State commits itself to ensure that the principle of equal pay for male and female workers for equal work is applied.

Last but not least, the rights of the European Parliament have been extended by the Maastricht Treaty As mentioned above, the EP now plays an important part in the decision-making process, Article 189b EC Treaty (see Chapter 6). The Treaty on European Union should have been ratified by the end of 1992 so that it could have come into effect with the establishment of the Common Market on 1 January 1993. However, numerous problems made it impossible to adhere to the schedule. The procedure of ratification in the different Member States turned out to be more difficult than expected.

The procedure in the British House of Commons was very tiring and often suspended before a positive decision was reached. The Irish plebiscite immediately brought a clear decision in favour of the Maastricht Treaty.

In Germany the Treaty on European Union was made subject to a ruling of the supreme court although the German parliament had already agreed on ratifying the Treaty. It was assumed that the Treaty of Maastricht would violate the German constitution, the Bonner Grundgesetz, and lead to an unconstitutional renunciation of sovereignty. However, on 12 October 1993 the supreme court in Karlsruhe decided that Germany's membership to the European Union would be compatible with the principles of the Grundgesetz and would not violate its sovereignty.

The ratification was particularly difficult in Denmark. Denmark was the first Member State of the Community that had its Community policy confirmed by its people in referendums. The first referendum in June 1992 brought a rejection of the Treaty of Maastricht by 50.7% of the population, a very narrow majority. Only 27,000 votes were missing for an approval. It was clear that special regulations were needed to gain a vote in favour of the Treaty. Denmark registered all its special requests in a Whitebook, most of which requests were approved by the Community. The second referendum in

May 1993 brought a clear majority (56.8%) in favour of the European Union. Now Denmark enjoys many special regulations concerning Union citizenship, economic and monetary union and defence policy. These special clauses do not alter the Treaty and concern Denmark only. Denmark's special situation is recorded in a separate agreement containing declarations of the other Community members.

The French referendum turned out to be tighter than expected: 51.2% decided in favour of the European Union. The French constitution does not stipulate a referendum but it was taken on the initiative of President Mitterand, who wanted France to again become the leading force in European integration and to also strengthen his internal political position.

The Treaty on European Union came into force on 1 November 1993. Article N of the Treaty states that the governments of the Member States or the Commission can propose amendments of the Treaties on which the Union is founded. Also "a conference of representatives of the governments of the Member States" shall be convened in 1996 to examine those provisions of the Treaty for which revision is provided.

During the late 1980s, Austria, Finland, Norway and Sweden applied to become members of the European Community. Negotiations of accession were formally opened on 1 February 1993 and concluded at the beginning of March 1994.

One of the criticisms levelled against the Community is that the three separate branches of government - legislative, executive and judiciary - are not clearly split between the four institutions. The judiciary branch is only held by the European Court of Justice. But the other two are exercised by the Commission, the Council and the European Parliament together.

A poll carried out in May 1992 on request of the Commission showed that 47% of the people questioned were discontent with the democratic functioning of the Community. The "democracy deficit" is to be primarily considered as a deficit of legitimization. A missing direct democratic authorization of those bodies which take political decisions and pass binding norms can be detected. Not only the Council as law-making body in the Community but also the Commission as initiating and controlling institution of the EC in some way represent a government. It is a government lacking direct democratic justification, which is essential to all Community countries.

The Council is made up of representatives of the Member States' national governments and the Commission consists of 17 members appointed by the member governments as opposed to the European Parliament, which is elected by direct universal suffrage since 1979.

If one transferred the model of parliamentarian democracy of the Member States to the supranational institution of the EC, the European Parliament would then be the only legislative body and control the other bodies as well. The Council and the Commission would then exercise executive powers only. Such a structure is considered a long-term objective for the Community.

The European Parliament was established as the Common Assembly of the European Coal and Steel Community in 1952. Its status was one of a pure assembly without many important functions. However, over the past few decades it has been slowly growing to a proper parliament with a certain democratic authorization and controls. Today it is being elected by the people of the Member States according to the principles of democratic voting. It therefore constitutes a democratically elected European representative body.

The Treaty of Maastricht has brought about a stronger position for the European Parliament in the decision-shaping process and more controlling powers (see Chapter 6). The democratic character of the EP is being strengthened continuously.

Another point of criticism is that too many decisions, especially those concerning the lives of people in the Community, are taken behind closed doors. More transparency or openness in the EC decision-making is being demanded. The Commission has already reacted. In 1992 it decided to announce, in advance, any new initiatives it is planning to take and to increase the amount of information it releases to the public. Because the Council of Ministers acts as the executive branch of government, it always meets in closed session. Otherwise, where the Council works as the legislative power, some formal sessions are televised. The European Parliament is an open institution just as legislatures in all democratic countries are. Plenary sessions and some committee meetings are public. Sometimes even public hearings on topical issues are organized.

This shows that criticism concerning the democratic structure of the institutions and the transparency of EC decision-making has been fruitful and that there is also a will to open Community functioning to the people.

PART TWO - ORGANIZATION AND INSTITUTIONS

CHAPTER 4: INTRODUCTION

Contrary to most of the other international organizations, the EC is based on a set of institutions that share the tasks of the Community. Some of their powers are autonomous; other powers must be exercised together with another institution. In the beginning their task was to supervise the economic integration of Europe. Over the years many changes have extended their roles and powers.

The four most important institutions were established by the Treaty of Paris and the Treaty of Rome. They are:

* the Council,
* the Commission,
* the European Parliament and
* the Court of Justice.

These four bodies are involved in the Community's decision-making process. Until July 1967 the three Communities had separate Councils and Commissions, which were then merged into a single Council and a single Commission. The European Parliament and the Court of Justice have been common to the three Communities since 1958. The purpose of these two merger treaties was to make the administrative work more efficient (out of 12 separate institutions at that time).

The Court of Auditors audits the accounts of the Community and the Community bodies. The European Investment Bank is the financial institution of the Community. It grants loans and guarantees for projects of common interest to several Member States and in order to assist less-developed regions.

As advisory bodies, the Economic and Social Committee as well as the Committee of the Regions were established. The Economic and Social Committee represents various sectors of economic and social life and is often consulted before decisions are taken. The Committee of Regions is a special body representing the interests of the various regions. Its function is only consultative.

The *separation of powers* is a typical feature of parliamentary democracies. According to Montesquieu's doctrine, all governmental powers are to be divided into three branches, namely the legislative, the executive and the judiciary. However, in the EC as a supranational organization this principle cannot be applied in full. Clearly separated and independent of the other institutions is the Court of Justice. With regard to the legislative and executive branches no delimitation can be detected, neither in a factual nor in an institutional way.

Since the Treaty of Maastricht *the principle of subsidiarity* has been discussed more often although it had already been a part of the EEC Treaty on environmental matters. Today, Article 3b EC Treaty quite generally states: "In areas which do not fall within its exclusive competence, the Community shall take action, in accordance with the principle of subsidiarity, only if and insofar as the objectives of the proposed action cannot be sufficiently achieved by the Member States and can therefore, by reason of scale or effects of the proposed action, be better achieved by the Community". This principle tries to coordinate the powers in such a way that - one day - not all of them will be cumulated in Brussels. The EC institutions shall only become active if the Member States do not declare themselves competent in a matter. This means a voluntary self-restriction on the Community level so that, on a lower level, the countries can decide on their own. It is not certain whether the subsidiarity principle will effectively reduce the tendency of growing centralism in the EC and thus of Euroscepticism.

The complexity of the institutions, their duties and the way decisions are taken demand a high grade of *cooperation and coordination.* (Cooperation means the contractual working together of governments, especially in particular fields of policy. Coordination is the commitment to mutual exchange of information and to match certain actions.) (See chapter 24.)

CHAPTER 5: THE COMMISSION

The Community Treaties have assigned the Commission a wide range of duties. Generally spoken, it is the Commission's role to initiate Community policy, to serve as the executive arm of the Communities, to defend the Community interest in the Council, and to act as the guardian of the Treaties.

Structure

At the moment, the Commission has seventeen *Commissioners.* One of them is the President, who is appointed by common accord of the governments of the Member States. The five largest countries of the Community - France, Germany, Italy, Spain and the United Kingdom - may appoint two each, the other Member States only one each. The Commissioners must have general competence, may not receive instructions from any national government, and must be nationals of a Member State. They are subject only to the supervision of the EP, which is the only body that can force them to resign collectively. Members are appointed for five years by mutual agreement of the governments of the Member States. The term of office is renewable. Depending on their individual political philosophies and the accord with the policy of the Member State of which they are nationals, it may happen that their appointment is not renewed. During their term of office, the Commissioners may not engage in any other occupation, whether gainful or not.

The *President* of the Commission is nominated by the governments of the Member States by common accord after having consulted the EP. The Commission may appoint one or two Vice Presidents from among its members. The President's main tasks are to chair the meetings of the Commission and to propose the allocation of portfolios to individual Commissioners. Every year he presents the Commission's legislative programme to the EP and replies to the debate on the programme. The President has the right to join the international summits of the Group of Seven and the European Council. He can be influential in promoting ideas that are adopted by the European Council.

According to an informal agreement of 1967, the term of the Commission's President would last two or at most four years and the nationality of the President would rotate among the Member States. An exception to this pattern is the presidency of the Frenchman Jacques Delors, who will serve for ten years, from January 1985 till January 1995.

Members of the Commission, the President, and the Vice President may be dismissed by the Court of Justice upon application by the Council or the Commission if s/he no longer fulfils the conditions required for the performance of his/her duties, or if s/he has been found guilty of serious misconduct. So far this has happened only once: following a poor prognosis after he had fallen into a coma, Commissioner Albert Borschette was replaced.

Otherwise the EP can dismiss the whole Commission if a motion of censure on the activities of the Commission is carried by a two thirds majority of the votes. The Parliament has never had to use this power because it usually is content with the work of the Commission. On the other hand, its wish for more legislative power has to be granted by the Council and the Member States, not by the Commission.

THE COMMISSION

☺☺ Germany
☺☺ Spain
☺☺ France
☺☺ Italy
☺☺ United Kingdom
☺ Belgium
☺ Denmark
☺ Greece
☺ Ireland
☺ Luxembourg
☺ Netherlands
☺ Portugal

1 President
6 Vicepresident
10 Commissioners
17 Members

} appointed by common accord of all Member States for a term of five years to be approved by the European Parliament

Main functions: * Community policy (development, draft legislation)
* Community law (guardian of Treaties)
* Executive function (representations in international organizations)

FisGrafX

Legislation

The *decisions* in the Commission must be taken by majority vote although the Commissioners often try to reach consensus. Once a decision has been taken, an unwritten rule requires that the Commission's decision is to be supported by all Commissioners in public, even by those who voted against it. The meetings are held in private though the Commission often invites the official who is responsible for a proposal.

For those matters which will not bring about a big discussion a separate written procedure has been developed: every Commissioner is sent a written proposal that will be adopted if none of them raises any objections within a specified period, usually one week. Some Commission members are responsible for one area where they work on the routine decisions. This way the weekly Commission meetings only deal with matters of importance and are not burdened with time-consuming routine matters.

Every Commissioner has his personal staff - his cabinet - and is responsible for one or more policy areas such as agriculture, budget, competition, energy etc. For each policy area a Director-General is assigned, who prepares proposals for new legislation. Before doing this, s/he often asks a committee of national experts or interest groups to consider a draft. Then s/he submits a proposal to the Commissioner's cabinet, the legal service, and the Commission for approval. This procedure, to a certain extent, allows consideration of national interests and reactions and, if necessary, amendments to the proposal so that it will be adopted by the Council without major problems.

It is usually the Commission's task to initiate the *legislative process* by making a proposal. Otherwise the Court can request the Council to determine the classes of action or proceeding (Article 168a EC). The Council may, on recommendation of the European Central Bank, conclude formal agreements on an exchange rate system for the ECU in relation to non-Community currencies (Article 109 EC). The EP can propose procedure for its elections to the Council (Article 106 EC). In most cases it is the Council that has the power to pass the legislation.

On some occasions the Council or a Member State may request the Commission to make a recommendation or a proposal. The Commission must then examine the request and submit its conclusions to the Council without delay (Article 109d), or the Commission must undertake any studies the Council considers desirable for the achievement of the common objectives and submit to it any appropriate proposals (Article 152 EC). This shows that the Council can request the Commission to take action in certain fields and to submit a proposal.

Although the sole power to initiate legislative proposals lies with the Commission, the major political initiatives of the Community come from the Council. When the Council meets to pass a Commission proposal a Commissioner will usually take part. The Council can amend the proposal on the basis of unanimity only. Thus, if the Council comes into a situation where neither the required qualified majority nor unanimity to accept the proposal can be attained, nor unanimity to amend the proposal, the Commissioner can break the deadlock by changing the proposal in such a way that it can achieve the required vote in the Council.

There are very few areas in which the Commission has powers to pass legislation. According to Article 48 (3) (d) EC, the Commission can draw up regulations determining conditions on the rights of workers. Workers shall have the possibility to remain in the territory of a Member State after having been employed in that state although they are nationals of another Member State. Based on this power, the Commission passed Regulation 1251/70 on 29 June 1970.

Under Article 90 (3) EC, the Commission can address directives to Member States to ensure the application of the Community's competition policy to public undertakings and undertakings to which Member States grant special or exclusive rights, e.g. a directive concerning the transparency of financial relations between Member States and public undertakings or a directive on the competition in the telecommunications terminal market.

Many legislative powers have been delegated to the Commission by the Council. Such a delegated power is, for instance, the possibility of passing regulations with respect to the common agricultural policy. A committee of representatives of the Member States is often established to advise and supervise the legislation of the Commission in areas of delegated legislative powers.

The power to decide on safeguard measures has been delegated to the Commission, too. However, before taking a decision, it must consult the

Member States and later notify the Council and the Member States of any outcome. Within a certain time limit any Member State can refer the Commission's decision to the Council.

Executive role

The Commission's executive powers are to implement Community policies on the basis of Council decisions or directly following Treaty provisions, above all in the field of competition policy under Articles 85-93 EC and safeguard measures under Article 115 EC. One of the important executive powers is that the Commission may even scrutinize documents and correspondence of a Member State or an undertaking with a view to compliance with competition policy. The Commission has wide powers in other sectors, too, such as coal and steel, and nuclear power. Otherwise, the Commission follows instructions from the Council, e.g. when negotiating trade agreements with non-member countries or the management of agricultural markets.

The Commission has executive powers in managing the Community's funds: the European Social Fund, the Guidance Section of the European Agricultural Guidance and Guarantee Fund, and the European Regional Development Fund. The last two structural funds were created by the Council, and their administration was delegated to the Commission.

The five prior objectives are:

(1) promoting the development and structural adjustment of the regions whose development is lagging behind (an objective of all the funds);
(2) converting the regions, frontier regions, or parts of regions seriously affected by industrial decline (an objective of the Regional Development Fund and the Social Fund);
(3) combating long-term unemployment (an objective of the Social Fund);
(4) facilitating the occupational integration of young people (an objective of the Social Fund);
(5) reforming the common agricultural policy (an objective of all the funds).

Other Community measures are aimed at promoting research, and various programmes of cooperation with non-member countries are financed from the Community budget (e.g. food aid) or by the European Development Fund.

In many cases the powers conferred to the Commission by the Council are to be exercised in close consultation with the governments of the Member States. For this reason the Commission is assisted by those committees consisting of government representatives:

(a) An Advisory Committee expresses its opinion to the Commission, which must take full account of these views but is in no way bound by them. The committee has no further influence on the procedure.
(b) A Management Committee for the agricultural policy. Here again, the committee remains entirely free to decide for itself.
(c) A Regulatory Committee, which is like the management committee but is being applied to other fields such as the adoption of common standards, environmental legislation, etc.

Commission as Guardian of Community Law

Article 169 EC gives the Commission the power to monitor whether the Member States are fulfilling their obligations under this Treaty. There are three formal stages of proceedings:

<u>First:</u>
The Commission sends a letter of formal notice to the Member State of which the Commission thinks it may have failed to fulfil certain Community law obligations and therefore asks such state's formal response.

<u>Second:</u>
The Commission delivers a reasoned opinion on the matter, giving the Member State the opportunity to submit its observations.

<u>Third</u>:
The Commission may bring the matter before the Court of Justice for a ruling on whether the Member State has breached its Community law obligations or not.

Most of these cases are resolved in the first or second stage.

The Commission also intervenes in all cases where the Court of Justice is asked for a preliminary ruling on the interpretation or validity of Community law. As Community prosecutor, the Commission plays an important role as neutral body which can take Member States to the Court of Justice. If legal prosecution owing to failure in complying with Community law was left to be initiated by Member States, it would be, by far, less effective.

Summary

The Commission's power to pass laws depends, above all, on the Council's willingness to delegate its legislative power to the Commission. The Commission has actual influence as initiator of legislation and participant in the Council, especially when it comes to amending its own proposal in order for the Council to be able to agree thereto. The Maastricht Treaty has introduced new powers of the European Parliament so that the EP is now also more actively involved in the legislative process.

The Commission's key area of executive powers is competition policy; apart from that, executive powers are vested with the Council. The Commission can also reform agriculture and improve the economic situation of the poorer regions, depending on the budget it is granted by the Council and the EP.

DIRECTORATES

DG I	External Relations
DG II	Economic and financial affairs
DG III	Internal market and industrial affairs
DG IV	Competition (cartels) and state aids
DG V	Employment, social affairs and education
DG VI	Agriculture
DG VII	Transport
DG VIII	Aid to developing countries
DG IX	Personnel, administration and translations
DG X	Information, communication and culture
DG XI	Environment, consumer protection and nuclear safety
DG XII	Science and research and development (including The Joint Research Centre)
DG XIII	Telecommunications, information industries and innovation
DG XIV	Fisheries
DG XV	Financial institutions and company law
DG XVI	Regional development and policy
DG XVII	Energy
DG XVIII	EC credit and investments (borrowing and lending)
DG XIX	EC budgets
DG XX	Budgets (internal financial control)
DG XXI	Customs Union and indirect taxation
DG XXII	Co-ordination of structural policies and instruments
DG XXIII	Enterprise policy, tourism, distributive trades and co-operatives. This DG is to be disbanded and its responsibilities redistributed.

FISGRAFX

CHAPTER 6: THE EUROPEAN PARLIAMENT

Structure

"The European Parliament ... shall consist of representatives of the peoples of the States brought together in the Community, ... ' states Article 137 EC Treaty.

The European Parliament originated from the Common Assembly of the ECSC, which used to have 78 members. In 1958, it became the Assembly of all three Communities (ECSC, EEC and Euratom) with 142 members. At that time the members were delegated from their national parliaments, which means that each member had a dual mandate. This was only changed in 1979, when the citizens of the Community elected their representatives directly to the European Parliament. In 1990, the number of delegates holding a dual mandate was 34 (6.5 per cent).

Although a direct universal suffrage was already envisaged in the founding treaties of the Community, it took more than 20 years to achieve this objective. The Assembly had submitted a draft convention to the Council in 1960, however, the heads of state or government did not agree to direct elections until 1974. Two years later, a new draft convention was adopted by Parliament and the Council finally signed the decision and the act on direct elections in Brussels on 20 September 1976. The act came into effect on 1 July 1978.

The first elections were held on 7 and 10 June 1979, with each state using its own national electoral system because the Council Act and Decision does not provide for a uniform electoral procedure. Such a procedure can be agreed upon by the Council on a proposal from the Assembly. Until then, each Member State must use its own national voting procedures, as they were again used when the following two Parliaments were elected in 1984 and 1989. All of the Member States use systems involving some sort of proportional representation, except for Great Britain, which uses a single ballot majority voting by constituency.

The elections are held every five years: 1979, 1984, 1989 and 1994. The Assembly called itself the European Parliament in 1962, however, it was not until 1987 that it was given this name legally by the Single European Act.

The members of the EP are not linked in national groups but in political ones. There are twelve groups altogether, of which the Socialist group was the largest (179 seats) after the elections in June 1989, followed by the Christian Democratic Group (122 seats).

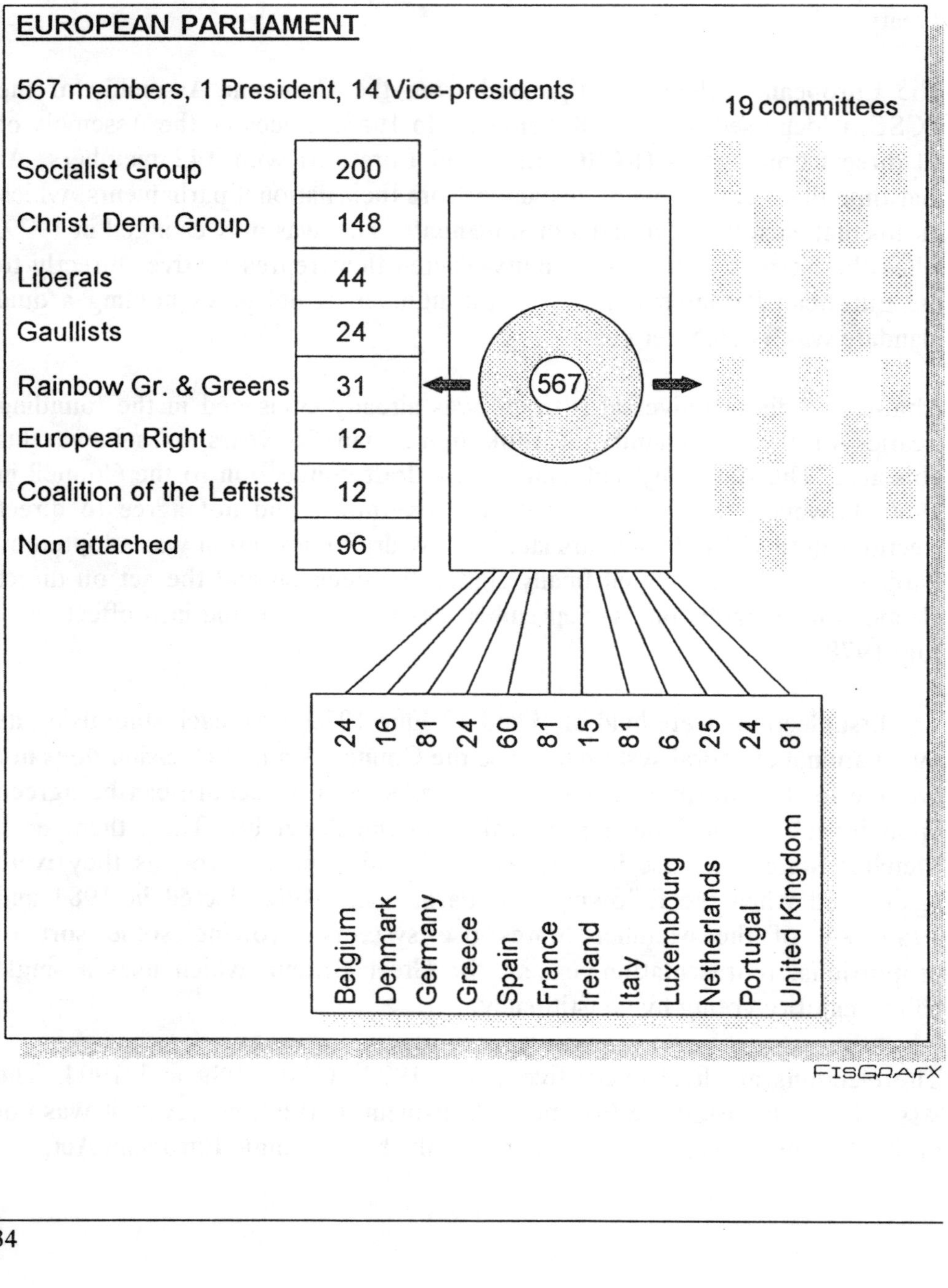

The EP elects its own President for two and a half years by absolute majority of the votes cast. He chairs the proceedings of Parliament in plenary session, performs administrative functions and represents the Parliament on ceremonial occasions. These functions can be delegated to one of the 14 Vice Presidents elected by the Parliament.

The President and the Vice Presidents form the Bureau, which also includes five quaestors elected by the Parliament. The quaestors do not have voting rights. The Bureau sets up and organizes the Secretariat and appoints its head, the Secretary General. It also proposes the memberships of the committees.

The enlarged Bureau consists of the Bureau and the chairpersons of the political groups. It takes decisions on Parliament's internal organization and on relations with non-Community organizations and plays an important role in the nomination process for the post of the President of the Commission (Article 158 (1) EC).

The Parliament's seat is in Strasbourg, although the committees and the political groups mostly meet in Brussels. Its Secretariat is based in Luxembourg.

The plenary sessions are held for one week each month and sometimes in between in order to discuss special issues. The parliamentary committees meet for two weeks and the political groups for one week.

There are 18 standing committees:

Political Affairs Committee
Committee on Agriculture, Fisheries and Rural Development
Committee on Budgets
Committee on Economic and Monetary Affairs and Industrial Policy
Committee on Energy, Research and Technology
Committee on External Economic Relations
Committee on Legal Affairs and Citizens' Rights
Committee on Social Affairs, Employment and the Working Environment
Committee on Regional Policy and Regional Planning
Committee on Transport and Tourism
Committee on Environment, Public Health and Consumer Protection

Committee on Youth, Culture, Education, the Media and Sports
Committee on Development and Cooperation
Committee on Budgetary Control
Committee on Institutional Affairs
Çommittee on the Rules of Procedure, the Verification of Credentials and Immunities
Committee on Women's Rights
Committee on Petitions

The committees prepare the Parliament's opinion on legislative proposals brought to the Council by the Commission. The assigned committee discusses the proposal and then suggests its acceptance, rejection or amendment in a plenary session. Within this process, independent experts and representatives of interest groups will be heard.

The parliamentary committee sessions are often held in public and are usually attended by the appropriate Commissioner.

Supervising the Community

Since 1973, when Question Time at each part-session of Parliament was introduced, questions can be directed to the Commission, the Council and the Conference of Foreign Ministers. The Commission must reply to questions asked by the Parliament or its members according to Article 140 EC. Pursuant to the EC Treaty, the Council has no such obligation, however, in practice, it answers most questions. The Conference of Foreign Ministers is usually asked on matters of European political cooperation. The President of the Parliament decides on the admissibility and order of the questions and whether oral questions should be put into writing. The Commission and the Council have a right to be heard by the Parliament - Article 140 EC.

The EP discusses the Commission's annual general report in open session - Article 143 EC. At the beginning of each year, the President of the Commission presents the annual legislative programme to the Parliament, on which a debate is then held. This is of greater importance than the annual general report, as the Parliament can try to influence the legislative programme of the coming year.

The Council also reports to the Parliament although it is not obliged to do so. As the presidency of the Council changes every six months, the Council's programme is presented at the beginning of the six months and a report is presented at the end of the presidency.

The most drastic power that the EP can make use of is a motion of censure on the activities of the Commission - Article 144 EC. A political group or one tenth of the members of Parliament can table such a motion. A debate on the motion can only be held after 24 hours. After the debate another 48 hours must pass before the vote can be taken. Such a motion needs a two thirds majority of the votes cast. If the motion passes, the Commission must resign as a body. Such a motion cannot be directed against an individual member of the Commission only. Although motions of censure were tabled on seven occasions, none of them was carried.

At the request of a quarter of its members the EP may set up a temporary committee of inquiry to investigate alleged contraventions or maladministration in the implementation of Community law - Article 138c EC. Within nine months, the committee must present a report. Such committees have been set up on a number of occasions investigating different matters, such as the problem stocks in the agricultural sector, the handling and transport of nuclear material, the problems of quality in the meat sector, racism and organized crime.

According to Article 138d: "any citizen of the Union, and any natural or legal person residing or having its registered office in a Member State, shall have the right to address ... a petition to the European Parliament on a matter which comes within the Community's fields of activity and which affects him, her or it directly." The petition is assigned to the committee responsible, which may conduct hearings and present a report.

In Article 138e, the Maastricht Treaty introduced the Ombudsman, who receives complaints. He can initiate an inquiry and then refer the matter to the institution concerned. The institution informs the Ombudsman on its views, who then forwards a report to the EP and the institution concerned. The person lodging the complaint is informed of the outcome of the inquiries.

(4*)

Budgetary Role

The two Budgetary Treaties of 1970 and 1975 extended the powers of the EP. Before these two treaties came into effect the Parliament's role was a purely consultative one.

A distinction in the budget is made between the compulsory expenditure and the non-compulsory expenditure (NCE). In a joint declaration of the EP, Council and Commission of 1982 compulsory expenditure was defined as "such expenditure as the budgetary authority is obliged to enter in the budget to enable the Community to meet its obligations, both internally and externally, under the Treaties and acts adopted in accordance therewith". Non-compulsory expenditure is such expenditure which is not the inevitable consequence of Community legislation.

A draft budget for the following calendar year must be submitted to the EP by the Council for its first reading no later than 5 October - Article 203 (4) EC. The Parliament has the right to amend the draft budget, acting by an absolute majority of the votes cast; however, it can only amend the NCE parts of the budget. It can only propose modifications to the compulsory expenditure parts of the budget. If the Parliament makes amendments and proposes modifications - which is usually the case - the draft budget is forwarded to the Council. After discussing the draft budget with the Commission, the Council may modify any of the amendments adopted by the EP and modify the other parts of the draft budget on the basis of the proposed modifications. Then the modified draft budget must be presented to the EP for a second reading. In this respect, the Parliament has no power to alter the parts of the budget relating to compulsory expenditure. It has, however, 15 days within which to amend or reject the modifications made by the Council to the Parliament's first reading amendments on NCE.

The Parliament can also ask for a new budget to be submitted after having rejected the draft budget. This happened in 1980, 1982 and 1985.

This shows that the EP has authorization over the NCE and the Council has authorization over compulsory expenditure.

Legislation

The Single European Act introduced a new procedure: the cooperation procedure according to Article 189c EC. It is applied to Articles 6 (2), 118a, 130c and 130o (2) EC. The Commission submits a proposal to the EP and the Council, which adopts a common position after the EP has expressed its opinion. The Council and the Commission shall fully inform the EP on the reasons which led the Council to adopt its common position and also of the Commission's position. The EP can accept, reject or amend the common position. The Commission shall re-examine the proposal considering the amendments proposed by the EP. The Commission is not obliged to accept any of Parliament's amendments but if it rejects them, it must forward them to the Council with its opinion on them. The Council can accept the Commission's re-examined proposal by qualified majority, or unanimously adopt any of the Parliament's amendments that were not accepted by the Commission.

The Parliament's influence has been strengthened by introducing the second reading in the cooperation procedure. The Parliament's amendments at the first reading are more likely to be adopted: 60 per cent by the Commission and more than 40 per cent by the Council. The amendments at the second reading are not so high: 46 per cent accepted by the Commission and 27 per cent by the Council.

At Maastricht, the legislative powers of the EP were strengthened by introducing the conciliation and veto procedure - Article 189b EC. This is a very complex procedure although parts of it are the same as the cooperation procedure. It provides a framework for dialogue between the three institutions during the legislative process. The Council no longer plays the major part but must seek a compromise with the other two institutions. Unfortunately, this procedure has not been developed for the important matters, such as competition policy, economic and monetary policy, etc. In these areas the EP remains relatively powerless.

Approving Accession and Association Agreements

Article O Maastricht Treaty defines the Parliament's role when European countries apply to become a member of the Union or only want to associate with it. Prior to Maastricht, this was established in Article 237 EEC Treaty. The new provision is identical to the old one.

The state must address its application to the Council. The application is referred to the appropriate committee of Parliament for consideration. Before negotiations with the applicant state commence a debate - if requested - may be held in Parliament. The Commission and the Council can be requested by a simple majority to take part in the debate. Once the negotiations are completed, the Parliamentary committee will present a report to the Parliament, where another debate will be held. At last, a vote on assent to the application will be taken and at least 260 votes are required to obtain the approval. Otherwise the EP can veto the accession of another country.

Prior to the elections in 1994 the EP had 518 members. After the German unification Germany was granted 18 representatives with observatory status. Today there are 567 members of the European Parliament (number of MEPs of aspiring members *in italics*):

Belgium	25	Greece	25	*Austria*	*21*
Germany	99	Italy	87	*Sweden*	*22*
Denmark	16	Ireland	15	*Finland*	*16*
Spain	64	Luxembourg	06	*Norway*	*15*
France	87	Netherlands	31		
Great Britain	87	Portugal	25		

CHAPTER 7: THE COUNCIL

The Council plays the leading role among the institutions in the Community and has the greatest legislative power. It consists of representatives of the governments of the Member States. Usually, each government sends one of its ministers, depending on which subject will be discussed. The transport ministers deal with transport matters, the agriculture ministers with agriculture and the finance ministers with financial issues. The foreign minister is regarded as the main representative of a country. This is why the Council can also be called "Council of Ministers".

The presidency of the Council rotates in alphabetical order every six months. The president initiates the Council meetings although they can be convened by one of the Council members or the Commission. The meetings are not held in public, except when the Council decides to do so unanimously. Such closed sessions are being criticized. Sometimes, when the Council works as the legislative power, formal sessions are televised.

Usually, the Commission takes part in the Council meetings unless the Council decides otherwise by simple majority. The Commission's participation in the legislative procedure is important in case the Council cannot agree on a Commission proposal. In such a case the participating Commissioner will alter the proposal so that the necessary majority or unanimity can be achieved.

Council and Commission officials and the ambassadors of the Member States will attend the meetings, too, however, they can be excluded if the ministers and the Commission want to negotiate on their own. The Council is assisted by a General Secretariat and its staff.

Decision-taking

The EC Treaty prescribes three different methods of voting: unanimity, qualified majority and simple majority.

Unanimity is required when the Council wants to amend a Commission proposal or to pass an issue which has been rejected by the European Parliament during the cooperation procedure.

The EC Treaty demands unanimity on several important measures:

* changes in the number of Commissioners, Article 157 (i) EC;
* changes in the number of judges and advocates-general in the Court, Article 165 and 166 EC;
* acceptance of a new Member State, Article 0 of the Treaty of the European Union;
* appointing members to the Court of Auditors, Article 188b (3) EC;

The Council Rules of Procedure require unanimity on procedural decisions:

* to hold a Council meeting in public;
* to appoint the Council Secretary-General;

Unanimity means that the decision can be prevented by only one vote against it. On the other hand, if only one minister votes for the issue and the others abstain from the vote, unanimity is attained, too.

"Save as otherwise provided in this Treaty, the Council shall act by a *majority* of its members", states Article 148 (i) EC. Simple majority is not used very often as a method of voting. It would be very easy for several smaller Member States to reach simple majority and overrule the Member States with a bigger population. In case of important matters this would not be very effective, so simple majority is only provided for in a limited number of cases.

The Council may deliver an opinion in favour of calling an international governmental conference for the purpose of determining the amendments to the Treaty, Article N (i) Treaty of the European Union. Once the conference has convened it must decide by common accord which amendments shall be taken.

According to Article 151 (3) EC, the Council may adopt its rules of procedure by simple majority. The Council may also, by simple majority, request to undertake studies it considers desirable for the achievement of the common objectives (Article 152 EC).

Since the early 1980s, *qualified majority* has developed into the main voting method. Before that time, decisions were mostly taken unanimously because most Members were not ready to give up sovereignty to the Community. They preferred operating by consensus.

Luxembourg Compromise

After the end of the transitional period it was intended to improve and accelerate the decision-making process by using qualified majority more often. France did not approve of this plan and consequently did not attend the Council's meetings for six months in 1965 - the so-called "empty chair policy".

France insisted that it could veto on matters of very important interest. The other Member States agreed that within a reasonable time they would try to achieve unanimity on such important matters. If they did not reach unanimity within a reasonable period, the majority voting system would be sufficient to adopt the measure. The Member States would have different positions but at least Community work could continue.

This was the content of the Luxembourg compromise. Today each state, not only France, is able to invoke a veto in the Council where important interests are at stake. If no very important interests are at stake, the veto may be rejected by the other Member States and the measure will be passed by qualified majority.

It is not a legally binding agreement but more of a gentlemen's agreement. It remains to be seen what is going to happen to the veto since the Single European Act has introduced the qualified majority for a number of areas.

The Single European Act made several amendments to introduce qualified majority. The qualified majority voting system is a bit unusual because one state has more than one vote, i.e. the votes are weighted (number of votes of aspiring members *in italics*).

Germany	10	Belgium	5	*Austria*	*4*
France	10	Netherlands	5	*Norway*	*3*
Italy	10	Portugal	5	*Finland*	*3*
UK	10	Denmark	3	*Sweden*	*4*
Spain	8	Ireland	3		
Greece	5	Luxembourg	2		

The distribution of votes does not depend on the population of a State. 54 votes are needed to obtain a qualified majority, which means at least seven countries have to be in favour of the measure being voted on. With 27 votes the decision can be blocked. The weighting of votes guarantees that a decision reaching the qualified majority represents the majority of the Community's population. If all aspiring members join, the total number of votes will amount to 90 and a qualified majority will then require 64 votes.

In March 1994, when the Council was discussing the accession of Austria, Finland, Norway and Sweden to the Community, the UK and Spain at first did not agree on increasing the amount of votes, from 23 to 27, which is the number required to block a decision being taken in the Council. A compromise was made: in principle, 27 votes are sufficient to block a decision for which a qualified majority is needed. If the measure concerns important issues of a specific State, the ministers shall agree on a compromise within an appropriate period of time. When, after some time, a Member thinks it is time to vote again, the Council will vote with simple majority on whether a new vote shall be held on the issue or not. In this case 27 votes are needed to form a blocking minority.

The *Committee of Permanent Representatives* (*COREPER*) is assigned to assist the Council. According to Article 4 of the Merger Treaty, COREPER shall prepare the work of the Council and carry out the tasks assigned to it by the Council.

Actually there are two committees: COREPER 1, made up of the deputy Permanent Representatives, the deputy ambassadors of the Member States to the Community, and COREPER 2, consisting of the Permanent Representatives, the ambassadors. Although both are equal, the ambassadors prepare the more important political issues.

COREPER can establish working parties which do the detailed preparatory work. There are about 100 such working parties. Every Permanent Representation of a Member State has an expert sitting in these working parties. They try to bring in the opinion of the governments they work for. On the other hand they advise and report to their ministers and governments and even to the Commission about a proposal.

If the working party has reached an agreement, COREPER will submit the proposal to the Council, which will pass it formally. If the working party cannot agree on a proposal, COREPER 1 or 2 will try to attain a common position, which it can then forward to the Council.

The civil servants often know more about specific areas than their ministers. They as well as the ambassadors attend the Council meetings in order to advise their ministers.

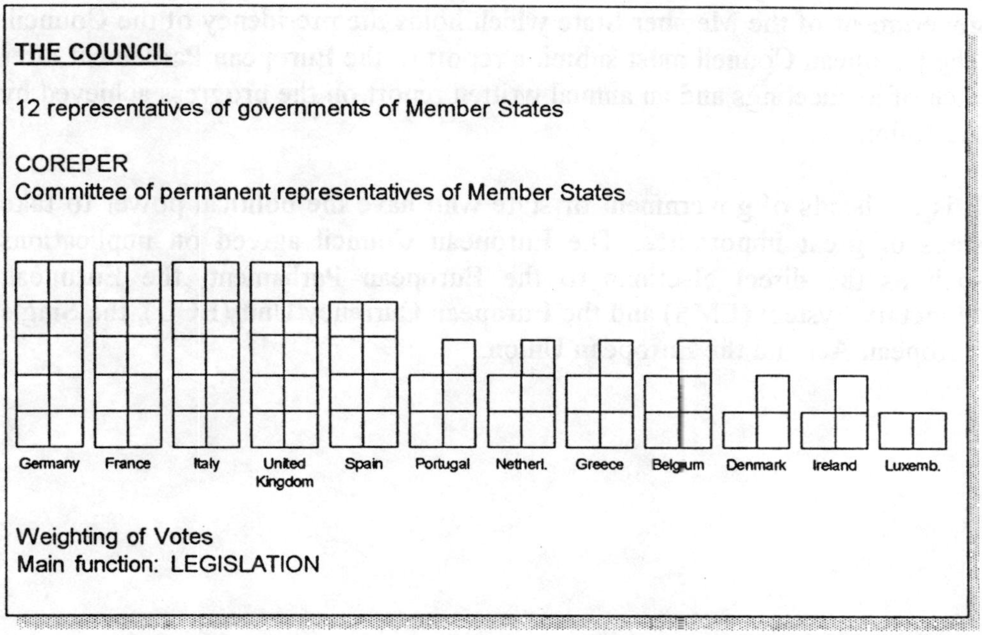

FISGRAFX

The European Council

The European Council was instituted in 1975; it was not an institution set up by the EEC Treaty. The European Council is a summit which brings together the heads of government or state, assisted by the foreign minister and the President of the Commission. It meets three times a year, trying to set objectives in Community affairs and seeking political cooperation. In 1986, the number of meetings of the European Council was reduced to two because it was slowly developing into a higher authority which could solve problems of the Council. The heads of government or state refused to take on such a role.

The Single European Act gave the European Council the position of a body established by the Treaty, but did not give it any specific role or framework. However, Article D of the Treaty on European Union states that "the European Council shall provide the Union with the necessary impetus for its development and shall define the general political guidelines thereof". It meets twice a year under the chairmanship of the head of state or government of the Member State which holds the presidency of the Council. The European Council must submit a report to the European Parliament after each of its meetings and an annual written report on the progress achieved by the Union.

It is the heads of government or state who have the political power to take steps of great importance. The European Council agreed on implications such as the direct elections to the European Parliament, the European Monetary System (EMS) and the European Currency Unit (ECU), the Single European Act and the European Union.

CHAPTER 8: THE COURT OF JUSTICE AND THE COURT OF FIRST INSTANCE

The existence of the Court of Justice underlines the Community's character as a system of law with a high grade of legal protection.

Its seat is in Luxembourg, where there are thirteen judges and six advocates-general. They are chosen from among persons whose independence is beyond doubt and who possess the qualifications required for the appointment to the highest judicial offices in their respective countries or who are jurisconsults of recognized competence (academic lawyers). They are appointed by common accord of the governments of the Member States for a term of six years.

Every Member State usually nominates a judge, and the thirteen judges are chosen by the four largest Community Members plus Spain; the seat of the thirteen judges rotates between these five countries. France, Germany, Italy, and the United Kingdom each nominate an advocate-general and the other two are appointed in rotation by the seven smaller countries plus Spain. Due to this rotation system, it is almost impossible to be renominated for another term.

Every three years, there is a partial replacement of the judges and the advocates-general. Seven and six judges will be replaced alternately and three advocates-general will be replaced, one on each occasion.

As the *President* of the Court of Justice does not have a decisive vote, there is an odd number of judges so that a majority decision can be reached. The President is elected from among the judges for a period of three years, which can be renewed. He directs the administration of the Court and appoints a judge rapporteur for every case.

The *advocates-general* act with complete impartiality and independence to make - in open court - reasoned submissions on cases brought before the Court of JusticeThe first advocate-general allocates a case to one advocate-general, who then prepares it and gives his opinion on how the Court should decide on the case. After he has presented the case, the judges will decide in a plenary session or a chamber without the advocate-general taking part. The judges are not bound by the advocates-general's opinion.

Being an advocate-general is considered to be a good training and springboard to become a judge of the Court. It has already happened on several occasions that an advocate-general became a judge. In the 1970s and 1980s the number of cases increased significantly. This was due to the accession of six new Members to the Community. The Court has adjusted to the increase in work in several ways. First of all, it has made more use of the possibility of assigning cases to a chamber. There are four chambers of three judges and two chambers of six judges. Each chamber has its own president. Cases of importance are decided in plenary session of the Court.

An uneven number of judges is needed to take a decision. The discussions are secret and held in French without interpreters. Each judge has the possibility of expressing his opinion on the case. After the discussion the judges vote, starting with the most junior judge and finishing with the most senior. Majority is needed to determine the decision of the Court.

COURT OF JUSTICE

	1992	1993
A. Judgements		
References for a preliminary ruling	112	128
Direct actions	88	69
Appeals	9	6
Special procedures	1	0
TOTAL	210	203
B. Cases dealt with		
By judgement	241	251
By order terminationg the proceedings	103	541[1]
By an Opinion	1	1
TOTAL	345	793
C. Cases Brought		
References for a preliminary ruling	162	204
Direct actions	251	265
Appeals	25	17
Opinions/Rulings	2	0
Special procedures	2	4
TOTAL	442[2]	490[3]

[1] of which 451 cases were transfered to the Court of First Instance

[2] including a series of 129 cases all concerning the non-contractual liability of the Community with regard to milk quotas

[3] including a series of 129 cases all concerning the non-contractual liability of the Community with regard to milk quotas

Proceedings of the Court of Justice and Court of First Instance of the European Communities

FISGRAFX

Secondly, the Court was relieved of a part of its work with the Single European Act by the establishment of the *Court of First Instance*. It took up its work in 1989. It has its seat in Luxembourg next to the European Court. There are twelve judges, one nominated by each Member State. The Council decision setting up the Court of First Instance did not plan any associated advocates-general, although the Court may ask any member to perform the task of an advocate-general. In such a case he does not take part in the decision of the case and has the same tasks as an advocate-general of the Court of Justice. The member who acts as an advocate-general in a special case is nominated by the President of the Court. There are three chambers which deal with staff cases, each with three judges deliberating, and two chambers dealing with competition cases where five judges deliberate. Sometimes the Court meets in plenary session. This is only the case when the assigned chamber requests that the case be heard in a plenary session. The decisions are taken in secret on the basis of a majority vote at the Court of Justice. The judges of the Court of First Instance were usually holders of national judicial office, academics, or legal civil servants. The requirements are not as high as those for appointment to the European Court.

The President of the Court of First Instance is elected by the judges for a renewable period of three years. He takes care of the judicial business and the administration of the Court. The President assigns each case to a chamber and appoints a judge-rapporteur to each case. He can be chosen as a president for a chamber.

The Court of First Instance can be called upon on staff cases and on cases implementing competition rules. Any party which takes action before the Court of First Instance can automatically appeal to the European Court. The appeal must be brought in within two months after the decision of the Court of First Instance. The Court of Justice can reverse a judgement of the Court of First Instance and decide the case or refer it back to the Court for a new decision.

COURT OF FIRST INSTANCE

	1992	1993
A. Judgements		
Direct actions	19	4
Staff cases	41	43
TOTAL	60	47
B. Cases dealt with		
By judgement	80	54
By order terminationg the proceedings	47	52
TOTAL	127	106
C. Cases Brought		
Direct actions	36	55
Staff cases	79	83
Special procedures	8	7
TOTAL	123	145[1]

[1] It should be noted that 451 cases (380 of which concerting the non-contractual liability of the Community with regard to milk quotas) were transfered to the Court of First Instance as of September 1993.

Proceedings of the Court of Justice and Court of First Instance of the European Communities

FISGRAFX

Interpretation

Working with legal texts always makes it necessary to find the right meaning of a word. The methods of interpretation can help us to find the right meaning. The four methods of interpretation - literal, historical, contextual and purposive or teleological - are not all used in the same way.

The literal interpretation tries to ascertain the words in their natural and ordinary meaning. This often does not bring a satisfying result because the EC Treaty, the regulations and directives are published in ten or nine languages, respectively. Translating a word from one language into another often brings out differing meanings in both languages although - technically - the same word is being used.

Historical interpretation uses documents trying to reveal the intention of the authors of the legal text. Often such preparatory work does not exist at all, and if it does, it has not been published. Since these documents are not generally accessible, the Court of Justice does not usually work with the historical interpretation method.

The Court prefers using the contextual and the purposive interpretations. Contextual means finding the overall context of the legal provision in which the words appear. The purposive method seeks the objectives stated in a provision and from there finds the correct meaning of the word being used. This is a more precise working method because the Court knows the exact aims and objectives of the Community.

As mentioned before, the Court can be called upon because of many different actions. Some of them will be explained here in detail, due to their importance in the legal system of the Community.

Article 169

"If the Commission considers that a Member State has failed to fulfil an obligation under this Treaty, it shall deliver a reasoned opinion on the matter after giving the State concerned the opportunity to submit its observations.

If the State concerned does not comply with the opinion within the period laid down by the Commission, the latter may bring the matter before the Court of Justice."

Before any legal steps are taken the Commission confers extensively with the Member State. This informal stage lasts about one year. The Member State has two possibilities: it must either change its law in accordance with the Community law or persuade the Commission that its laws do not violate Community regulations.

If the Commission and the Member State cannot agree on this matter, the Commission will send a letter of formal notice to the State. The addressed State may then answer and bring up its reasons to justify its laws.

Most of the cases being pursued under Article 169 are solved in these first two stages. Only a few cases reach the stage where the Commission delivers a reasoned opinion as to how it considers that a Member State has failed to fulfil a Treaty obligation. In the reasoned opinion the Commission expresses its legal arguments as to why the State is violating the Community law. The Commission must bring all of its arguments forward in the reasoned opinion because later, before the Court, it is not able to raise new grounds or submissions. If it did, the Court would reject them.

The Commission gives the Member State a short period of time to comply with its opinion, otherwise the case is referred to the Court. The Court of Justice then gives a judgement on the case, deciding if the State is in violation of its obligations under Community law or not. The State cannot defend itself by arguing that the national law prevents from complying with Community law. Such an argument would be rejected by the Court.

A Member State failing to comply with a Community directive, regulation or decision is confronted with the proceeding of Article 169, too. Infringements of Community law must be punished by the legal system of the Member State in the same way as if a national law had been broken. Article 169 also applies if a nationalized industry or a private body under government control breaches Community law.

Article 170

"A Member State which considers that another Member State has failed to fulfil an obligation under this Treaty may bring the matter before the Court of Justice.
Before a Member State brings an action against another Member State for an alleged infringement of an obligation under this Treaty, it shall bring the matter before the Commission."

This form of action against a fellow Member State is not used very often because the Member State carries the burden of proof and the costs. It could further lead to diplomatic embarrassment if the action failed. The Member States of the Community prefer the Commission coming up with such actions rather than initiating them on their own.

Article 171

"If the Court of Justice finds that a Member State has failed to fulfil an obligation under this Treaty, the State shall be required to take the necessary measures to comply with the judgement of the Court of Justice."

Unlike the judgements of national courts, the Court's judgements are only declaratory. Thus, it can happen that a Member State may not comply with the Court's judgements at all, or only very slowly. If this is the case, the Commission can lay down a time limit within which the Member State has the possibility to comply with the Court's judgement. The Commission also specifies the amount of the lump sum or penalty payment to be paid by the Member State if it does not obey. If the Court of Justice finds that the Member State concerned has not complied with its judgement, it may impose the lump sum or penalty payment on it. The Court is not limited to the amount suggested by the Commission. It is not even obliged to sentence the State to pay a penalty.

Before the possibility of imposing such financial penalties was introduced by the Treaty of Maastricht, more than five per cent of all the judgements effected against the Member States in infringement proceedings had not been complied with. What is still missing is a system to ensure that these financial sanctions are paid.

Article 93(2)

According to Article 93, the Commission shall keep all systems of aid existing in the Member States under constant review. If the Commission finds that aid granted by a State or through State resources is not compatible with the common market or that such aid is being misused, it shall decide that the state concerned must abolish or alter such aid within a determined period of time. If the state concerned does not comply with the decision within the prescribed period, the Commission or any other interested state may refer the matter directly to the Court of Justice.

In order to avoid such actions, any Member State may apply to the Council for consideration that the aid being granted by the State is compatible with the common market.

Articles 169, 170, 171 and 93(2) all deal with cases that are brought before the European Court of Justice to check the compliance of Member States with Community law. However, the Court of Justice has other tasks as well, such as reviewing the legality of acts adopted by the Community institutions (Article 173), taking action if an institution fails to act (Article 175), or pleading for the inapplicability of a regulation (Article 184).

Article 173

"The Court of Justice shall review the legality of acts ... It shall for this purpose have jurisdiction in actions brought by a Member State, the Council or the Commission on grounds of lack of competence, infringement of an essential procedural requirement, infringement of this Treaty or of any rule of law relating to its application, or misuse of powers.

Any natural or legal entity may under the same conditions institute proceedings against a decision addressed to that person or against a decision which, although in the form of a regulation or a decision addressed to another person, is of direct and individual concern to the former."

According to Article 173, the Member States, the Council and the Commission have unlimited *locus standi*, which means they do not have to prove that they have an interest in bringing the proceedings. The European Parliament can bring an action to the Court to protect its own prerogatives. They are considered as privileged applicants. On the other hand, natural and legal persons are known as non-privileged applicants, meaning they can only take actions against decisions addressed to them. The applicants must show that the decision is of direct and individual concern to them or that a regulation is in reality a decision.

In the case of *Plaumann v. Commission*, the Court defined individual concern in the following way: "Persons other than those to whom a decision is addressed may only claim to be individually concerned if that decision affects them by reason of certain attributes which are peculiar to them or by reason of circumstances in which they are differentiated from all other persons and by virtue of these factors distinguishes them individually just as in the case of the person addressed." This definition has been used in many subsequent cases.

Four grounds of review are stipulated in Article 173

1) Lack of competence: this is the case when a Community institution passes a measure on an issue in a way that exceeds its power given by the Treaty.

2) Infringement of an essential procedural requirement: this ground comes into play if a measure has been passed although the correct legislative process was not applied.

3) Infringement of the Treaty or of any rule of law relating to its application.

4) Misuse of powers is defined as illegality, which occurs when a decision is taken for purposes other than those stated.

The actions of annulment must be instituted within two months of the publication of the measure, or of its notification to the plaintiff or, in absence thereof, of the day on which it came to the knowledge of the latter. This is a rather short time-limit but it can be extended in case "unforeseeable circumstances or force majeure (which) might have prevented the applicants from instituting proceedings within the prescribed period", (according to case 352/87 *Farzoo and Kartmann v. Commission*).

If the Court agrees with the action, it declares the measure or only part of a measure to be void.

Article 175

"Should the European Parliament, the Council or the Commission, in infringement of this Treaty, fail to act, the Member States and the other institutions of the Community may bring an action before the Court of Justice to have the infringement established."

The action can only be brought before the Court if the institution concerned has first been called upon to act. The institution has two months to define its position or take a decision. It can say that it is not going to act or that it is going to act in a different way than expected by the applicant.

If the Community institution concerned does not define its position, the action may be brought before the Court of Justice within a further period of two months. All the Court can demand is that the institution which failed to act according to the Treaty takes the necessary measure to comply with the judgement (Article 176).

Article 177

"The Court of Justice shall have jurisdiction to give preliminary rulings concerning:

a) the interpretation of this Treaty;
b) the validity and interpretation of acts of the institution of the Community and of the ECB;
c) the interpretation of the statutes of bodies established by an act of the Council, where the statutes so provide.

Where such a question is raised before any court or tribunal of a Member State, that court or tribunal may, if it considers that a decision on the question is necessary to enable it to give judgement, request the court of Justice to give a ruling thereon."

National courts and tribunals may request a decision from the Court on matters of Community law. The Court of Justice rules how provisions of Community law are to be understood so that the national court or tribunal can then reach its decision on its own case based on the Court's ruling.

The preliminary rulings stated in Article 177 make up half of the work of the Court. The average waiting period for the Court of Justice to decide is more than 17 months, which is definitely too long.

According to subparagraph (a), the Court can be asked questions on the interpretation of the EC Treaty. Subparagraph (b) leaves the scope of the Court's jurisdiction open when it speaks of "acts of the institutions of the Community". Evidently this refers to the legally binding provisions referred to in Article 189, i.e. regulations, directives and decisions. The Court reviews the validity and the interpretation of these acts. Subparagraph (c) is of no major importance.

Only a national court or a tribunal may request the Court to give a ruling. If, for instance, two contract partners decide to settle disputes between themselves by arbitration, then such a case cannot be referred to the Court of Justice according to Article 177 unless a national law requires to settle such disputes before it. The decisive factor is that the law or the public authorities can to a certain extent control the composition of such a body (see *Vaassen v. Beambtenfonds Mijnbedrijf*).

Although Article 177(2) requires that an ECJ ruling is required to enable the national court to give judgement, the Court of Justice has taken a liberal approach in the interpretation of this requirement. Based on the doctrine of a division of judicial functions between the ECJ and the national court or tribunal the latter is to assess whether a case or issue is to be heard by the ECJ and a preliminary ruling is sought.

The functions of both courts are clearly separated: the national courts investigate the facts of the case and the Court of Justice gives a ruling on how the Community law should be read and interpreted.

The third paragraph of Article 177 states that a national court against whose decision there is no judicial remedy under national law can bring a question concerning the interpretation of a Community provision before the Court of Justice.

Article 178

Articles 178 and 215(2) regulate the non-contractual liability. If an institution causes damage to a person the latter can bring an action for compensation before the Court of Justice.

Three requirements must be fulfilled for the Court to grant liability:

(i) The institution must have acted unlawfully.

(ii) The person bringing the action has to have suffered damage.

(iii) A direct link in the chain of causality must exist between the wrongful act and the damage caused.

The damage must be specified. If the parties do not agree on the amount of damages, the Court will impose an amount.

The plaintiff has five years time to take the action. The limitation period begins on the occurrence of the damaging event.

Article 179

"The Court of Justice shall have jurisdiction in any dispute between the Community and its servants within the limits and under the conditions laid down in the Staff Regulations or the Conditions of Employment".

Before a staff member takes his/her case to the Court of First Instance s/he has to run through an administrative procedure. The member of staff brings his/her complaint to the authority concerned, which has taken an action affecting him/her. The limitation period for an action under Article 179 amounts to three months. After the complaint has been tabled the authority has four months time within which it delivers a reasoned decision to the person concerned. If the authority rejects the complaint or does not reply to it the member of staff can file an appeal with the Court of First Instance.

An appeal can be lodged to the Court of Justiceagainst the decision of the Court of First Instance.

Article 180

This Article ensures that the European Investment Bank and the Member States in their activities with the Bank operate according to the provision of Community law. Furthermore, the European Central Bank (ECB) can take an action against a national central bank which has failed to fulfil an obligation under the EC Treaty. Before filing an action the ECB asks the national central bank to take position against the accusation of infringing a Community obligation. Upon receipt of the answer of the national central bank the ECB issues a reasoned opinion with which the national central bank must comply. If it does not adhere to the opinion, the ECB may bring an action before the Court of Justice.

Article 181

"The Court of Justice shall have jurisdiction to give judgement pursuant to any arbitration clause contained in a contract concluded by or on behalf of the Community, whether the contract be governed by public or private law."

It is up to the Community institutions whether they want to appoint the Court of Justice as arbitrator in any disputes which arise after a contract has been concluded. Such clauses are not agreed upon very often.

An arbitration clause must specify which state's law shall be applied in case of a dispute. Article 215(1) requires that "the contractual liability of the Community shall be governed by the law applicable to the contract in question."

Article 182

According to this Article disputes between Member States can be carried out before the Court of Justice if the parties have a special agreement which makes the Court competent for such arbitration cases. Article 182 has been used only once so far because disputes between Member States usually fall under Article 170.

AVERAGE LENGTH OF PROCEEDINGS (including judical vacations)[1]

	1992	1993
Court of Justice		
References for a preliminary ruling	18,8 months	20,4 months
Direct actions	25,8 months	22,9 months
Appeals	17,5 months	19,2 months
Special procedures	2,7 months	
Court of First Instance		
Direct actions		23,3 months
Staff cases		17,0 months

[1] The figures relating to the average length of proceedings have been arrived at by calculating only the cases brought to an end by judgements and excluding cases where the proceedings have been formally stayed.

Proceedings of the Court of Justice and Court of First Instance of the European Communities

FISGRAFX

CHAPTER 9: THE ECONOMIC AND SOCIAL COMMITTEE

The Economic and Social Committee consists of representatives of the various categories of economic and social activity, in particular representatives of manufacturers, farmers, carriers, workers, dealers, craftsmen, professional occupations and representatives of the general public.

Belgium	12	Ireland	9
Denmark	9	Italy	24
Germany	24	Luxembourg	6
Greece	12	Netherlands	12
Spain	21	Portugal	12
France	24	United Kingdom	24

The members of the Committee are appointed by the Council for a period of four years. They may be reappointed for a second term. The members are independent. Before they are appointed by the Council every Member State will submit a list containing twice as many candidates as the amount of seats the state is granted. When the members of the Committee are appointed a balance between employers and employees must be kept.

The Committee elects its chairman and officers from among its members for a term of two years. The chairman convenes the Committee at the request of the Council or the Commission. The Committee may also meet on its own initiative.

Specialized sections have been established, i.e. an agricultural section and a transport section. They operate within the general terms of reference of the Committee but they may not be consulted independently of the Committee.

Sub-committees can be set up to prepare on specific questions or in specific fields and draft opinions to be submitted to the Committee for its consideration.

The Economic and Social Committee must be consulted by the Council or by the Commission where the Treaty provides for it; it must be consulted

* when the Council adopts provisions for the harmonization of legislation concerning turnover taxes, excise duties and other forms of indirect taxation (Article 99);
* when the Council adopts incentive measures in the field of public health (Article 129);
* when the Council adopts specific action which supports and supplements the policy pursued by the Member States to protect the health, safety and economic interests of consumers (Article 129a);
* in the fields of industry, economic and social cohesion as well as research and technological development.

In other cases the Council or the Commission may - if they consider it appropriate - consult the Committee. Whenever necessary a time limit may be set within which the Committee must submit its opinion. The time limit may not be less than one month from the date on which the chairman receives notification of it. The Committee and the specialized section each forward their opinion to the Council and the Commission.

The Economic and Social Committee is a purely advisory body and it is rather difficult to judge its influence on the legislative process.

CHAPTER 10: THE COMMITTEE OF THE REGIONS

The Committee of the Regions was established by the Maastricht Treaty. The 189 members of the Committee are representatives of regional and local bodies with advisory function.

The members of the Committee are appointed by the Council, acting unanimously. Their term of office is renewable. They must be completely independent in the performance of their duties and may not be bound by any mandatory instructions.

The Council and the Commission must consult the Committee of the Regions where the Treaty so provides and in all other cases in which one of these two institutions considers it appropriate. This is the case

* in adopting measures on education, vocational training and youth (Article 126);
* in taking steps concerning cultural aspects in the Community (Article 128);
* when the Council takes measures ensuring a high level of human health protection (Article 129);
* when the Council decides on specific measures ensuring the competitiveness of the Community's industry (Article 129d);
* in the field of economic and social cohesion (Article 130b).

Within this procedure the Council or the Commission can impose a time-limit of not less than one month on the Committee. If the Committee does not submit an opinion upon expiry of the time-limit, the absence of an opinion does not prevent further action.

The Committee of the Regions may also issue an opinion on its own initiative in cases in which it considers such action appropriate.

CHAPTER 11: THE EUROPEAN INVESTMENT BANK

The European Investment Bank is governed by Articles 198d and 198e EC Treaty. It has legal personality and consists of the Member States. Its task is "to contribute to the balanced and steady development of the common market in the interest of the Community". The Bank operates on a non-profit-making basis, grants loans and gives guarantees which facilitate the financing of projects in all sectors of the economy. They include

* projects for developing less-developed regions;
* projects for modernizing or converting undertakings;
* projects of common interest to several Member States which are of such a size or nature that they cannot be entirely financed by the various means available in the Member States.

"In carrying out its task, the Bank shall facilitate the financing of investment programmes in conjunction with assistance from the structural funds and other Community financial investments."

The Bank can borrow money on the capital markets and lend it to private and public undertakings. Most of the loans are granted for projects within the Community, but some are meant to provide aid to other countries all over the world. The loans are used to finance infrastructure and industrial and agricultural projects in the Mediterranean countries, the countries of Africa, the Caribbean and the Pacific. The Bank's financial aid to the countries of Central and Eastern Europe, especially Hungary and Poland but also the Czech Republic, Bulgaria and Romania is of great importance.

CHAPTER 12: THE COURT OF AUDITORS

The Court of Auditors was established by the Treaty of 22 July 1975 and took up its work in 1977. Since the Treaty of Maastricht, the Court of Auditors has been governed in its own section, Articles 188a, b and c EC Treaty.

The Court consists of twelve members who are unanimously appointed for a term of six years by the Council. Reappointment is possible. However, four members of the Court of Auditors, chosen by lot, are appointed for a term of office of four years only. From among its members the Court of Auditors elects a President for a term of three years. The President may be re-elected, too.

The requirements for becoming a member of the Court of Auditors are special qualifications for this office or previous work in an audit body in the respective countries. The members' independence must be beyond doubt. During the performance of their duties they may neither seek nor take instructions from any government or from any other body.

A member of the Court of Auditors may be deprived of his/her office or of his/her right to a pension or other benefits only if the Court of Justice, at the request of the Court of Auditors, finds that s/he no longer fulfils the requisite conditions or meets the obligations arising from his/her office.

The Court examines the accounts of all revenue and expenditure of the Community and its bodies. It checks whether all Community receipts have been collected and expenditure incurred in a lawful and regular manner and whether the financial management has been sound.

The Court of Auditors can extend its investigations into the Member States where it can work in cooperation with national audit bodies or with the competent national departments on such issues as the collection of customs duties or the expenditure on agriculture.

At the end of each financial year the Court draws up an annual report. It is published in the Official Journal of the European Communities, together with the replies of the other institutions of the Community to the annual report.

The Court may also undertake observations on individual or special issues and then submit a special report. It may also deliver opinions at the request of one of the other institutions of the Community. The annual reports, special reports or opinions are adopted by a majority of the Court members. The Court of Auditors assists the European Parliament and the Council in exercising their powers of control over the implementation of the budget.

PART THREE - PRIMARY SOURCES OF EC LAW

CHAPTER 13: INTRODUCTION

The Community's legislation can be compared to the legal structure of a democratic country: a constitution establishing the legal foundation and a system of laws based thereupon. The constitutional documents of the Community are the Treaty that established the European Community and all of its amendments, the Treaty that established the European Coal and Steel Community and the Treaty on the European Atomic Energy Community Treaty. According to these Treaties, the Council and the Commission are supposed to make regulations, issue directives, take decisions, make recommendations, or deliver opinions (Article 189 EEC Treaty, Article 161 Euratom Treaty, and Article 14 Treaty on Coal and Steel Community). Regulations, directives, decisions, recommendations, and opinions are considered as secondary legislation.

Several leading principles characterize the Community. They are of a general nature but have provided guidelines for establishing the Common Market and are helpful in legislation. Other primary sources of EC law are Community external treaties such as the Lomé Conventions, GATT, and the agreements with EFTA. The European Community and EFTA joined to establish the European Economic Area (see chapter on the European Economic Area and relations with EFTA).

CHAPTER 14: CONSTITUTIONAL PRINCIPLES

Economic integration of Europe is the first goal to be achieved. This is why most of the provisions of the EC Treaty concern the elimination of customs duties and quantitative restrictions on the import and export of goods. Furthermore, the Treaty pursues the establishment of the four freedoms as stated in Article 3c:

free movement of goods

free movement of persons

free movement of services

free movement of capital

These four freedoms are essential for the setting up of a well functioning European market that is not limited by national borders.

The free movement of goods is the most important of the four freedoms and has produced a significant number of cases. Based on Articles 12 and 95 EC, fiscal trade barriers have been reduced or even abolished between Member States (see chapter on taxation and single market). Article 30 prohibits quantitative restrictions on imports between Member States. The term "quantitative restriction" is well known in international trade law, meaning that a state will only import a certain amount of a commodity from another country to protect its own commodity of the same kind. These numerical limits are a more vigorous instrument because they ban trade completely instead of making imported goods more expensive. An absolute ban on importation is also established by Article 30.

The Article also states that "measures having equivalent effect" to quantitative restriction (MEQR) are forbidden and must be abolished. The meaning of this expression was rather difficult to determine until - in 1974 - MEQR was subject to a ruling of the European Court. In the case *Procureur du Roi v. Dassonville*, the Court defined MEQRs as "all trading rules enacted by Member States which are capable of hindering, directly or indirectly, actually or potentially, inter-Community trade". According to this definition, the restrictive effect of the national regulation is the decisive factor and not its form. Many of the Court's rulings concern Article 30.

The free movement of persons can be applied to workers (Article 48) and self-employed persons (Article 52), who may establish themselves in any Member State. Workers may accept offers of employment, move freely within the territory of Member States for this purpose, stay in a Member State for the purpose of employment in accordance with the provisions governing the employment of nationals of that State, and remain in the territory of a Member State after having been employed there. In the case *R v. IAT* the Court ruled that there is a right of entry and residence in order to look for work. Limitations are justified on grounds of public policy, public security, and public health. Article 48 does not apply to employment in public service. Such barriers must be interpreted narrowly, even those concerning the other freedoms. Many workers in the EC- several millions - are not nationals of a Member State and therefore cannot claim rights from Article 48.

The free movement of persons also includes the right of establishment (Article 52), which is the right to take up and pursue activities as self-employed persons and to set up and manage undertakings, in particular companies or firms. The right of establishment must be compared to the right to provide *services* within the Community pursuant to Article 59 because a distinction between the two is often difficult to make. Articles 52 and 59 are directly effective (see *Reyners v. Belgian State*) but many directives amplifying these rights have also been passed.

The free movement of capital is fundamental to the establishment of market integration. Capital is a key factor of production and its movements are closely connected to the national economic policies of the Member States. Due to the different currencies in the Community, free movement could harm the proper functioning of the common market. Sudden flows of considerable amounts of capital could affect national economies and economic policies of Member States.The movement of capital is freed only "to the extent necessary to ensure the proper functioning of the common market". This makes Article 67 not directly effective. According to Article 69, it was up to the Council to issue the necessary directives for the progressive implementation of the free movement of capital. However, the Court did not make much progress because many States would not loosen their strict exchange controls.

A distinction must be made between the movement of capital and the movement of payments. As mentioned before, the movement of capital can be restricted because of the close connection to the economic and monetary policy of the Member States. Money transactions arising out of tourism or travel for business purposes are considered as movement of payments and are treated in a similar manner as the other key freedoms.

These four freedoms are of such fundamental importance to the common market that they can be considered as Community principles. However, they were not sufficient to make the customs union become reality. In addition, supporting measures were introduced: prohibition of discrimination on grounds of nationality (Article 6), regulations against the distortion of competition, a ban on subsidies, and the alignment of laws and economic policies.

A further constitutional principle is that of *subsidiarity*, which has already been mentioned in Chapter 4.

Article 3b EC refers to the subsidiarity principle in three paragraphs. The first paragraph does not bring anything new, as the Community has always been able to act only in those fields in which the Treaty is a legal basis for its actions.

The second paragraph is the subsidiarity principle itself:

> In areas which do not fall within its exclusive competence, the Community shall take action, in accordance with the principle of subsidiarity, only if and in so far as the objectives of the proposed action cannot be sufficiently achieved by the Member States and can therefore, [...], be better achieved by the Community.

The Commission issued some guidelines on how a matter should be examined and put into the competence of the Member States or of the Community. If a matter falls clearly into the exclusive competence of the Community, the subsidiarity principle cannot be applied.

The third paragraph of 3b EC states:

> Any action by the Community shall not go beyond what is necessary to achieve the objectives of this Treaty.

This paragraph is based on the principle of *proportionality*, which has been developed by the Court of Justice. Whenever the Community takes action, the measures should be proportionate to the objective to be achieved and burdens should be minimized. Regulations should not be used when a directive is sufficient. Detailed measures are not necessary in those matters where framework directives will achieve the objective. This shows a tendency to stray away from detailed Community law and to move towards looser measures. Now, before the Commission proposes any legislation, it must go through a wider consulting process to ensure that the proposed measures conform with the principle of subsidiarity. The Commission is even obliged to submit an annual report to the European Council and the European Parliament on matters where the subsidiarity principle was applied.

Community law has *direct effect* on the Member States and even on its courts. This was the European Court's ruling in the case *Van Gend en Loos*: the Dutch government increased the customs duty on a specific chemical being imported into the Netherlands. Van Gend en Loos objected to paying the higher rate, as it was inconsistent with Article 12 EC, and went to court. The court requested a preliminary ruling from the European Court according to Article 177 as to whether Article 12 was directly applicable to individuals. The Court's opinion was that the Treaty had created a new legal system which "not only imposes obligations on individuals" but also confers rights upon them. The EC Treaty is not just an international agreement but also the constitutional charter of a Community based on the rule of law. The European Court ruled that the imposed increase in the customs duty had been unlawful and that Van Gend en Loos did not have to pay the increased amount. Since this decision of the Court, individuals can refer to the direct effect of Treaty provisions on other individuals and even on a Member State.

CHAPTER 15: CONSTITUTIONAL DOCUMENTS

This chapter on constitutional documents is more of a summary in combination with a few new aspects, since the treaties establishing the European Community have been dealt with in detail in the first three chapters.

The most important constitutional document is the Treaty establishing the European Economic Community. It is divided into six parts stipulating the principles, the citizenship of the Union, Community policies, the Association of Overseas Countries and Territories, the institutions of the community, and general and final provisions. In 1987, the Single European Act came into effect, extending the applicability of qualified majority voting, increasing the Parliament's influence, and introducing new Community powers. The Treaty on European Union brought additional changes to the Treaty of Rome and a new element, separate from the legal order of the Community. The new element is based on a Common Foreign and Security Policy as well as on Justice and Home Affairs. Article G of the Treaty on European Union amended large parts of the EEC Treaty. Articles 102a-109m are especially important because they establish a timetable for progress towards economic and monetary union. Maastricht also altered the name from EEC to EC, i.e. the treaty established the European Community.

The first constitutional document was the Treaty establishing the European Coal and Steel Community (ECSC) in 1951, also known as the Treaty of Paris. It has not undergone similarly major amendments as the EEC Treaty for the simple reason that it lost importance once the Economic Community had been founded. The second Treaty of Rome established a European Atomic Energy Community (Euratom) in 1958. Its scope of activities was very limited compared to the activities of the EEC.

Further constitutional documents are:

* Treaty of 25 March 1957 for a joint European Parliament, a joint Economic and Social Committee and a joint Court of Justice
* Merger Treaty of 8 April 1965 for a joint Council and a joint Commission
* Treaty of Accession of Denmark, Ireland and the UK to the EEC of 1972
* Treaty of Accession of Greece of 1981
* Treaty of Accession of Portugal and Spain of 1986.

CHAPTER 16: COMMUNITY EXTERNAL TREATIES

"The Community shall have legal personality" (Article 210 EC). According to international law, the Community is also regarded as a legal person. This status can be recognized by other states either directly or indirectly. In practice, this is usually done by taking up diplomatic relations with the EC. Today more than 120 missions are accredited to the EC.

It is not sure how far the Community's ability to act reaches but according to the implied powers theory, it has the competence for all external cases in those matters for which it is competent within the Community. So there is a parallel between internal and external competence. The negotiations with the states or international organizations are conducted by the Commission. The agreements are concluded by the Council (Article 228).

As the EEC was established in 1958, the six founding countries were already members of the General Agreement on Tariffs and Trade (*GATT*). GATT has been in use since 1 January 1948 and includes more than 80 per cent of world trade. Many of the former bilateral trade agreements have been replaced by the multilateral GATT regulations. According to Article XXIV GATT, all agreements on the establishment of free trade areas or customs unions must comply with GATT law and especially follow the very detailed GATT regulations on non-discrimination of trade competition. GATT itself is not yet in effect; it is only "in use for the time being".

The ECSC has left the competence of foreign trade policy in matters of coal and steel with its Members. It established a common market for coal and steel which is neither a free trade area nor a customs union. The ECSC managed to attain an exception (a so-called "waiver") from several GATT duties according to Article XXV:5 GATT.

After signing the EEC Treaty the six Member States notified GATT before ratifying it according to Article XXIV:7(a) GATT. The EEC countries assured "that as long as the six would remain contracting parties to the General Agreement they would scrupulously observe their obligations under this Agreement." The EC Treaty itself stipulates in several regulations that the established customs union and the common trade policy of the EC (Articles 110-116) must be carried out in compliance with GATT. According to Article 234 EC Treaty, "rights and obligations arising from agreements concluded before the entry into force of this Treaty between one or more

Member States on the one hand, and one or more third countries on the other, shall not be affected by the provisions of this Treaty". And Article 229 EC Treaty determines that the Commission shall ensure "the maintenance of all appropriate relations with the organs ... of the General Agreement on Tariffs and Trade".

The twelve Member States of the Community have - pursuant to international law - kept their membership in GATT. Since the Dillon Round (1960/1961), the Commission is represented in almost all GATT organs (like a party to the Treaty) and exercises most of the rights and duties of the EC Member States in the name of the EC. The Commission is not represented in the budget committee because all contributions to the budget of GATT are paid by the Member States. This double-membership of the EC and its Member States has not led to any difficulties so far.

Many regulations, directives and decisions have been passed by the EC for the implementation of GATT law; they must be interpreted in a way which is compatible with GATT law. The question whether a citizen of the EC may refer to obedience of explicit GATT duties before a court is only then of importance when the relevant GATT regulations have not been taken over into Community law. The European Court of Justice and the Member States reject the direct effectiveness of GATT although GATT itself does not mention anything about it.

Apart from numerous bilateral agreements with developing countries the EC has concluded multilateral treaties with states of the Third World, of which the Lomé Conventions with the ACP countries - countries of Africa, the Caribbean and the Pacific - are the most important ones.

On 20 July 1963, the first Yaoundé Convention was agreed on between the EEC, eighteen African countries and Madagascar; in 1969, it was replaced by the second Yaoundé Convention. These two conventions only concerned the francophile African states, but in 1968 and 1969 they were expanded by the two Arusha Conventions with the anglophile African countries. In 1975, the first Lomé Convention (Lomé I) was concluded, which contained the four mentioned treaties plus an agreement with 46 ACP countries. In 1979, Lomé II replaced Lomé I and since 8 December 1984, Lomé III has been in effect.

In comparison with other multilateral agreements, Lomé III is the most intensive form of economic cooperation between the EC and the developing countries. Goals of these cooperation conventions are both the support and acceleration of the economic, cultural and social development of the ACP states as well as the extension and diversification of relations between the EC and the ACP countries. This model of cooperation is intended to create a more just and balanced economic order between industrial and developing countries. The main areas of cooperation are agriculture and industrial development. A further important goal is the increase of self-sufficiency in the food sector. Many ACP countries export agricultural goods and raw materials.

Not only the trade relations between the EC and the ACP states are supported by Lomé but also those between ACP countries. Almost all goods originating in the ACP countries are exempt from customs duties or any charges having equivalent effect when imported into the Community. (99 per cent of the commercial and 95 per cent of the agricultural goods.) Only a few agricultural products are subject to small restrictions. On the other hand, the ACP countries are not obliged to grant similar concessions for goods coming from the EC. Only if serious disturbances occur on the Community's market, may it impose preventive measures. A system to stabilize the export proceeds of 44 agricultural products (STABEX) has been established as well as a balance and aid system for mining products (SYSMIN).

Most of the financial aid is granted by the European Development Fund. Credits are given by the European Investment Bank. The total amount of aid for the ACP countries came to 8.5 billion ECU by 1990. Technical cooperation contains different forms of advice, studies and administrative services. In the field of industrial cooperation a centre for industrial development has been set up. Regular payments and the movement of capital shall not be obstructed by foreign exchange restrictions. Bodies of the Convention are the Council of Ministers, the Committee of Ambassadors, and the Assembly.

According to Article 238 EC Treaty, the "Community may conclude with one or more states or international organizations agreements establishing an association involving reciprocal rights and obligations, common action and special procedure". Such agreements usually establish free trade zones or customs unions and sometimes only regulations for economic and financial cooperation.

The association with European states is usually a preparatory stage for a later accession to the Community. Such association agreements have been concluded with Cyprus, Malta and Turkey. Many have been set up with non-European countries, mostly under the aspect of foreign aid, e.g. Algeria, Egypt, Israel, Jordan, Lebanon, Morocco, Syria and Tunisia.

CHAPTER 17: RELATIONS WITH EFTA - THE EUROPEAN FREE TRADE ASSOCIATION

In 1960, the European Free Trade Association (EFTA) was established by Austria, Denmark, Norway, Portugal, Sweden, Switzerland and the United Kingdom. It was not only considered a reaction to the economic disadvantages expected from not being members of the European Economic Community but also a basis for a future membership as well as for arrangements for a free trade association with the EEC. Later on Iceland joined EFTA, and Finland associated with the Association, while Denmark, Portugal and the UK became members of the EEC.

Goals of EFTA are: the increase in economic activity between the Member States, full employment, increase in productivity, financial stability, steady improvement of the standard of living and just competition conditions. When comparing EFTA with other economic organizations it can be noticed that its structure is rather simple: the EFTA Council as a representative body is responsible for the implementation of the agreement and is the highest decision authority when it comes to solving disputes between members. All decisions must be taken unanimously by all EFTA member states. The office and a number of committees and working groups are further bodies of EFTA. EFTA's seat is in Geneva.

Object of EFTA is the gradual reduction of customs and quantitative restrictions on industrial and commercial products. Agriculture and fishing are, however, exempt from this free trade system. The export customs duties were already removed by January 1962.

A number of protective clauses to protect the free trade zone against disturbances and competition distortion were introduced. Such precautionary measures can be taken by any member state in the interest of its public morality and in order to prevent disturbances of public safety as well as in case of dumping practices.

EFTA's competition policy is oriented towards the prevention of public and private restraints of trade. Taxes and customs to protect products from foreign competition were removed step by step. State subsidies are forbidden.

Relations between EFTA and EEC

In the 1970s, the EFTA states of Austria, Iceland, Norway, Sweden, Switzerland and the associated state of Finland concluded several free trade agreements with the EEC and the ECSC but none with Euratom. There were also bilateral agreements and agreements between EFTA and the EEC as economic organizations. Effective 1 July 1977, seventeen Western European countries formed an extensive free trade organization in which the trade with goods was fully liberalized in 1984.

CHAPTER 18: EEA - THE EUROPEAN ECONOMIC AREA

In the late 1980s, it became clear that the European Community would complete the common market by 1993. The EFTA countries feared serious disadvantages in trade with the Community, its most important trade partner. For this reason solutions were searched for. In 1984, the ministers of the then 16 EEC and EFTA states suggested the creation of a European Economic Area. Jacques Delors, President of the Commission, brought this idea up again in a speech before the European Parliament in 1989. From the point of view of the EEC this improved form of association might prevent potential candidates from applying for accession. Some EFTA countries considered this offer as the golden mean between isolation and full membership, allowing them to participate in the internal market.

Negotiations were taken up in 1990 but turned out to be difficult and were often in danger of breaking off. Originally, the negotiations should have been finished before the summer of 1991, but several questions of political importance - e.g. differences in the question of fishing, financial contributions of EFTA and the bilateral transit negotiations - delayed the completion. By November 1991 all issues had been agreed upon. However, several weeks later, on 14 December 1991, the European Court published an expert report that labelled the EEA jurisdiction as not compatible with EC law. The Court considered it impossible that the planned EEA Court would take decisions influencing the EC's jurisdiction. This made new negotiations necessary and delayed the conclusion of the agreement once more. Eventually, the agreement was signed on 2 May 1992 in Porto.

After the signing the EEA Treaty had to be approved by the national parliaments of the EFTA member states and by the European Parliament. In Liechtenstein and Switzerland plebiscites had to be carried out. The Swiss plebiscite did not achieve the required majority. At a diplomatic conference of all EEA member states all changes were made to adapt the agreement after Switzerland had dropped out. The EEA Treaty came into effect on 1 January 1994, one year later than scheduled. Members of the EEA are Belgium, Denmark, France, Germany, Great Britain, Greece, Italy, Ireland, Luxembourg, the Netherlands, Portugal, and Spain (EC), Austria, Finland, Iceland, Liechtenstein, Norway and Sweden (EFTA).

The European Economic Area constitutes an improved and more specialized free trade area compared to the former association agreements between the EC and EFTA states. It is the largest economic area of the world in which 40 per cent of the world's trade take place. The EEA includes 380 million consumers.

EEA Institutions

As regards institutions, the agreement names the EEA Council, the EEA Joint Committee, the EEA Parliamentary Joint Committee and the EEA Consultative Committee. An EFTA Court and an EFTA Surveillance Authority have been established by an EFTA internal agreement on 2 May 1992. In addition, a Permanent Committee for the EFTA states has been created in which the EFTA countries are to coordinate their positions before taking up work in the EEA Joint Committee. The Parliamentary Committee of the EFTA states advises them in all EEA matters.

The EEA Council (Article 89 EEA) consists of members of the EC Council, members of the Commission and a member of each EFTA member state government. Its function is to determine the political guidelines, to give new impetus for the implementation of the agreement and to take political decisions concerning the amendment of the Treaty. The EEA Council takes its decisions by mutual agreement between the EC and EFTA member states.

The EEA Joint Committee is in charge of the effective implementation and application of the agreement and takes the decisions on the extension of new Community legislation to the EEA. It consists of representatives of both parties to the Treaty and makes its decisions by consensus between the Community and the EFTA states.

The EEA Parliamentary Joint Committee (Article 95 EEA Treaty) contributes to a better communication between the EC and the EFTA states in all matters which fall under this agreement. It does not, however, have any supervisory or decisive rights although it may express its views in the form of reports or resolutions. The EEA Parliamentary Joint Committee is composed of 33 members of the European Parliament and 33 members of the parliaments of the EFTA states. The President of the EEA Council may appear before the EEA Parliamentary Joint Committee in order to be heard by it.

The EEA Consultative Committee (Article 96 EEA Treaty) brings social partners together in order to support the awareness of the economic and social aspects of the growing reciprocal interdependence of the national economies and the interests of the parties to the Treaty within the EEA. It is composed of an equal number of members of the Economic and Social Committee and the EFTA Consultative Committee.

The Agreement on the European Economic Area seeks to strengthen the trade and business relations between the 18 EEA member states to establish a uniform economic area. On the basis of Community law, the EEA extends the four fundamental freedoms of the EC to the six EFTA states. Furthermore, cooperation in various fields is planned, e.g. environment, education, social policy, research and development.

In order to achieve similar conditions for the internal market in the EEA, the substantive EEA regulations must correspond to the EC legislation ("mirror legislation"). This has led to a take-over of all relevant primary and secondary EC legislation. However, as the EEA is only a free trade zone, not all of the acquis communautaire will be taken over. In addition, it was agreed that the EC agriculture and fishing policies as well as the harmonization of tax laws would not be matters falling under the EEA Treaty.

The EEA is not a customs union, which means that the border checks are not completely removed and the present tax frontiers remain. The *Cassis de Dijon* principle is applicable in the EEA: any commodity produced anywhere in the EEA may be sold in every EEA member state unless specific requirements stand in the way, e.g. for health or environmental reasons (free movement of goods).

Regulations of the EEA Treaty concerning the movement of workers (Article 28 EEA Treaty) and the freedom of establishment (Article 31 EEA Treaty) are to a large extent identical with those of the EC Treaty. Thus, any discrimination due to nationality between citizens of the EC or EFTA with regard to employment, payment or other working conditions must be abolished. Every EEA citizen may move freely in the sovereign territory of an EC or EFTA member state to apply for a job and also to be gainfully employed. This freedom does not apply to employment in the public sector.

Every citizen of an EEA country may establish him/herself as a self-employed person in any other EC or EFTA state, as long as s/he fulfils the requirements for such occupations in the relevant country. The right of residence also applies to students, retired people and those who are not economically active.

The EEA regulations which concern the freedom of services are very similar to the regulations of Articles 59, 60 and 61 EC Treaty. The possibility of providing or claiming services in the commercial, industrial, technical or self-employed field must not be submitted to restrictions depending on discrimination. For this reason the regulations on recognition of diplomas and exam certificates may be used to lighten the implementation of this freedom. Thus, every EEA citizen may conclude an insurance or claim bank services completely independent of his/her domicile.

The free movement of capital forbids any restrictions for natural or legal persons (within the EEA). It includes direct investments, investments in real estate and transactions with stocks, shares and loans. The cooperation goes beyond the four fundamental freedoms, e.g. it also covers social policy, consumer protection and environmental protection.

PART FOUR - SECONDARY SOURCES OF EC LAW

CHAPTER 19: LEGISLATION

"In order to carry out their task and in accordance with the provisions of this Treaty, the European Parliament acting jointly with the Council, the Council and the Commission shall make regulations and issue directives, take decisions, make recommendations or deliver opinions." (Article 189 EC)

The different types of legislation are used for different purposes depending on what the institution wants to regulate, how important the matter is and to whom it is directed. In important matters, for instance, the Commission would issue a regulation to bind all Member States. In other cases a directive may be sufficient if only one Member State or even only one or more undertakings are concerned. Thus, the form of legislation depends entirely on the subject matter. Most of the provisions in the Treaty stipulate which form is to be used. In some cases the institution may even have a choice. The effect of the Court's decisions on Community legislation is very interesting and important. In several judgements, the Court has explained how a certain provision of the Treaty is to be understood.

CHAPTER 20: REGULATIONS

"A regulation shall have general application. It shall be binding in its entirety and directly applicable in all Member States" (Article 189 EC).
The Council, the Commission, and the European Parliament acting jointly with the Council have jurisdiction to pass regulations The Commission may exercise the powers conferred on it by the Council for implementation of the rules laid down by the latter by issuing regulations (Article 155 EC).

The fact that the regulation has general application is indicated by its generally abstract character. The wording "[...] shall be binding in its entirety [...]" is not intended to emphasize the binding character of the regulation but rather to show the difference between regulations on the one side and directives and decisions on the other side. The statement that regulations are "[...] directly applicable in all Member States" means that they are automatically part of each national legal system without a necessity of any implementing legislation. Regulations are the most powerful part of Community legislation because they become part of the national legal systems without any intervention by the national governments. All regulations must be published in the Official Journal of the Community. According to Article 191 EC, regulations enter into force on the date specified in them or, if there is no date mentioned, on the twentieth day following that of their publication.

The political institutions are often given a choice as to whether they should pass a regulation, a directive or a decision. Usually, it is the Commission who exercises this right to choose. The EC Treaty names only three occasions on which regulations must be used:

(i) regulations embodying the conditions according to which people may remain in the territory of a Member State after having been employed in that state (Article 483d EC),
(ii) regulations relating to state aids (Article 94 EC), and
(iii) financial regulations specifying in particular the procedure to be adopted for establishing and implementing the budget and for presenting and auditing accounts (Article 209a).

A very good example is Regulation 17/62, designed to give effect to the principles of Articles 85 and 86. This regulation enables the Commission to apply and administer the competition rules and to observe their uniform use in every Member State of the Community. Most sectors of the economy, except for air and sea transport, are now controlled.

The Commission may initiate an investigation or wait until Member States or natural or legal persons apply to it to take action. Natural or legal persons must claim a legitimate interest. The Commission has interpreted the term "legitimate interest" very broadly so that complaints from rival firms, consumer representative organizations and customers are accepted. It may, however, happen that the Commission declines to pursue the complaint. In such a case the Commission must name the reasons for the refusal of the complaint. In practice, the complainant then pursues the matter under Article 173.

If a company is suspected of acting in violation of the competition rules, the Commission may investigate by requesting information or even visiting such company. The regulation confers on the Commission the power to investigate sectors of the economy which are suspected of anticompetitive conduct. The business enterprise is given the possibility to comply with the competition rules. Otherwise the Commission will move to the formal stage of procedure, where hearings can be held and fines can be imposed.

Regulation 1612/68, regarding the workers' right to free movement within the Community, is also of importance. It is divided into three titles dealing with eligibility for employment (Articles 1-6), employment and equality of treatment (Articles 7-9), and workers' families (Articles 10-12). The first title repeats the principle that jobs are open equally to nationals of all Member States. Exceptions can be made where the particular post requires linguistic competence. The second title determines that the conditions of employment taken up must be the same for everybody. Furthermore, the migrant "shall enjoy the same social and tax advantages as national workers". This covers equal availability of benefits arising outside the contract of employment. Equal access to housing and equality of membership of and participation in trade unions are stressed, too. The third title of the regulation confers rights to family members of the worker. The spouse, descendants under 21 or dependants may migrate with the worker and settle in the state in which s/he is employed.

Two more regulations worth mentioning are:

Regulation 1251/70, which covers the right of a worker to remain permanently in a Member State after having been employed there. This regulation applies to workers who have retired and workers who are no longer able to work as well as to frontier workers. This right covers family members in the same way as Regulation 1612/68.

The Merger Control Regulation (4064/89), which provides rules for the event that two or more previously independent undertakings merge. Large mergers are controlled at Community level, smaller mergers are regulated by national authorities.

CHAPTER 21: DIRECTIVES

"A directive shall be binding, as to the result to be achieved, upon each Member State to which it is addressed, but shall leave to the national authorities the choice of form and methods" (Article 189 EC).
A directive is not necessarily addressed to all Member States; it may only apply to one EC state. The countries may choose the form and methods of implementing the directive in their national laws. The directives are binding as far as the result that is to be achieved is concerned.

The EEC Treaty did not require that directives be published in the Official Journal but only required that those Member States be notified to whom they were addressed. Since Maastricht, directives which are addressed to all Member States must be published in the Official Journal of the Community. According to Article 191(2) EC, directives enter into force on the date specified in them or, if no date is specified, on the twentieth day following that of their publication. If a Member State fails to implement the directive within the specified period of time, individuals or legal persons may nevertheless rely on the provisions of the directive.

In some cases, the Treaty leaves open the choice of form of legislation to the institutions, in others it determines exactly whether a regulation or a directive must be used. Sometimes directives are more appropriate to achieve the result, e.g. when harmonization rather than uniformity is intended.

The following table shows how long it takes the individual Member States to implement the directives applicable to them.

IMPLEMENTATION OF DIRECTIVES AS AT 31 DECEMBER 1990

Member state	Directives applicable	Directives acted upon	Percentage
Belgium	889	816	91.8
Denmark	872	842	96.5
France	885	828	93.5
Germany	886	845	95.4
Greece	907	775	85.4
Ireland	862	787	91.3
Italy	884	723	81.8
Luxembourg	874	788	90.2
Netherlands	895	834	93.2
Portugal	917	771	84.1
Spain	885	828	93.5
United Kingdom	852	806	94.5

Source: Eigth Annual Report to the European Parliament on Commission Monitoring of the Application of Coummunity Law 1990 (1991) Com(91) 321, Annex B.

FISGRAFX

Appended below we have listed a few examples of directives.

Directive 64/221 contains provisions specifying the principle of the free movement of workers determined in Article 48(3) EC. It also includes derogations from the principle, defining the nature of public policy, public security and public health. This directive limits the possibilities of Member States that are trying to refer to exceptions. All diseases or disabilities which may cause the refusal of entry or of granting a residence permit are enumerated in directive 64/221 as an exception to the principle of free movement of workers for reasons of public health. The personal conduct of an individual may limit the right of free movement due to public security. Previous criminal records may not lead to a limitation of his/her rights.

Directive 68/360 covers the function of authorities with regard to the rules on free movement. Rights of entry, residence and equal treatment derive directly from the EC Treaty but must be proved. A Member State may therefore ask the migrant for relevant documents - identity card or passport - which prove his/her citizenship of an EC country. An authority may not require visas except if a family member of a worker is not a national of a Member State. A worker who produces these documents must be granted the right of residence and a residence permit must be issued. The residence permit is proof of the right of residence. It is usually valid for five years, automatically renewed after expiry and may be used throughout the territory of the issuing state.

Directive 70/50, based on Article 33(7) EEC, focuses on Article 30 EC. It describes measures passed by a Member State which favour home produced goods to imported products. Article 2 of the directive lists such possible measures, nineteen altogether, e.g. rules demanding that imported goods must show a certain size or shape and rules fixing the prices on imports, etc. Initially, this directive was thought to last only for a certain period of time, applying to measures which were abolished at the end of 1969. However, it has proved to be very useful in understanding the nature and purpose of Article 30, so the Court still refers to it in its judgements. .

Directive 90/366 grants students, their spouses and dependent children the right to reside in the host state as long as the student is enrolled in vocational training courses at recognized educational institutions. This directive applies only to those students who earn their living themselves so that they do not become a financial burden for the state.

Directive 90/365 goes in the same direction as directive 90/366. It grants the right of residence to those who have stopped their occupational activity.

In several provisions, the Treaty stipulates the use of directives:

* Articles 54, 56(2): directives to be issued on the freedom of establishment;
* Article 57: directives to be issued on the mutual recognition of diplomas, certificates and other formal qualifications to make it easier for persons to take up and pursue activities as self-employed persons;
* Article 63: directives to be issued on the freedom to provide services;

* Article 100: the Council to issue directives for the approximation of laws affecting the establishment and functioning of the common market.
* Article 101: directives to be issued regarding the elimination of distortions of competition in the common market;
* Article 113(3): the Council to issue directives which set the guidelines for negotiations of the Commission with third countries in matters of common commercial policy;
* Article 118a(2): directives to be issued on the working environment, especially regarding health and safety of workers.

CHAPTER 22: DECISIONS

"A decision shall be binding in its entirety upon those to whom it is addressed" (Article 189). A decision is more of an administrative than a legislative measure. It comes into effect when those to whom it is addressed have been notified. Important decisions are often published in the Official Journal but decisions adopted in accordance with the procedure referred to in Article 189b must be published (Article 191(1)).

The Treaty demands the use of decisions in many provisions, e.g.

* Article 73g(2): the Council may decide that a Member State shall amend or abolish its measures against a third country with regard to capital movements and payments;
* Article 76: the Council may approve of a Member State giving less favourable treatment for carriers of other Member States until common rules in transport have been laid down;
* Article 93(2): the Commission may decide that aid granted by a Member State is not compatible with the common market and that it must be abolished or altered;
* Article 100b: in 1992, the Council decided that certain provisions in force in a Member State must be recognized as being equivalent to those applied by another Member State in order to complete the internal market.
* Articles 70(2), Article 73, Article 79(4), 80, 89(2), 92(3), Article 103(2), 104c(4), and (9), 108(3), 109(3), 125 EC and 130d-e Article EEC.

According to Article 145, the Council may confer on the Commission the power to take decisions on matters which fall in the competence of the Council.

Decisions do not have general application but are issued to one or more Member States or one or more companies. They have direct effect on and are binding for the national courts and authorities, even if the states have not complied with the decision.

CHAPTER 23: RECOMMENDATIONS AND OPINIONS

Article 189 stipulates: "Recommendations and opinions have no binding force." Recommendations are issued by the competent institution whenever necessary. Unlike recommendations, opinions are reactions to someone else's conduct, which means they can only be delivered if something happens. Both recommendations and opinions are not binding and not revisable.

Recommendations and opinions are provided for under the following provisions of the Treaty:

* Article 81: the Commission may make recommendations on charges or dues in respect of the crossing of frontiers:
* Article 102: the Commission may recommend measure to avoid the distortion in competition in the common market:
* Article 104c(7): the Council may make recommendations to the Member States concerned on possibilities how to stop excessive government deficits.
* Article 113 (3): the Commission makes recommendations to the Council, which authorizes the Commission to negotiate with non-EC countries or international organizations.
* Article 118b: the Commission can issue opinions concerning the dialogue between management and labour at European level.
* Article 126 (4): the Council shall adopt recommendations related to education.
* Article 128 (5): the Council can adopt recommendations on cultural matters.
* Article 129 (4): the Council can make recommendations on public health.
* Article 155: the Commission can formulate recommendations or deliver opinions on matters dealt with in the EC Treaty if it expressly so provides or if the Commission considers it necessary.

According to Article 228, "the Council, the Commission or a Member State may obtain the opinion of the Court of Justice as to whether an agreement envisaged is compatible with the provisions of this Treaty". The agreements referred to in this provision are those between the Community and one or more non-Community states or international organizations.

The Court has stressed that opinions under Article 228 are - like all other Court judgements - binding and not advisory. Thus, if the Court considers an agreement to be incompatible with the Treaty, it must be altered to correspond with the Treaty.

Few opinions have been delivered by the Court although a very important one was given in 1991, namely the *Opinion on the draft Agreement on a European Economic Area* (Opinion 1/91). The Court found the draft agreement to be incompatible with the Treaty for several reasons. It pronounced that the direct effect and supremacy of Community law were effected. The proposed European Economic Area Court would not be accepted because its judgements would influence Community law. The draft agreement was altered in order to comply with the Court's opinion. The European Court's opinion (1/92) on the revised draft agreement stated its compatibility with Community law.

CHAPTER 24: THE LEGISLATIVE PROCESS IN THE COMMUNITY

"Regulations, directives and decisions adopted jointly by the European Parliament and the Council and such acts adopted by the Council or the Commission, shall state the reasons on which they are based and shall refer to any proposals or opinions which were required to be obtained pursuant by the Treaty " (Article 190).

According to this Article, the Court requires that legislation must contain a statement of the reasons and facts leading to the necessity to adopt it. This way the Court has the possibility to review the facts and the reflections of the institution which adopted the act. It can happen that the Court declares the measure null and void because the statement of reasons that led to the adoption of the act was not clear enough or did not include sufficient reasons.

There are several procedures for the making of Community law. The *cooperation procedure*, introduced by the Single European Act (Article 189c/former Article 149 EEC) is a very important one. The Commission submits a proposal to the Council which adopts a common position after obtaining the opinion of the European Parliament. There are no time limits on the Parliament for the first reading but it usually takes six months. To adopt the common position Article 189c requires a qualified majority from the Council. Sometimes the Parliament demands the application of the provisions for consultation and conciliation between the first and the second reading stage but the Council opposes to this idea by arguing that a second reading is sufficient.

After the common position has been adopted, the Council must inform the Parliament thereof and explain the reasons which led the Council to adopt its common position. The Parliament must also be informed of the Commission's position. Then the Parliament has a second reading. It can approve the common position within three months; if it does not act within such time period, the Council will definitely adopt the act in question in accordance with the common position. However, the Parliament may, by an absolute majority, reject the Council's common position or propose amendments. If the European Parliament has rejected the Council's common position, then the Council can pass the act by unanimity only. In such a case the Council

must pass the decision within three months, otherwise the Commission proposal shall be deemed not to have been adopted.

If the Parliament has amended the Council's common position, the Commission must, within a period of one month, re-examine the proposal, taking into consideration the amendments proposed by the Parliament. The Commission forwards the amendments of the European Parliament, which have not been accepted by it, to the Council and expresses its opinion on them. Then the Council, acting by a qualified majority, adopts the proposal as re-examined by the Commission. Again, the Council is required to act within a period of three months. If no decision is taken within this period, the Commission shall be deemed not to have been adopted. However, until the Council has adopted the proposal, the Commission may at any stage submit a new proposal, altering the first one. By introducing the second reading as part of the cooperation procedure, the Parliament's influence has been increased. The Parliament now has more time to work on the legislation.

The cooperation procedure applies to

* legislation designed to prohibit any discrimination on grounds of nationality (Article 6 (2) EC);
* legislation for the multilateral surveillance procedure in matters of economic policy (Article 103(5) EC);
* measures specifying definitions for the application of the prohibition of access to financial institutions by Community institutions and national authorities (Article 104a EC);
* measures specifying definitions for the application of the prohibition of the Community's or a Member State's liability for commitments of other Member States or public undertakings (Article 104b EC);
* measures harmonizing the denominations and technical specifications of all coins intended for circulation within the Community after the adoption of a single currency (Article 105a EC);
* directives on minimum requirements and improvements of health and safety of workers (Article 118 EC);
* decisions relating to the European Regional Development Fund (Article 130e EC);
* measures necessary to further Community policy in the sphere of development cooperation (Article 130w EC).

At Maastricht, the *conciliation and veto procedure* was newly introduced in Article 189 b, also strengthening Parliament's powers. The first reading stage is the same as that in the cooperation procedure. The two procedures differ in the second reading in Parliament. After the Council has fully informed the Parliament of the reasons which led to the common position and the Commission has forwarded its position, the European Parliament has several possibilities of acting:

(i) If the Parliament accepts the common position or takes no decision at all within three months, the Council will adopt the act in question in accordance with its common position.

(ii) When the Parliament indicates - by an absolute majority of its members - that it will reject the common position, it must immediately inform the Council accordingly. The Council may agree to a meeting of the Conciliation Committee. At this point the European Parliament either confirms its rejection of the common position or it proposes amendments by an absolute majority of its component members. If the rejection of the common position is confirmed, the proposed act is deemed not to have been adopted. This is the Parliament's veto on Community legislation.

(iii) The Parliament may also propose amendments to the common position by an absolute majority of its component members. The proposed amendments are forwarded to the Council and then to the Commission. Within three months the Council may approve all the amendments of the Parliament and adopt the act. If the Commission has not delivered a negative opinion, the Council must adopt the measure by qualified majority. Otherwise - in case the Commission has expressed a negative opinion - the measure can only be passed by unanimity. Where the Council does not adopt all of the Parliament's amendments, the President of the Council shall, in agreement with the President of the European Parliament, convene a meeting of the Conciliation Committee. The Conciliation Committee is composed of the members of the Council or their representatives and an equal number of representatives of the European Parliament. Its task is to reach an agreement on a joint text by a qualified majority of the members of the Council or their representatives and by a majority of the representatives of the European Parliament. If within a period of six weeks the Conciliation Committee approves a joint text, the

European Parliament and the Council are given a period of six weeks from that approval within which to adopt the act in question in accordance with the joint text. If one of the two institutions fails to approve the proposed act, it is deemed not to have been adopted. This creates a second possibility for the European Parliament to raise a veto.

Where the Conciliation Committee fails to approve a joint text, the Council can - within a period of six weeks - confirm the common position to which it agreed before the conciliation procedure was initiated. If the Council does confirm its original common position, acting by qualified majority, the measure is adopted unless the European Parliament rejects it by an absolute majority within six weeks of the date of confirmation by the Council.

Article 189b prevents the Council from passing legislation without the assent of the Parliament. The Parliament always has the last word and may block legislation whenever it wants.

The conciliation and veto procedure applies to:

* legislation on the freedom of movement for workers (Article 49);
* directives on the freedom of establishment (Article 54(2));
* measures for the approximation of laws establishing the internal market (Article 100a);
* incentive measures contributing to the development of quality education (Article 126(4)),
* incentive measures contributing towards the flowering of the cultures of the Member States (Article 128(5)),
* incentive measures contributing towards ensuring a high level of human health protection (Article 129(4));
* specific action which supports and supplements consumer protection policy (Article 129a(2));
* guidelines achieving the objectives in matters of trans-European networks (transport, telecommunications and energy infrastructures) (Article 129d(1));
* multiannual framework programmes on research and technological development (Article 130i(1));
* general action programmes setting out priority objectives on environmental policy (Article 130s(3)).

An intergovernmental conference will examine certain provisions of the EC Treaty in 1996. Article 189b (e) states that the provision on the conciliation and veto procedure is one of them. By 1996, the Commission must submit a report to the Council on how the scope of the procedure may be widened.

In another legislative procedure the consultation of the European Parliament is essential. The Commission comes up with a proposal and submits it to the Council, which sends the proposal to the Parliament, asking for its opinion. Once the Parliament has delivered its opinion, the Council can pass legislation according to the provision which provides the legal basis for the proposal. The Council is not bound by the Parliament's opinion.

However, there are several occasions where - according to the EC Treaty - the Commission can make proposals which are then adopted by the Council without Parliament being consulted, e.g. measures on commercial policy in accordance with Article 113.

LEGISLATIVE PROCEDURE IN THE EC

Cooperation procedure according to Article 189c
Conciliation and veto procedure according to Article 189b

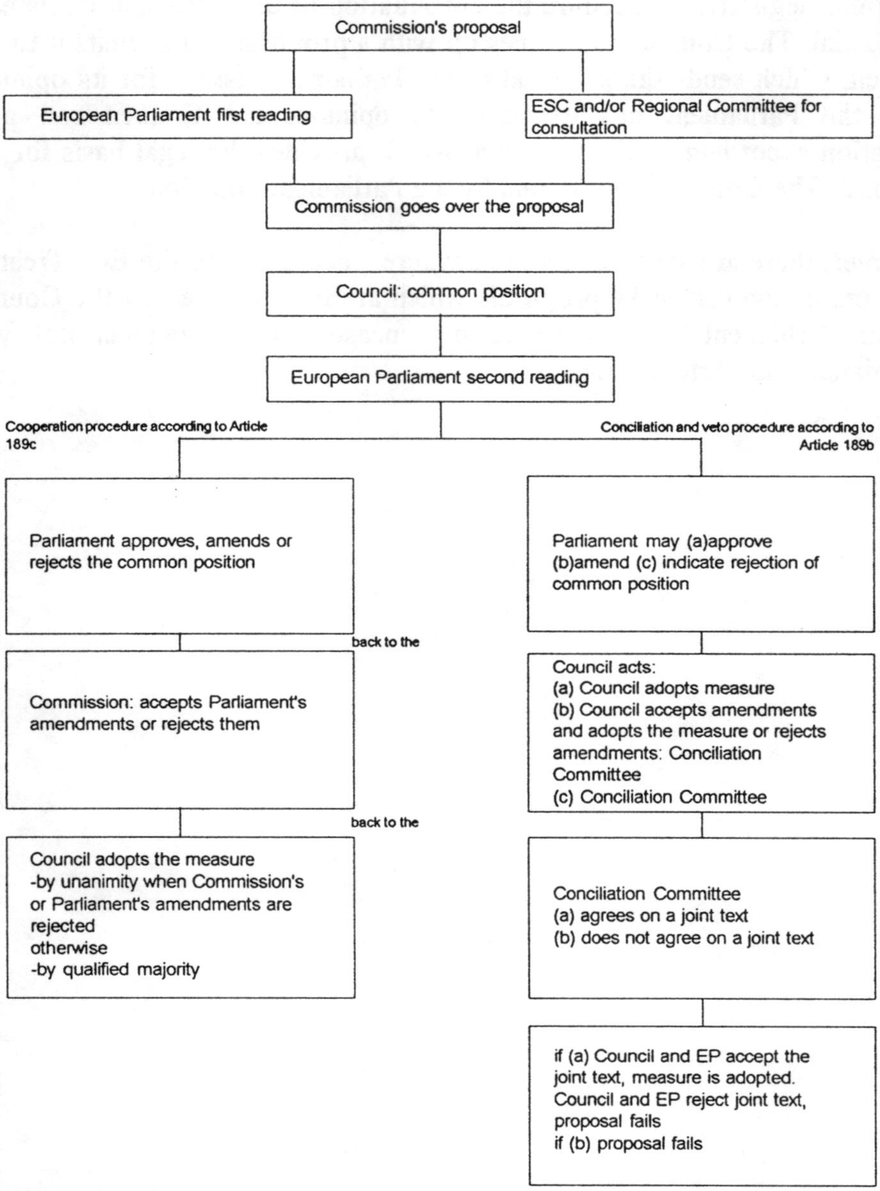

FISGRAFX

CHAPTER 25: THE RELATIONSHIP BETWEEN COMMUNITY LAW AND NATIONAL LAW

The Treaties establishing the European Communities did not explicitly stipulate the supremacy of EC law. However, there is not doubt that Community law has priority over the laws of Member States and in case of a conflict between both, the latter does not apply. By referring to the objectives and purposes of the Treaties, the European Court of Justice shares this opinion. The Court firmly established the primacy of Community law in its decision *Costa v. ENEL*, in which the Italian government did not accept the application of certain provisions of Community law in Italy. The Court's ruling on the nature of the Community and its legal system is famous:

> **By creating a Community of unlimited duration, having its own institutions, its own personality, its own legal capacity and capacity of representation on the international plane and, more particularly, real powers stemming from a limitation of sovereignty or a transfer of powers from the States to the Community, the Member States have limited their sovereign rights, albeit within limited fields, and have thus created a body of law which binds both their nationals and themselves.**
> **The integration into the laws of each Member States of provisions which derive from the Community, and more generally the terms and the spirit of the Treaty, make it impossible for the States, as a corollary, to accord precedence to a unilateral and subsequent measure over a legal system accepted by them on a basis of reciprocity.**

The European Court's view on the supremacy of Community law was extended in other cases. In the *Internationale Handelsgesellschaft* case the Court stated that Community law takes primacy over the constitutions of Member States. In the *Simmenthal* case the question arose whether a national court had the power to refuse the application of conflicting provisions of national law in favour of Community law. The European Court decided that every national court was obliged to apply Community law and, if necessary, to refuse the application of conflicting national law. The national

(8)

courts must not annul such provisions or wait until legislation has repealed them but only state that they will not apply them.

Most of the Community Member States accept the primacy of Community law. Some national constitutions (Greece, the Netherlands) explicitly state that international treaties have priority over national law; other countries reach the same result through judicial interpretation (Spain and Portugal). For a long time, the highest court on public law in *France*, the Conseil d'Etat, did not accept the supremacy of Community law. Once it even failed to comply with a judgement of the European Court (*ONIC v. Huileries de Pont-a-Mousson,* 1980). However, the Conseil d'Etat is slowly converging towards an acceptance of the priority of Community law.

Italy has gone a similar way. In the past it refused to acknowledge the supremacy of Community law. Nowadays Italy does accept the supremacy of Community law over subsequent national law but only as long as the Community ensures Italian fundamental rights. So, if the European Court were not able to uphold fundamental rights within the Community legal order, Italy would not accept the supremacy of Community law in the field of fundamental rights.

In *Germany* the constitutional court, the Bundesverfassungsgericht, accepts the supremacy of Community law. However, initially, when Community law violated fundamental German rights, the German constitutional court would reject the principle of priority over national law. At that time it argued that the European Parliament was not directly elected and that Community law did not have a catalogue of fundamental rights. Today the German constitutional court fully accepts the supremacy of Community law because it trusts the European Court on upholding fundamental rights.

When the *United Kingdom* joined the European Community in 1973, it clearly spoke out the supremacy of Community law over laws in the United Kingdom.

The Community law is not only superior to the national law of the Member States but it may also have *direct effect* in the Member States. Community law may confer rights on individuals which national courts must protect without the Member State having to implement any legislation. In order to produce direct effect a Community provision must be unconditional and sufficiently precise. A Community provision is unconditional if the right being granted is independent of the judgement or discretion of a Community institution or a Member State. The provision is sufficiently precise if it supplies "workable indications to the national court" (Case 43/75 [1976] ECR 455, 473).

Community law having direct effect enables individuals to rely on it before national courts. In this way Community law can be applied more quickly because the Member States do not have to implement legislation. Additionally, the enforceability of Community law is also increased. If a Member State does not comply with Community law having direct effect, the Commission will not have to proceed according to Articles 169 or 170 because at some point an individual will take action before his own national court.

In the *Van Gend en Loos* case the Court stated that a provision of the Treaty had direct effect in the Member States and in the national courts. In its decision the European Court explained that the institution's powers affected both Member States and individuals. The Court decided that Community law is a new legal order in which "independently of the legislation of the Member States, Community law ... not only imposes obligations on individuals but is also intended to confer upon them rights which become part of their legal heritage".

According to Article 189, regulations are "directly applicable in all Member States". This means that the Member States do not have to implement any legislation. However, "directly applicable" does not necessarily mean directly effective. All regulations are directly applicable but they only have direct effect if they are unconditional or sufficiently precise. Directives and decisions can have direct effect.

CHAPTER 26: CASE LAW

Case law has developed to be a very influencing part of Community law. Several judgements of the European Court have established fundamental principles and explained many important provisions of the Treaty. We have selected only a few that turn up again and again in literature on Community law. Some of the cases mentioned below will be explained in more detail in Section B of this book.

In the case *Procureur du Roi v. Dassonville* the Court defined the scope of Article 30 by explaining the meaning of measures having equivalent effect to quantitative restrictions (abbreviated: MEQR). These are "all trading rules enacted by Member States which are capable of hindering, directly or indirectly, actually or potentially, inter-Community trade" (case 8/74 [1974] ECR 837, [1974] 2 CMLR 436, paragraph 5 of the judgement). This quotation from the Court's judgement is known as the *Dassonville formula.* In addition, the Court stated that it does not depend on the legal form of the national practice but on its effect in order to be interpreted as an MEQR. In several subsequent decisions the Court has referred to this formula when it had to dismantle restrictive national rules. The Court prefers using its own judicial interpretation of MEQRs although directive 70/50 was issued in order to explain Article 30.

In the case *Rewe Zentrale v. Bundesmonopolverwaltung für Branntwein,* commonly known as *Cassis de Dijon,* the Court extended its interpretation of Article 30. The Court established a new principle, the *Cassis de Dijon principle,* by saying: "Obstacles to movement in the Community resulting from disparities between the national laws relating to the marketing of the products in question must be accepted in so far as those provisions may be recognized as being necessary in order to satisfy mandatory requirements relating in particular to the effectiveness of fiscal supervision, the protection of public health, the fairness of commercial transactions and the defence of the consumer". On the one side, this decision created an exception to Article 30, allowing regulations which restrict the movements of goods in the Community. On the other side, It is at the same time an extension of Article 36 which must be interpreted narrowly. The Cassis de Dijon principle has influenced many following cases before national courts and the European Court, e.g. *Gilli and Andres,* and *Commission v. Germany (Reinheitsgebot).*

PART FIVE - SUBSTANTIVE LAW

CHAPTER 27: THE FINANCIAL COMMON MARKET

In Articles 67-73, the Treaty of Rome described the establishment and objectives of the free movement of capital belonging to persons resident in the Member States. The free movement of capital is one of the fundamental freedoms. It covers financial services such as banking and credit, insurance, brokerage and securities.

The free movement of capital cannot be treated in the same way as the free movement of goods, persons or services. Sudden shifting of large amounts of capital may influence financial markets or even national economies in a dangerous way. The fact that every Member State has its own currency made it difficult to set up a common market in this field.

Although the first half of the 1960s was a period of positive and harmonious economic development in the European Community, the second half was not quite as prosperous and successful. The loss of confidence in the leading currency, the US Dollar, and the two oil crises in the 1970s delayed the initial lifting of restrictions on the movement of capital. Instead, many Member States reintroduced controls in that respect.

The Articles covering the other three freedoms have direct effect but Article 67 states:

> **During the transitional period and to the extent necessary to ensure the proper functioning of the common market, Member States shall progressively abolish between themselves all restrictions on the movement of capital belonging to persons resident in Member States and any discrimination based on the nationality or on the place of residence of the parties or on the place where such capital is invested.**
> **Current payments connected with the movement of capital between Member States shall be freed from all restrictions by the end of the first stage at the latest.**

The clause "to the extent necessary to ensure the proper functioning of the common market" deprives Article 67 of its direct effect. This leaves the power to control the economic and monetary policy to the Member States.

In 1970, the Luxembourg Prime Minister at that time, Werner, submitted a plan for the establishment of an economic and monetary union. Because of the dollar and oil crises of the following years the plan never became reality. Only the exchange rate system remained, in which the rates could rise or fall by up to 2.25 per cent. This system was not very stable due to the temporary withdrawal of several Member States.

However, nine years later, on 13 March 1979, the European Monetary System (EMS) and other binding agreements came into effect. The designers believed that the EMS would do two things: help governments fight inflation and promote trade throughout Europe. The exchange rates could still fluctuate up to 2.25 per cent, which is called the Exchange Rate Mechanism (ERM). Only Italy was granted a margin of fluctuation of 6 per cent because of economic problems. The United Kingdom did not take part in this system. The introduction of the European Currency Unit (ECU) as part of the EMS was an extraordinary event. The European Monetary Cooperation Fund (EMCF) was set up to carry out all EMS transactions. The EMCF consists of the governors of the central banks. It holds 20 per cent of the gold and dollar reserves of each Member State in exchange for ECU.

The EMS exchange rate system turned out to be very successful: it overcame several crises, exchange rates remained more stable in comparison with the rest of the world, inflation rates were reduced and economic policies gained stability.

At the beginning of 1985, the Commission published a White Paper which proposed many measures for the removal of physical, technical and fiscal barriers. The attainment of the internal market was aimed at by enabling the free movement of persons, goods, services and capital. In June 1988, a committee, chaired by Jacques Delors, President of the Commission, was set up to study and propose concrete steps towards an economic and monetary union. The Delors Report was published in April 1989 and proposed the following steps in the economic field:

* removal of all physical, technical and fiscal barriers within the Community for the completion of the internal market by the end of 1992;
* promotion of regional development and correction of regional imbalances;
* strengthening of economic and fiscal policy coordination;

and in the monetary field:

* complete freedom of movement of capital;
* freedom to provide banking, financial and insurance services;
* participation of all Community currencies in the exchange rate mechanism of the European Monetary System;
* full private use of the ECU;
* more coordination of decisions on monetary policy and exchange rate policy.

CHAPTER 28: THE EUROPEAN CURRENCY UNIT (ECU)

For the creation of an economic and monetary union the European Currency Unit - the ECU - was introduced in 1979. The name derives from a French coin used in the Middle Ages. The ECU is like a basket consisting of weighted amounts of the Member States' currencies. (See *chart*: Composition of the ECU) The extent of influence of each currency on the ECU depends on the size and economic power of a Member State. The ECU plays an important role in the European Monetary System: it is a reserve unit and an instrument for joint exchange rate support operations on the currency market. It is also used to set the central rates in the exchange rate mechanism and as a reference for the divergence indicator. The divergence indicator warns Member States when their currencies diverge from the central rate by a specified percentage. In such a case the Member States may take economic measures to stabilize their currencies.

Citizens may also use this currency. They can open bank accounts in ECU, take up ECU loans, pay with ECU cheques or even buy ECU bonds. In this way a private ECU market has been established alongside the official ECU market. Especially on the bond market the ECU has developed into a very important currency. It is more stable than a single currency because it represents the average value of the individual currencies of the Member States, i.e. 80 per cent of its value consists of stable currencies. Initially, investors came from hard currency countries whereas borrowers mainly came from weak currency, high interest countries. Now multinational companies are using the ECU in external trade. In the Treaty of Maastricht it was agreed to try to establish the ECU as a single European currency before the year 2000. A single European currency would bring about many advantages: it would eliminate exchange costs, boost trade and produce welfare gains. It would also generate more stability and influence vis-à-vis the US Dollar and the Japanese Yen. A single European currency would also have symbolic importance for the identity of a unified Europe.

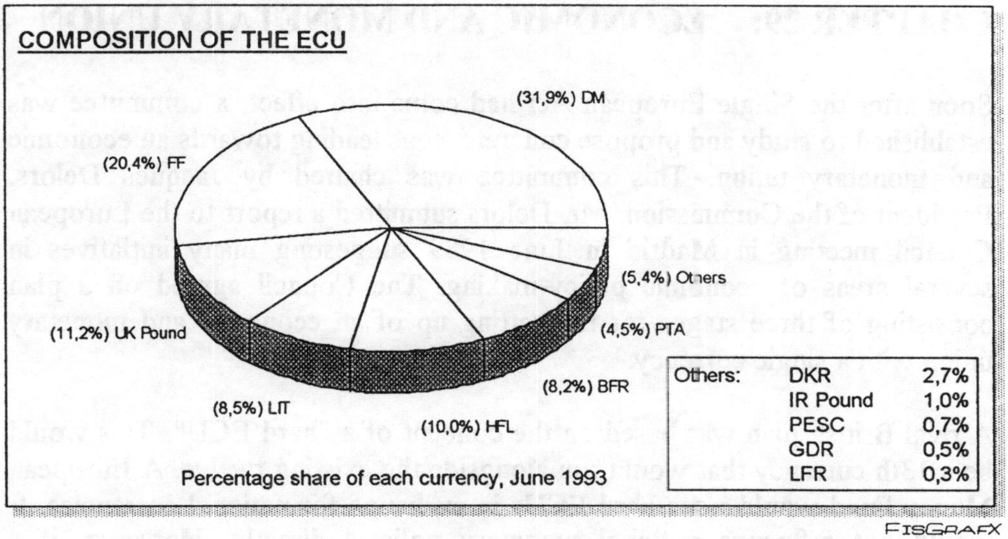
COMPOSITION OF THE ECU
(31,9%) DM
(20,4%) FF
(5,4%) Others
(11,2%) UK Pound
(4,5%) PTA
(8,2%) BFR
(8,5%) LIT
(10,0%) HFL
Percentage share of each currency, June 1993
Others:
DKR 2,7%
IR Pound 1,0%
PESC 0,7%
GDR 0,5%
LFR 0,3%
FISGRAFX

CHAPTER 29: ECONOMIC AND MONETARY UNION

Soon after the Single European Act had come into effect, a committee was established to study and propose concrete steps leading towards an economic and monetary union. This committee was chaired by Jacques Delors, President of the Commission. Mr. Delors submitted a report to the European Council meeting in Madrid in June 1989 suggesting many initiatives in several areas of economic policy-making. The Council agreed on a plan consisting of three stages for the setting up of an economic and monetary union with a single currency.

A rival British plan was based on the concept of a "hard ECU". This would be a 13th currency that would run alongside the existing twelve. A European Money Fund would issue hard ECUs in exchange for national currencies. It would not influence national monetary policies directly. However, if a national currency became weak, the national central bank could be forced to buy its own currency back from the fund with hard ECUs. This British draft was not accepted.

The *first stage* of EMU already began on 1 July 1990 and focused on completing the internal market as described in Article 7a. It was officially completed on 1 January 1993 with the implementation of the free movement of capital, goods, services and people. By the beginning of 1992, all Member States had entered the Exchange Rate Mechanism (ERM), except for Greece. At the time, Portugal, Spain and the United Kingdom were granted a margin of fluctuation of 6 per cent of the central rate and not 2.25 per cent like the other Member States. Due to difficulties on the international capital markets the sterling and the lira had to leave the ERM in September 1992. Later, Spain was forced to devalue the peseta. It took quite some efforts for France and Germany to remain in the ERM. However, the deepening recession forced Europe's governments to loosen the ERM by widening the margins within which currencies fluctuated from plus or minus 2.25 per cent to plus or minus 15 per cent.

As expected, the *second stage* of EMU (Maastricht's programme for economic and monetary union) started in January 1994. During this phase, the newly established European Monetary Institute (EMI), which is seated in Frankfurt, will prepare the way for the final stage, in which - presumably - several European currencies and monetary policies will be united. The EMI formulates opinions or recommendations to Member States on the overall orientation of monetary policy and exchange rate policy, recommendations on improving payment systems, planning for ECU bank notes and coinage and developing the use of the ECU. Additionally, the EMI will strengthen cooperation between the national central banks, monitor the functioning of the European Monetary System and prepare the instruments and the procedures necessary for carrying out a single monetary policy in the third stage. By 31 December 1996, at the latest, the EMI must specify the regulatory, organizational and logistical framework necessary for the European Central Bank (ECB) to perform its tasks in the third stage. This framework will be submitted for decision to the ECB at the date of its establishment. Actually, the French wanted the EMI to be as strong as possible, whereas the Germans preferred the opposite.

In phase three, EMI will become the European Central Bank (ECB). The EMI has legal personality and is directed and managed by a council consisting of a president and the governors of the national central banks. One of the governors is the vice-president according to Article 109f. During this second stage, Member States must try to avoid excessive government deficits. Each Member State shall start the process leading to the independence of its central bank.

During the *third stage,* a single currency will be established. This phase of economic and monetary union shall begin no later than 1 January 1999, even if only a minority of the Member States meet the convergence criteria. If a majority of Member States meets the requirements, the third stage may already commence on 1 January 1997. The five convergence criteria are:

(1) *Price stability*: The inflation rate of a successful Member State should be no more than 1.5 per cent above the average of the three EC countries with the lowest price rises.
(2) *Interest rates*: Long-term interest rates should be within 2 per cent of the average of the three members with the lowest rates.
(3) *Debts*: The public debt ratio must be less than 60 per cent of GDP.
(4) Deficits: National budget deficits must not exceed 3 per cent of GDP.
(5) *Currency stability*: A national currency must not have been devalued in the previous two years and must have remained within the normal margin of plus or minus 2.25 per cent. Since 1 August 1993 the fluctuation may even be plus or minus 15 per cent.

This progress towards a single currency is irrevocable. It is possible that Treaty amendments to the timetable may be agreed upon at the next intergovernmental conference in 1996.

At Maastricht an opt-out protocol was negotiated with the United Kingdom. This protocol gives the United Kingdom the right not to take part in the third stage of economic and monetary union, even if it meets the requirements to enter the third phase. If the United Kingdom does decide to take part in the single currency policy later on, it may opt in if it satisfies the convergence criteria. Meanwhile, the United Kingdom would be treated like a Member State with a derogation.

The *European Central Bank (ECB)* will replace the EMI. The governments of member sates without a derogation will appoint the President, the Vice-President and the other members of the Executive Board of the ECB. The members being appointed must be of recognized standing and professional experience in monetary or banking matters. Their term of office is eight years and not renewable. The full exercise of their powers will commence from the first day of the third stage. The ECB will take over tasks of the EMI, while the EMI will go into liquidation. At the beginning of the third stage, the Council will, on a proposal from the Commission and after consulting the ECB, adopt the conversion rates at which the Member States' currencies shall be irrevocably fixed and at which irrevocably fixed rate the ECU shall be substituted for these currencies. From this point on, the ECU will be a currency in its own right.

The ECB will have to be completely independent and take no instructions from Community institutions or bodies, from any government of a Member State or from any other body. The members of the Executive Board are joined by the governors of the national central banks of the Member States to form the Governing Council of the ECB. The Governing Council elaborates the monetary policy of the Member States taking part in the single currency.

The ECB's main task will be to control the ECU and maintain price stability. Additionally, it defines and implements the monetary policy of the Community, conducts foreign exchange operations, holds and manages the official foreign reserves of the Member States and promotes the smooth operation of payment systems. The ECB has the exclusive right to authorize the issue of bank notes within the Community. It will be consulted on any proposed Community act and by national authorities regarding any draft

legislative provision in its fields of competence. The ECB must submit an annual report on its activities and on the monetary policy of both the previous and the current year to the European Parliament, the Council, the Commission and the European Council.

CHAPTER 30 - COMPETITION POLICY

Competition policy plays a key role in the European Community. Consumers are provided with a wide choice of goods and services from companies in all Member States of the Community. Competition makes companies give more attention to the needs and wishes of the consumers and keeps prices of manufacturers and suppliers as low as possible.

On the other hand, companies sometimes like to avoid competition as much as possible by cooperating in anti-competitive cartels. They fix prices and divide markets between themselves. This gives companies the possibility to increase their revenue and plan further steps with more certainty. Such a system does not leave much choice for the consumer who can only accept what the cartel decides on.

Some big firms abuse their dominant position on a market by asking for higher prices or pushing other competitors out of the same market. This is not compatible with EC law. In addition to the four freedoms, competition policy was needed to establish a common market free of barriers and, furthermore, an economic union. Competition guarantees that prices reflect the actual relationship between supply and demand. The competition rules as per the EC Treaty apply to undertakings, dumping and aids granted by states.

Article 85

> 1. The following shall be prohibited as incompatible with the common market: all agreements between undertakings, decisions by associations of undertakings and concerted practices which may affect trade between Member States and which have as their object or effect the prevention, restriction or distortion of competition within the common market, and in particular those which:
>
> (a) directly or indirectly fix purchase or selling prices or any other trading conditions;
>
> (b) limit or control production, markets, technical development, or investment;
>
> (c) share markets or sources of supply;

(d) apply dissimilar conditions to equivalent transactions with other trading parties, thereby placing them at a competitive disadvantage;

(e) make the conclusion of contracts subject to acceptance by the other parties of supplementary obligations which, by their nature or according to commercial usage, have no connection with the subject of such contracts.

2. Any agreements or decisions prohibited pursuant to this Article shall be automatically void.

3. The provisions of paragraph 1 may, however, be declared inapplicable in the case of :

-- any agreement or category of agreements between undertakings;
-- any decision or category of decisions by associations of undertakings;
-- any concerted practice or category of concerted practices;

which contributes to improving the production or distribution of goods or to promoting technical or economic progress, while allowing consumers a fair share of the resulting benefit, and which does not:

(a) impose on the undertakings concerned restrictions which are not indispensable to the attainment of these objectives;

(b) afford such undertakings the possibility of eliminating competition in respect of a substantial part of the products in question.

Article 85 is the first of many competition rules which apply to undertakings. It prohibits cooperation which influences the effectiveness of competition in the common market. Paragraph 2 adds that prohibited practices are void. This means that prohibited agreements can neither be referred to before national courts nor can they be enforced. Yet, according to Article 85(3), some agreements between undertakings may be applied, even if they suppress competition. Such agreements must contribute to improving the production or distribution of goods or to promoting technical or economic progress. It is up to the Commission whether such an exemption may be granted or not (the Commission is responsible for the administration of the Community's competition rules).

Different types of practice which fall within the scope of prohibitions are listed in Article 85 (1). However, this list is not exhaustive. An agreement does not violate competition rules because of its legal form or its content but because of its effect on other producers or distributors.

A practice may only then be prohibited if it has as its "object or effect the prevention, restriction or distortion of competition within the common market". Furthermore, such practice must "affect trade between Member States". If an agreement or practice does not "affect trade between Member States", Article 85 cannot be applied. Such cases must be solved according to national law.

The EC Treaty does not specify what is to be understood by undertakings, agreements or concerted practices. Over the years, the Commission, as administrator of the competition rules, and the Court have developed the effect and exact meaning of Article 85.

Agreements are contracts set up between companies. In such contracts the parties divide commercial markets and fix prices to which they stick. The Commission and the Court interpret the notion of "agreement" broadly because many of them are not written or expressed to be informal or non-binding. It would not serve the purpose of competition if Article 85 only applied to written agreements. Most cartels are set up in secrecy to avoid detection. Not only is the legal form irrelevant for an agreement but, likewise, the motive which leads to it. An agreement is set up when the contracting parties have reached consensus about action they want to take on the market.

Concerted practice is a loose form of cooperation which goes further than the agreement. Although the parties may never have reached an agreement, they might cooperate and achieve the same effect, e.g. the coordination of their price policies or the sharing of markets.

Sometimes it might be difficult to find out if the parties have an agreement or are acting according to a concerted practice. In reality such a distinction is not necessary because both the agreement and the concerted practice fall within the scope of Article 85 (1). So as soon as a concerted practice has been detected there is no need to search for an agreement.

The notion "*undertaking*" is not defined in the Treaty either. However, in the case *Italy v. Council and Commission* the advocate-general proposed a definition for this term: "[...] apart from legal form or the purpose of gain, undertakings are natural or legal persons which take actively and independently part in business and are not, therefore, engaged in a purely private activity [...]" This definition has proven to be very useful. It is very broad and even includes individuals acting independently in business. It does not matter whether the firm is privately or state owned. Article 90 stipulates that public undertakings also fall within the ambit of Article 85.

Article 85 does not apply if the agreement or concerted practice between undertakings does not have an effect on trade between Member States. If such agreement or practice effects one Member State only, then it is not a matter at Community level but at national level.

Article 85 (3) stipulates that exceptions are possible. For an exemption to be granted four conditions (two positive, two negative) must be complied with. The two positive conditions are contained in the middle paragraph: an agreement can only then be allowed if it contributes to improving the production or distribution of goods or to promoting technical or economic progress. This first positive condition is also known as the economic benefit criterion, aiming at a general economic point of view. The requirement of consumer benefit demands that the contract bring a fair share of the resulting benefit to the consumers.

The two negative conditions state that an exemption can only be granted if certain results do not follow. The first negative condition insists that the agreement does not impose restrictions which are not indispensable to the attainment of the objectives. This means that restrictions of competition which are not strictly necessary may not be allowed according to Article 85 (3). The second negative condition requires that the deal shall not permit the elimination of competition in respect to a substantial part of the products in question. A reduction of competition can be accepted, but not an elimination.

In reality, the Commission cannot examine whether every agreement or concerted practice is captured in Article 85(3). The amount of work would not be manageable. So in order to secure the effective administration of

Article 85 the Commission uses block exemptions. The Commission therefore issues regulations which contain a block exemption to several categories of cooperation. Every block exemption has a list of clauses which may or may not be used in agreements. This makes it easier for the Commission to fulfil its duties referred to it by Article 85. Some major block exemptions are:

Regulation 1983/83	Exclusive Distribution agreements
Regulation 1984/83	Exclusive Purchasing agreements
Regulation 123/95	Motor Vehicle Distribution agreements
Regulation 4087/88	Franchising agreements

Abuse of dominant position - Article 86

> Any abuse by one or more undertakings of a dominant position within the common market or in a substantial part of it shall be prohibited as incompatible with the common market in so far as it may affect trade between Member States.
>
> Such abuse may, in particular, consist in:
>
> (a) directly or indirectly imposing unfair purchase or selling prices or other unfair trading conditions;
>
> (b) limiting production, markets or technical development to the prejudice of consumers;
>
> (c) applying dissimilar conditions to equivalent transactions with other trading parties, thereby placing them at a competitive disadvantage;
>
> (d) making the conclusion of contracts subject to acceptance by the other parties of supplementary obligations which, by their nature or according to commercial usage, have no connection with the subject of such contracts.

Article 86 aims at forbidding the abuse of a dominant position. It is also known as the monopoly provision. A producer holds a monopoly when it is the only producer in a certain market. The consumer does not have much of a choice: either s/he buys this product or no product at all. The normal conditions of a competitive market are not existent and do not influence the producer. The monopolist can do whatever it wants to do: it may raise prices and does not need to improve or innovate its product. Article 86 forbids such a dominant position.

Similar to Article 85, Article 86 focuses on the effect of a dominant position. Article 86 also has a non-exhaustive list of practices which fall within the notion of the abuse of a dominant position: unfair purchase or selling prices (see (a) supra), limiting production, markets or technical development (see (b) supra), applying dissimilar conditions to equivalent transactions (see (c) supra) and restricting the conclusion of contracts (see (d) supra).

Generally, the Community accepts the existence of dominant firms but it will not accept such a company abusing its dominance. Such firms are subject to strict supervision.

On the other hand, competition is forbidden in certain fields, e.g. water and electricity supply. Competition would not work, so here the Member States have established natural monopolies to secure the efficient supply for the consumers. For this reason price controls and safety measures are set up by law. Due to the lack of competition in such fields strict controls are necessary.

Once again the Treaty does not specify what a *dominant position* is. In the case *United Brands v. Commission*, the Court defined the term of a dominant position as "a position of economic strength enjoyed by an undertaking which enables it to prevent effective competition being maintained in the relevant market by giving it the power to behave to an appreciable extent independently of its competitors, customers and ultimately of its customers." Such a dominance cannot be influenced by normal competitive measures on the market.

A company's dominant position can only be related to the specific market in which the firm operates. So before a company is recognized as being dominant, the market must be identified and analysed. Only then can one determine the dominance and find out if it is subject to the supervision of Article 86. At first the market must be asserted, and only thereafter whether the firm has a dominant position on the relevant market.

A company dominates a market if it can act independently of competitive pressures. The market share of a company indicates its strength but it must be compared with the shares of other competitors. If a firm holds 100 per cent of a market, its dominance is obvious. Even if market shares do not reach 100 per cent, a company could still be dominant. However, as soon as a company has an equally strong competitor, market dominance is not likely, for example, when two companies each hold about 40 per cent of the market. If a firm has 45 per cent and the next largest competitor holds only 10 per cent of the same market, the first one can withstand attacks from his competitors without losing market shares. The Court would consider such a position as dominant.

This shows how thoroughly a market and its players (the competitors) must be examined before a company can be asserted as holding monopoly control over a certain market. However, a dominant position alone is not enough; the company must abuse its dominance, otherwise it does not act unlawfully.

Article 86 does not define the notion of abuse but it does give several examples. Abuse can be the *unfairly high or low pricing* of products. The Court compares the selling price with the cost of production and then calculates the profit made. A price "which is excessive because it has no reasonable relation to the economic value of the product supplied" would be abusive (Court's ruling in *United Brands*). However, on the other hand, unfairly low pricing may also constitute a form of abuse. By asking for extremely low prices, which a strong company is able to endure, smaller and weaker competitors are pushed out of the market because they just cannot afford to follow drastic price reductions. Then other competitors do not exist anymore and the strong firm is able to raise the prices. If low pricing has such an effect on competition, it is considered as an abuse according to Article 86.

Another form of abuse is when a producer asks for different prices from the distributors for the same goods. Such *discriminatory pricing* also falls within the scope of Article 86. United Brands, for example, was a firm importing bananas into the European Community. The bananas arrived in Rotterdam where distributors took over and sold them to retailers. UBC asked for different prices from distributors from different states: Danish banana distributors ended up paying much more than Irish distributors. Although prices must be adjusted to local market conditions, UBC had been acting abusively because the market conditions in Rotterdam had been the same for everybody. Furthermore, UBC was not subject to local market conditions in other areas of the EC.

Another possibility of a company to abuse its dominant position is to choose its customers. By controlling supply the company can maximize its own power and squeeze potential competitors out of the market.

Example (d) of Article 86 states that making the conclusion of contracts subject to acceptance by the other parties of supplementary obligations which have no connection with the subject of such contracts may be abusive. For instance, a firm will only conclude the agreement if the other partner not only buys product I but also product II from it at the same time. If the selling firm has a dominant position on the market, such contracts can exclude existing or potential competitors. Or a company may have customers with low discount prices if the customers bind themselves to a business relationship over a long period of time. The Commission and the Court consider such conduct by a dominant firm as anti-competitive and a violation of Article 86.

Regulation 17/62, which is based on Article 87, gives the Commission the power to enforce and administer the competition rules. This regulation is an important source for the Commission's control of most sectors of the economy. Initially, the sectors of air and sea transport were excluded from the Commission's supervision but today even these sectors are controlled by the Commission.

The Commission may start an investigation on its own initiative. Alternatively, Member States and natural or legal persons may ask the Commission to take action. Natural or legal persons must claim a legitimate interest. The Commission may decline to pursue a complaint but the applicant has a right to be informed of the reasons.

Whenever the Commission suspects a firm of acting in violation of the Community competition rules, it may investigate the firm by asking for information or even by visiting the premises. According to Article 11 of the Regulation, the Commission may submit an informal *request for information* to the firm. This request needs to state the legal basis, the purpose of the request, the time limit for answering and the penalties provided for in Article 15(1)(b) for supplying incorrect information. If the firm does not comply with the request within the time limit fixed by the Commission or supplies insufficient information, the Commission may require the information by means of a *decision.* This decision will again specify the request, fix an appropriate time limit and indicate the applicable penalties. Finally, the decision will inform the recipient that it has a right to challenge the decision in the Court of Justice (Article 11 Regulation 17/62).

Article 14 of Regulation 17/62 is a more powerful provision, which gives the Commission the power to do "all necessary investigations" in the undertakings, e.g. visiting premises, even without announcement, examining the books and asking for explanations on the spot ("*dawn raids*"). Such visits will only have to be tolerated by the firm if the visit has been ordered by decision of the Commission which decision will have to specify the subject matter and the purpose of the investigation, appoint the date on which it is to begin and indicate the penalties applicable. Again, such decision may be reviewed by the Court of Justice upon request of the firm. Member State governments will have to be informed in advance and will have to grant assistance to the authorized officials in case the firm concerned opposes an investigation duly ordered.

Article 19 gives the firm that is being investigated the possibility of being presented a statement of objections. This statement informs the firm of the objections raised against it. Then a hearing is arranged in which the firm can submit its arguments and complaints before the Hearing Officer.

Most of the investigations are settled informally, i.e. without a formal decision. The firm either amends or abandons its practice. The Commission may also issue a comfort letter which declares that no further procedural steps will be taken because Article 85 or 86 do not apply in the matter.

On the other hand, the Commission might decide that Article 85 or 86 has been violated. The Commission will then try to end the infringement in an informal way, which will save both time and paperwork. The Commission expresses its view informally in a recommendation and the firm concerned usually complies with it. But some cases cannot be solved informally. Then a formal decision is needed, requiring that the violation of the competition rules be brought to an end. Sometimes, if the matter is important, the Commission will issue a formal decision which then serves as a guide for future cases.

In addition to the end of an infringement, fines may be imposed. Fines follow two means: first to remove profits gained through anti-competitive actions and secondly to prevent other firms from doing the same. Fines are a powerful and effective enforcement strategy. In 1991, for example, the Commission imposed a fine of 75 million ECU on *Tetra Pak* for abuse of a dominant position.

A firm being investigated by the Commission may seek review by the Court according to Article 173 EC (action for annulment). The applicant must make sure that proceedings be instituted within the two-months time limit of Article 173. When the Commission requests information based on a decision, the firm may challenge such a decision according to Article 11 of Regulation 17/62. If the Commission wishes to undertake investigations or requires that an unlawful practice must be ended, the company being investigated may take steps according to Article 14 of the same regulation.

CHAPTER 31: SOCIAL POLICY

The Community has committed itself to social policy since its foundation. At that time, the Community was eager to establish a common market, therefore social policy only focused on employment. There were no signs of linking social policy with education, health or cultural policy. Although social policy has often been subject to heavy political opposition, it has gradually developed over the years. Most of the provisions are very general and vague:

Article 117 speaks of "the harmonization of social systems".

Article 118 promotes the

> close cooperation between Member States in the social field, particularly in matters relating to:
> -- employment;
> -- labour law and working conditions;
> -- basic and advanced vocational training;
> -- social security;
> -- prevention of occupational accidents and diseases;
> -- occupational hygiene;
> -- the right of association, and collective bargaining between employers and workers.

Article 119 is the most precise of these provisions:

> Each Member State shall during the first stage ensure and subsequently maintain the application of the principle that men and women should receive equal pay for equal work.
>
> For the purpose of this Article, 'pay' means the ordinary basic or minimum wage or salary and any other consideration, whether in cash or in kind, which the worker receives, directly or indirectly, in respect of his employment from his employer.
>
> Equal pay without discrimination based on sex means:
>
> (a) that pay for the same work at piece rates shall be calculated on the basis of the same unit of measurement;

(b) that pay for work at time rates shall be the same for the same job.

Article 119 establishes the principle of equal pay for equal work regardless of the sex. This Article was subject of the Court's decision in *Defrenne v. SABENA*, in which two main characteristics of Article 119 were set up: first, Article 119 is directly effective and second it applies to all employees irrespective of whether s/he is employed by a private party or a public body.

However, Article 119 even goes further and forbids *indirect discrimination*. Indirect discrimination occurs when an employer hires workers of both sexes but clearly disadvantages one sex. This way many unlawful practices which were sexually biased have been stopped. For example, in *Rinner Kuhn v. FWW* the Court ruled that Article 119 had been violated: employees who did not work more than ten hours weekly or forty-five hours monthly were not granted sick pay. As more women used the advantage of part-time work and no objective factors justifying the differential treatment were submitted, the Court decided that a breach of Article 119 was obvious.

Or in *Jenkins v. Kingsgate Ltd.* the hourly rate of pay of part-time employees was lower than that of full-time employees although both did the same work. Almost all of the part-time working employees were female. Officially the number of hours of work was the criterion but indirectly women were being disadvantaged. According to the Court, this constituted a violation of Article 119.

In such cases it is very difficult for the employee to prove his/her complaint, so the Court usually orders the employer to explain how wages are calculated and to make the payment system transparent. Thus, the employer bears the burden of proof. Several directives have already been issued in the field of social policy.

Directive 75/117 establishes the principle of equal pay for work of equal value. This directive gives the courts the possibility to compare the economic worth of jobs. If a woman is doing a job and she feels that her pay is less than that of a man doing a job which is different but of comparable economic worth, she can submit a complaint before a national tribunal. As already mentioned this is also a directly effective right. This directive makes the practical application of Article 119 easier.

Directive 76/207 goes even further than the demand for equal pay as laid down in Article 119 and requires equal treatment of both sexes. This way the equality of men and women has become a general principle of Community law. Article 2 of the directive defines "that there shall be no discrimination whatsoever on grounds of sex either directly or indirectly by reference in particular to marital or family status". Men and women shall be treated equally, for instance, in recruitment, promotion and when it comes to redundancies. The treatment of a pregnant women is controversial. The Court considers discrimination due to pregnancy as direct, as it is a purely female characteristic. Another possible approach would be to compare how the employer treats a man who is not capable of going to work over the same time period. If the employer treats the man and the pregnant woman in the same way, no discrimination has occurred. On the other hand, if s/he disadvantages the woman just because she is pregnant, then s/he has clearly violated the equal treatment principle under Directive 76/207. However, this directive also stipulates exceptions in case the nature of a certain job requires a specific sex of the worker (Article 2(2)). Article 3(3) allows provisions which protect women.

Directive 79/7 demands equal treatment in the sphere of social security, e.g. unemployment, occupational diseases, sickness, accidents at work, disability and old age. It is aimed at the working population, which Article 2 defines as "self-employed persons, workers and self-employed persons whose activity is interrupted by illness, accident or involuntary unemployment and persons seeking employment" as well as "retired or invalid workers and self-employed persons".

In December 1989, the Community Charter of the Fundamental Social Rights of Workers was adopted in Strasbourg. This charter is considered to be a policy commitment to future initiatives. All Member States except for the United Kingdom signed the charter. Mrs. Thatcher thought that the charter would diminish the flexibility of the market.

At Maastricht the Member States wanted to extend and deepen the Community's social policy. This was agreed upon without the United Kingdom participating in the advanced social policy. The new provisions focus on better working conditions, social protection and more dialogue between management and labour. Thus, today the United Kingdom does not take part in negotiations concerning new proposals or provisions on social policy and it is not bound by such acts.

CHAPTER 32: PUBLIC PROCUREMENT

According to Friedl Weiss, public procurement "occurs whenever states or certain of their territorial or functional subdivisions acquire goods or services needed for their own operations or secure the construction of works, buildings and amenities for public use. Thus, procurement means acquisition for public consumption". In the EFTA practice the notion of public procurement is broader. The comparison with other international agreements shows that the terminology differs (GATT, OECD, UNCTAD); thus, there is no settled or internationally recognized term.

In his report of 1986, Cecchini illustrated the importance of public expenditure: in 1986, central and local governments, their agencies and enterprises spent 530 billion ECU for purchasing supplies and works. At the time, this was about 15 per cent of the Community's GDP. With the integration of Spain and Portugal in 1986 and the accession of the German Democratic Republic in 1990 these figures have increased.

The figures also show how important government contracts are. They form a large sector of the economy. Until recently governments and other local authorities have been purchasing their supplies of goods and their services from domestic suppliers. By opening this field to the competition of all firms from all Member States, the government has a bigger choice of goods and services. By letting companies from other Member States compete with domestic contractors, prices are reduced and thus taxpayers' money is saved.

When the White Paper was published in 1985, it contained a programme to complete the opening up of government procurement and large public-sector construction projects in the single market by the end of 1992. This was necessary because the Treaty establishing the EEC had no provision on public procurement because it actually made no difference between private and public vendors or purchasers. Secondly, the EEC Treaty is only a framework agreement. Several directives were issued in the 1960s and 1970s, but they only covered a fraction of public contracts:

* Commission Directive of 17 December 1960, which only dealt with goods, although it should have focused more on the supplier bidding for public contracts;
* Commission Directive of 7 November 1966;

* Commission Directive 70/32/EEC concerning the supply of goods to the government authorities of a Member State;
* Council Directive 71/304 concerning public works;
* Council Directive 71/305 concerning public works;
* Council Directive 77/62 concerning public supplies.

The structure and principles of the last three directives mentioned above are the same: contracts must be advertised in the Official Journal, foreign bidders may not be discriminated against, and there must be objective criteria for the tendering and award procedures.

Unfortunately, these directives were not adequately applied by the Member States; often they were even ignored because governments preferred to buy domestic products. So in the Single European Act the twelve Member States of the Community committed themselves to liberalizing public purchasing and construction, as presented in the White Paper. In March 1987, the Commission forwarded a reform package which suggested the application of the free trading principles of the common market to the public sector of purchasing goods and services:

* more transparency in tendering and award procedures;
* rules for EC-wide tendering, even for those sectors which had been excluded;
* more public procurement of services;
* to ensure enforcement.

In the late 1980s, two new directives governing supply and works contracts were adopted:

Council Directive 88/295 For Public Supplies - 22 March 1988

This new directive was concluded after twenty months of negotiations and is considered the successor of Directive 77/62. It brought important changes, especially increasing transparency and clarifying rules on public procurement. Article 1(a) of the Directive stipulates that:

> "public supply contracts" shall be contracts for pecuniary interest concluded in writing involving the purchase, lease, rental or hire purchase, with or without option to buy, of products between a supplier

> (a natural or legal person) and one of the contracting authorities..[...]. The delivery of such products may, in addition, include siting and installation operations.

The scope of application of the directive is limited, geographically and by sectors of economic activity. The sectors of telecommunications, energy, water and transport are excluded. These sectors will be opened for competition by separate directives. In reference to Article 223(1)(b) arms, munitions and war material are also excluded from public procurement.

This directive uses contract value thresholds of ECU 200,000.00 and ECU 130,000.00 (to comply with GATT rules). In order to calculate the contract values a method of valuing was introduced which considers all types of contract, lease, rental or hire purchase. This was necessary because the authorities used to avoid the Community rules by splitting a contract into several smaller contracts. Each one of these contracts did not exceed the threshold of Directive 77/62. Today this practice is forbidden.

The most important part of Directive 88/295 is comprised of the provisions on the procurement procedures. The more open and clearer these procedures are, the more stimulated competition will be. There are three types of different procedures:

(a) The *open procedure* is the rule. An authority puts a contract out to tender with the invitation that every interested contractor shall put in a bid for the contract by a certain date. From the presented offers the authority must choose one.

(b) The *restricted procedure* is an exception to the open procedure and must be justified by the Commission. The authority selects from among the contractors who reply to the tender notice. Then only the selected contractors are invited to submit an offer.

(c) The *negotiated procedure* must also be justified by the Commission. After having published a notice in the Official Journal of the EC, the contracting authority chooses one or several suppliers which have presented an offer. Then the contracting authority and the suppliers negotiate the terms of contract. The award of the contract must also be published in the Official Journal of the EC.

The restricted procedure and the negotiated procedure may only be used under certain circumstances. The new Article 6 (2) of Directive 77/62 enumerates the cases where the negotiated procedure may be used. The directive also requires that whenever a contracting authority uses the restricted or the negotiated procedure it must write a report stating the reasons justifying the use of such procedure. Such reasons are, for instance, "a need to maintain a balance between contract value and procedural costs" or "the specific nature of the products to be procured". The first of these examples tries to avoid that high costs for a contract of low value are incurred. The second sample justification refers to cases where the authority concerned needs a particular commodity which can only be supplied by specialized tenderers.

Several new provisions require the authorities to publish information on future procurement and projects. Additionally, all results of an award procedure must be published as well. This gives all interested suppliers an opportunity to gather all information for future bids they want to present. This kind of information is published in the Official Journal of the European Communities. Furthermore, the Commission is able to monitor the award procedures more easily because it knows the plans of the different authorities.

Council Directive 89/440 For Public Works - 18 July 1989

Expenditure for public works constitutes a major part of the economy of a Member State and is often used for policy making and economic regulation. This directive amends Directive 71/305 and aims at greater accessibility of public works contracts to intra-Community competition.

The award procedures - the open, restricted and negotiated procedures - are the same as those of the award of public supply contracts. The differences are small: there are two additional justifications for the use of the negotiated procedure. The threshold values are much higher than in Directive 88/295: 5 million ECU net of VAT for public works contracts and public works concessions.

Public works contracts "are contracts for pecuniary interest concluded in writing between a contractor and a contracting authority ... which have as their object either the execution, or both the execution and design, of works related to one of the activities referred to in Annex II ...", according to new Article 1(a) of Directive 71/305 incorporated therein by Directive 89/440. The notion "work" is defined as "the outcome of building or civil engineering works taken as a whole that is sufficient of itself to fulfil an economic and technical function", new Article 1(c) of Directive 71/305.

According to new Article 1(b) a *contracting authority* is [...]

> any body:
>
> -- established for the specific purpose of meeting needs in the general interest, not having an industrial or commercial character, and
>
> -- having legal personality, and
>
> -- financed, for the most part, by the State, or regional or local authorities, or other bodies governed by public law; or subject to management supervision by those bodies; or having an administrative, managerial or supervisory board, more than half of whose members are appointed by the State, regional or local authorities or by other bodies governed by public law. [...]

Annex I of the directive contains a list of such bodies. This list is supposed to be as exhaustive as possible and is subject to review. The Commission may amend this list.

So whenever a contracting authority - as defined above - decides to conclude a contract of public works, the directive applies. Furthermore, the directive is applied when the State covers more than 50 per cent of the cost of a public works contract, even if the body is not a public body. In addition, the fire, police, health and education authorities are bodies that are subject to this directive.

A *public works concession* is a contract of the same type as that indicated in (a) except for the fact that the consideration of the works to be carried out consists either solely in the right to exploit the construction or in this right together with payment", new Article I (d) of Directive 71/305. The growing importance of concession contracts is the reason they were included in the directive. Here the threshold value is also 5 million ECU.

Public Procurement of Services

The White Paper also contained a proposal for procurement in services. On 18 June 1992, the Public Services Directive 92/50 was adopted. It covers public service contracts which are defined as contracts for pecuniary interest concluded in writing between a service provider and a contracting authority. Contracting authorities "are the State, regional or local authorities, bodies governed by public law, associations formed by one or several authorities or bodies governed by public law". The directive applies to public service contracts with a minimum value net of ECU 200,000.00. This value threshold already includes the remuneration of the supplier.

At the beginning of each budgetary year, every authority planning to purchase a service must publish a notice in the Official Journal. After the authority has awarded the contract, it must publish another notice on the conclusion of the contract. The lowest price and the most economically advantageous tender are criteria for the award of contract.

Summary

These directives show the Community's effort to develop legislation in the field of public procurement. They may also be regarded as a success over the Member States' hostility towards certain provisions. Negotiations were long and difficult because national legislation of public procurement in the Member States varied greatly. The further legal development in this field will most likely be orientated with regard to GATT rules.

CHAPTER 33: COMPANY LAW

The fundamental freedoms of the Community, such as the free movement of persons or the right of establishment, do not only apply to individuals. Article 58 EC Treaty extends them to all companies which pursue an economic objective; Article 58 states:

> Companies or firms formed in accordance with the law of a Member State and having their registered office, central administration or principal place of business within the Community shall [...] be treated in the same way as natural persons who are nationals of Member States.
> 'Companies or firms' means companies or firms constituted under civil or commercial law, including cooperative societies, and other legal persons governed by public or private law, save for those which are non-profitmaking.

Laws concerning companies differed considerably from one country to another. For the development of an internal market these differences would have been very inconvenient and would not have secured the necessary protection of the interests of shareholders, employees, creditors and third parties. The need for equivalent protection throughout the Community made the harmonization and coordination of company law necessary.

Based on Article 54(3)(g), the Council issued directives co-ordinating the legislation on company law in the Member States:

* Directive 68/151 on a system of public disclosure applicable to all companies in the Community;
* Directive 77/91 on the raising, maintenance and alteration of the capital of public limited companies;
* Directive 78/855 on a common procedure for company mergers;
* Directive 78/660 on the harmonization of the annual accounts of public limited companies. Altered by the Directives 83/349, Directive 89/666, Directive 90/605 and Directive 90/604;
* Directive 82/891 concerns the scission of a public limited company into several undertakings;

* Directive 83/349 concerns the consolidated accounts of groups of undertakings - parent companies and subsidiaries; altered by Directives 90/605 and 90/604 Directive;
* Directive 84/253 defines the qualifications to be held by those responsible for the statutory audit of accounts required under Community legislation;
* Directive 89/666 on the creation and operation of limited liability companies by a single person;
* Directive 90/604 concerns public limited companies as partners incorporated in another company with share capital;
* Directive 90/605 on the statement of accounts of small and medium-sized companies.

In 1985 Regulation 2137/85 on the *European Economic Interest Grouping* was issued. The EEIG is an EC corporate structure enabling companies to cooperate within the Community. It permits companies in several Member States to jointly pursue certain activities while keeping their national legal incorporation and economic independence. An EEIG must be registered in the country in which it has its seat. The seat, though, can be moved. It may not employ more than 500 employees, nor offer any participation to the public. According to Article 4 of the Regulation natural persons, companies pursuant to Article 58(2) EC Treaty or another legal body of public or private law may be a partner of an EEIG.

However, the EEIG is only a step towards the European Company or Societas Europaea (SE). Such an SE will be registered with the European Court in Luxembourg according to a specific EC company statute although it can have its headquarters in any Member State of the Community. An SE would make cross-border mergers and cooperation much easier. In May 1991, the Commission submitted a proposal for the adoption of a regulation and a directive on the SE, based on Article 235 EC.

CHAPTER 34: DIPLOMAS AND PROFESSIONS

One of the Community's main objectives is the free movement of persons within the Member States. It is not only necessary to be able to exercise the profession of one's choice but also to receive education at institutions of other Member States. The principle of equal treatment must be applied to the practice of a profession in another Member State, too. Thus, since about 1970, any job discrimination against Community citizens on grounds of nationality has been forbidden except for limitations justified on grounds of public policy, public security or public health. Interestingly, there is no directly applicable provision in the EC Treaty which requires a Member State to recognize professional qualifications of a person coming from another Member State.

Article 57 stipulates: "In order to make it easier for persons to take up and pursue activities as self-employed persons, the Council shall [...] issue directives for the mutual recognition of diplomas, certificates and other evidence of formal qualifications". Following this Article, the Council issued many directives, trying to regulate every profession separately: Directive for doctors (1975), Directive for nurses (1977), Directive for dentists (1979), Directive for veterinary surgeons (1980), Directive for midwives (1983) and a Directive for pharmacists (1985). However, issuing directives for every single profession overloaded the Council with work. For this reason, and in order to make legislation easier and clearer, the *Mutual Recognition Directive 89/48* was adopted. This directive provides a general system for the recognition of diplomas obtained in any Member State and covers all diplomas which are not affected by sectoral directives:

(1) A diploma must be awarded by a competent authority in a Member State after the completion of a course of at least three years at university level or equivalent institution.

(2) The holder of a diploma must pursue a regulated profession in a Member State.

(3) If a diploma is considered to be a condition for exercising a regulated profession in a Member State, then a diploma awarded in another Member State is sufficient.

Lawyers

In 1977, *Directive 77/249* concerning lawyers was adopted. This enables a lawyer of a Member State to practise his/her profession in another Member State on a temporary basis. While performing his/her work as a lawyer, s/he must use the title of the country where s/he comes from. In general, a foreign lawyer can do the same work as a local lawyer but the Member State can reserve specific services for its national lawyers. In such a case the foreign lawyer must hire a local lawyer. Directive 77/249 does not concern the right of establishment but only the provision of services.

The Mutual Recognition Directive 89/48 applies to the profession of a lawyer because it is listed as a regulated profession. According to Article 3 of the directive, a diploma obtained in a Member State must be recognized in any other Member State. A lawyer working in another Member State may use the title of the Member State in which s/he practices as long as s/he exercises the right of establishment. Furthermore, a Member State can require that a foreign national practise under supervision for a certain period of time or pass a qualification test before s/he is registered.

Vocational Training

In the case *Gravier v. City of Liège*, the Court defined the notion of vocational training as "any form of education which prepares for a qualification for a particular profession, trade or employment or which provides the necessary training and skills for such a profession, trade or employment [...] even if the training programme includes an element of general education". In *Blaizot v. University of Liège,* the Court decided that only "certain courses of study [...] intended for persons wishing to improve their general knowledge rather than prepare themselves for an occupation" do not fall within the scope of vocational training. This case also confirmed that a student may claim equal access to a course and on the same basis as nationals of a Member State.

CHAPTER 35: AGRICULTURAL POLICY

Due to the importance of agriculture in every country and the concern to secure food supplies, the Community established the concept of the common agricultural policy (CAP). The Community succeeded in creating a single market in agriculture as early as in 1962: food was made available for consumers in all Member States at affordable prices and the EC has reached self-sufficiency in nearly all major products. However, this was not an easy objective to attain. Agriculture had to be set up as a special regime because normal economic rules do not work in this sector. Article 42 already mentions that "rules on competition shall apply to production of and trade in agricultural products only to the extent determined by the Council". Moreover, the interests of the different Member States often brought about heavy conflicts.

The Treaty of Rome stipulates the main objectives of the agricultural policy in Article 39:

* to increase agricultural productivity;
* to ensure a fair standard of living for the agricultural community;
* to stabilise markets;
* to assure the availability of supplies;
* to ensure that supplies reach consumers at reasonable prices.

These objectives are aimed at in the interests of both the producer and the consumer.

As mentioned above, these main objectives were attained by the creation of a single market for agriculture in 1962. Since 1968, common prices have been applied. Farmers did not have to accept cuts because prices were set in such a way that each product was rated at the price of the country where the product was most expensive. This made the prices for EC agricultural products even higher than world market prices. EC products, however, had to remain cheaper than imported agricultural products: import duties or levies were and still are imposed on imports, which made imported products more expensive than products of the Member States. In addition, EC products are subsidized so that they can compete on world markets when exported.

In 1960, a special Committee for Agriculture was established, which enabled the Council to get information and incentives for legislation. The first Council regulation on agricultural policy, Regulation 19/62, contained the market organization in cereals such as wheat, oats, maize, barley, buckwheat, hard wheat, rye, etc. It was replaced by Regulation 2727/75, which is still in use for the market in cereals. It also concerns the common price system of the Community and must be applied for trade with non-Community members. The price system encompasses a target price, an intervention price and a threshold price.

Each year before 1 August, the Council agrees on the *target price*. With this price the farmers can plan their production and know which price they can expect on the market for their product during the next year (from 1 August to 31 July). The target price always includes costs of transport so that cereals can be traded from Community surplus areas to Community deficit areas.

If producers are not able to sell their product on the market, the national authorities must pay the producers the *intervention or guarantee price* for their surplus products. This guarantees the farmers the sale of the remaining products. This price is not the same throughout the Community - unlike the target price - because the circumstances of the areas are different. The intervention price is lower than the target price.

For cereals which are imported into the EC the Council determines an import price, the so-called *threshold price*. The reason is that imported cereals shall not be sold lower than the target price because EC producers would not be able to sell their products on the market. It is calculated by deducting the price of transport from Rotterdam to the area of greatest deficit from the target price. Target prices, intervention prices and threshold prices are reviewed every month. If necessary, they can be increased during the marketing year.

The Community has adopted other regulations as well:

* Regulation 2771/75 on eggs;
* Regulation 2777/75 on poultry;
* Regulation 1035/72 on fruit and vegetables;
* Regulation 337/79 on wine and vines;
* Regulation 804/69 on milk and dairy products.

The Common Agricultural Policy has been very successful. During the past decades it responded to new priorities and developments in markets. Albeit this success some reforms were and still are necessary.

The system of guaranteed prices for unlimited production got farmers a minimum price for their products even if they were not able to sell them on the market. In such a case intervention authorities bought the surpluses and resold them at subsidized prices on the world markets. This way the Community met its self-sufficiency targets.

Farm output rises by an average of two per cent a year. Since demand does not but is either stable or falling the Community had to react. In 1984 milk quotas were introduced: if production exceeds a certain fixed level (the maximum guaranteed quantity - MGQ), support payments to farmers are automatically reduced. This system was also introduced for other agricultural products. These limits reduce Community spending on each product area.

In 1991 the Commission presented reform proposals which were adopted by the Council in June 1992. These reforms are necessary to cut the high prices and the excessive overproduction. The five main objectives are:

(1) To make farmers more competitive on home and export markets and to maintain the Community's position as a major agricultural producer and exporter.
(2) To reduce the rural exodus and encourage younger farmers to remain on their land.

FARMERS IN THE COMMUNITY

(1000)

	1960	1975	1990
B	367	140	119
DK	-	177	147
D	2216	1234	1081
GR	-	-	889
E	-	-	1496
F	3426	1950	1394
IRL	-	325	173
I	4007	2826	1913
L	22	12	6
M	363	254	289
P	-	-	840
UK	-	626	577
EUR 6	10402	6414	4802
EUR 9	-	7542	5699
EUR 12	-	-	8923

FisGrafX

(3) To approximate production with market demands.
(4) To focus support for farmers' income where it is really needed.
(5) To develop the natural potential of the countryside and protect the environment.

The 1992 reform will reduce the EC budget costs on agriculture by about ECU 3 billion by 1997. This money is intended to support the farmers directly and will be used less on stocking surpluses or subsidizing exports on world markets. This should make the farmers more competitive within the Community and on world markets.

CHAPTER 36: CONSUMER POLICY

According to paragraph 1 of Article 129a

> The Community shall contribute to the attainment of a high level of consumer protection through:
> (a) measures adopted pursuant to Article 100a in the context of the completion of the internal market;
> (b) specific action which supports and supplements the policy pursued by the Member States to protect the health, safety and economic interests of consumers and to provide adequate information to consumers.

Furthermore, any action referred to in Article 129a(1)(b) and adopted according to Article 129a "shall not prevent any Member State from maintaining or introducing more stringent protective measures. Such measures must be compatible with this Treaty. The Commission shall be notified of them."

The Treaty on European Union agreed upon at Maastricht added consumer protection as a new competence to the already existing ones. As in the area of environment, the Community acts in order to contribute to the attainment of a high level of consumer protection, but such action does not prevent any Member State from maintaining or introducing more stringent protective measures. Thus, even if the Community has passed legislation in this field, a Member State may adopt rules which protect the consumer further. Such national rules must be justified under Article 36.

Before consumer protection was included in the Treaty, the Community focused on harmonizing legislation with a continuing action programme:
The *First Programme* (1975-1981) stipulated five basic rights which serve the interests of consumers:

* the right to protection of health and safety;
* the right to protection of legal and economic interests;
* the right of redress;
* the right of information;

* the right of representation.

Soon after this First Programme was published (Annex to Council Resolution of 14 April 1975), about 80 directives were issued on the protection of consumers' health and safety. These directives covered provisions on food stuffs, fruit, vegetables, animal health, motor vehicles, chemical substances, household goods and cosmetics. The right to protection of legal and economic interests aims at fighting "against the abuse of power by the seller, in particular against one-sided standard contracts, the unfair exclusion of essential rights in contracts, harsh conditions of credit, demands for payment for unsolicited goods and against high-pressure selling methods" (OJ 1975, C92, Article 19). Furthermore, the consumer must have the right to complain about defective products or unsatisfactory services and be awarded redress for injury or damage deriving from them. The right to information should enable the purchase of goods or services to recognize differences between competing products and services and to make a rational choice. The consumer should have access to information about the safe use of dangerous products. Organizations representing the consumers' interests have been established, e.g. the Consumers Consultative Committee in 1973.

The *Second Programme* (1981-1985) added the protection of consumers in the field of services to the general action programme. Several directives of the First Programme were amended and new legislation was passed.

The *Third Programme* (1985-1988) criticized the slow progress and pointed out significant problems, e.g. the coordination of consumer protection with other Community policies, economic interests, and health and safety. Moreover, the Community set up common standards ensuring higher quality of products. The Community also changed its objectives: instead of harmonizing all the legislation, it decided to set standards only in the "essential" fields. This way the rest is left to the discretion of the Member States. Essential fields of harmonization are: the telecommunication sector, the food sector, the construction and civil engineering sector and the pharmaceutical sector. Legislation in the Third Programme focused on product liability, unfair terms in contracts, consumer credit and doorstep selling.

The *Fourth Programme* (1988-1992) expressed its objective as completing the internal market. A resolution on consumer education in primary and secondary schools was adopted by the Council and the Commission as well as a policy for improved food product quality. The major legislation comprises directives on package holidays, cosmetics, foodstuffs and food labelling, cleaning substances and detergents.

For the purpose of illustration, two major Council directives in the field of consumer protection shall be dealt with here:

Council Directive 85/734 on Defective Products of 25 July 1985

This directive envisages the approximation of the laws of the Member States concerning the liability of the producer for damage caused by the defectiveness of its products. This is necessary because the divergences may entail a differing degree of protection of the consumer against damage caused by a defective product to his/her health or property.

According to Article 1 of the directive, a producer is liable for damage caused by a defect in its product. "Product" means all movables, with the exception of primary agricultural products and game, even when incorporated into another movable or into an immovable. Product includes electricity. "Producer" is defined as the manufacturer of a finished product, the producer of any raw material or the manufacturer of a component part and any person who, by putting his/her name, trademark or other distinguishing feature on the product, presents himself as its producer. An injured person must prove the damage, the defect and the causal relationship between defect and damage. However, there is a limited period of time for bringing an action of compensation, namely 10 years from the date on which the producer put the actual product which caused the damage into circulation unless the injured person has, in the meantime, instituted proceedings against the producer.

Article 6 states that "a product is defective when it does not provide the safety which a person is entitled to expect ... including:

(a) the presentation of the product;
(b) the use to which it could reasonably be expected that the product would be put;
(c) the time when the product was put into circulation."

The liability of the producer is not reduced when the damage is caused both by a defect in product and by an act of a third party. However, the liability of the producer may be reduced in certain cases: e.g. if the damage is caused both by a defect in the product and by the fault of the injured person.

However, the producer is not liable if s/he proves, for example:

(a) that s/he did not put the product into circulation; or
(b) that it is probable that the defect which caused the damage did not exist at the time when the product was put into circulation by him/her or that this defect came later; or
(c) that the product was not manufactured by him/her for sale.

Damage means death, personal injury or damage to or destruction of any item of property. The liability of the producer may not be limited or excluded by a provision limiting his/her liability or exempting him/her from liability.

Council Directive 93/13 on Unfair Terms in Consumer Contracts of 5 April 1993

First of all, it should be noted that a Member State is responsible for ensuring that contracts concluded with consumers do not contain unfair terms. The laws of the Member States relating to unfair terms in consumer contracts have shown divergences. However, for the internal market it is essential that a consumer buying a product from a seller of another Member State, must also be protected against unfair terms in his/her contract. That is why the purpose of this directive is to approximate the laws, regulations and administrative provisions of the Member States relating to unfair terms in contracts concluded between a seller or a supplier and a consumer. According to Article 2 of the directive, "'consumer' means any natural person who, in contracts covered by this Directive, is acting for purposes which are outside his trade, business or profession. A 'seller or supplier' is any natural or legal person, who, in contracts covered by this Directive, is acting for purposes relating to his trade, business or profession, whether publicly owned or privately owned."

A contractual term which has not been individually negotiated is regarded as unfair if, contrary to the requirement of good faith, it causes a significant imbalance in the parties' rights and obligations arising under the contract, to the detriment of the consumer. A term is regarded as not individually negotiated where it has been drafted in advance and the consumer has, therefore, not been able to influence the substance of the term, particularly in the context of a pre-formulated standard contract. If a seller or supplier claims that a standard term has been individually negotiated, the burden of proof, in this respect, lies with him/her.

The Annex to Directive 93/13 contains an indicative and non-exhaustive list of the terms which may be regarded as unfair, e.g.:

* excluding or limiting the legal liability of a seller or a supplier;
* permitting the seller or supplier to retain sums paid by the consumer where the latter decides not to conclude or perform the contract, without providing for the consumer to receive compensation of an equivalent amount from the seller or supplier where the latter is the party cancelling the contract;
* requiring the consumer who fails to fulfil his obligation to pay a disproportionately high sum in compensation;
* authorizing the seller or supplier to dissolve the contract on a discretionary basis where the same facility is not granted to the consumer;
* obliging the consumer to fulfil all his obligations where the seller or supplier does not perform his/her part.

If they are offered to the consumer in writing, contract terms must always be drafted in plain, intelligible language. Where doubt occurs about the meaning of a term, the interpretation most favourable to the consumer must prevail.

CHAPTER 37: TRANSPORT

It is not very likely that a frontier-free single market can function well without efficient transport networks. Two basic principles of the European Community depend on the transport sector: the free movement of goods and of people. During the last few years, several laws have been passed to liberalize the main modes of transport: air, inland waterway, rail, road and sea.

Article 75(1) lists the objectives of a common transport policy:

(a) common rules applicable to international transport to or from the territory of a Member State or passing across the territory of one or more Member States;
(b) the conditions under which non-resident carriers may operate transport services within a Member State;
(c) measures to improve transport safety;
(d) any other appropriate provisions.

In a memorandum of 10 April 1961 the Commission proposed to establish a "Common Market in Transport" organized according to Community rules, able to respond to the needs of transport in the Community and ensuring elimination of discrimination based on nationality". Additionally, the Commission wanted competition to develop between the different modes of transport and between the carriers. Furthermore, environmental aspects, energy and regional needs were added to the transport policy of the Community.

However, from the establishment of the European Community until the late 1980s little progress was achieved in the transport sector. The Council had failed to adopt a common transport policy (see case 13/83: *European Parliament v. EC Council*). In the 1985 White Paper, the Commission acknowledged the slow progress and set up new priorities and specific measures to be taken in this field. This is what had been implemented anyway: tariff measures had been introduced to harmonize charges which had been bilaterally agreed upon between the Member States. These tariffs were applied to transport by rail, road and inland waterways. Technical harmonization required for directives which set up technical standards for safety, pollution, equipment and comfort. Directive 70/156 on the standard-type approval of motor vehicles and Directive 74/150 on agricultural and forestry tractors contributed to technical harmonization as well. Working conditions in internal and inter-state transport were harmonized in regulations. These regulations contain common standards for working conditions, resting periods for drivers, recording equipment and penal sanctions.

Road Transport

Frontier checks and quota restrictions on goods crossing from one Member State to another were lifted on 1 January 1993. Many regulations and directives concerning road transport have been issued:

* a Community driving licence, Directive 80/1263;
* the approximation of national laws concerning insurance against civil liability due to the use of motor vehicles, Directive 84/5;
* technical characteristics such as weights and dimensions of certain road vehicles, Directive 85/3;
* harmonization of national laws regulating the tread depths of tyres of vehicles and trailers, Directive 89/459;
* vocational training of drivers who transport dangerous goods in their vehicles, Directive 89/684.

The Commission has drawn up a plan of a trans-European network for the year 2002. The aim is that every Member State sets up a national network which is then linked to neighbouring networks by motorways. Outlying regions like Greece, Ireland and Portugal shall be connected to the Community's main roads and motorways. A further objective is to relieve congestion on the roads and to extend the application of tolls in order to cover traffic costs.

Air Transport

Community legislation on air transport only started in the 1980s. However, since then much has been achieved. There are no more price controls on air fares. Revenue-sharing agreements between national carriers flying a particular route have been eliminated. Today, consecutive cabotage is no longer forbidden and full cabotage will be allowed effective 1997. Consecutive cabotage means that a British airline may operate between two German cities as long as they are connected to a flight originating outside Germany.

Rail Transport

Until now only little has been achieved in the fild of transport by rail: e.g. rates for the international carriage of goods by train have been established, Decision 82/529. There is a plan to establish a European high-speed train network by 2010. France, Germany, Spain, Italy and Denmark already offer certain routes in high-speed trains. The United Kingdom is currently developing a new generation of fast electric trains.

Sea Transport

Legislation on maritime transport has eliminated national quota restrictions and unfair pricing practices. The competition rules of Articles 85 and 86 may be applied to maritime transport, too. Except for shipping services to islands cabotage is allowed.

Inland Waterways

Since 1 January 1993, there have been no controls at inland EC frontiers. Cabotage on inland waterways has become possible. Further Community legislation concerns:

* reciprocal recognition of navigability licences for vessels, Directive 76/135;
* certain technical requirements for inland water vessels, Directive 82/714;
* conditions for the navigation of the Rhine, Regulation 2919/85;
* improvements in inland waterway transport, Regulation 1101/89.

One of the aims of the Maastricht Treaty is to establish a trans-European network (TEN). From the twelve national networks, a single European network shall be created. Outlying regions of the Community shall also be integrated, making it easier for people living in these regions to travel to other parts of the Community. This shall be achieved by modernizing the existing networks and by making their use more attractive to the consumer. The exchange of information between the systems shall also be improved.

CHAPTER 38: AUDIO-VISUAL POLICY

In October 1989, the Council adopted the "Television without frontiers" Directive concerning the freedom of movement for television broadcasting in the Community. This directive harmonizes specific rules regulating:

(a) *Advertising and sponsorship.* Advertising may not exceed 15 per cent of the daily transmission time. Advertising for certain medicinal products and tobacco products is prohibited and limited for alcoholic beverages.

(b) *Protection of minors* must be respected. Programmes on pornography, racism or violence should be shown later in the evening if at all. Advertising must consider the development of children and adolescents and not encourage them to buy certain products.

The Community has established a policy to try to attain certain cultural objectives in the European audio-visual industry. For this reason, the Council adopted a five years programme (1991-1995) with a financial support of ECU 200 million. This cultural media programme is also open to the EFTA countries, since European culture cannot be bound by frontiers. The programme may even be extended to East European countries. The measures of the programme pay attention to national differences and try to maintain them, avoiding cultural uniformity. Presently more than 20 projects are being supported:

* Several training projects designed for professionals in the field of media management, e.g. the Media Business School in Madrid.
* Projects supporting the distribution of European films in the cinemas, promoting independent television and multilingual television programmes.
* Institutions throughout Europe improving media technologies or supporting the writing and development of screenplays.

In May 1992, the Council adopted a directive on the standards for satellite broadcasting of television signals. The Community has developed a high definition standard which shall be promoted world-wide, namely the HD-MAC.

CHAPTER 39: COMMUNITY BUDGET

The European Coal and Steel Community (ECSC) has its own operational budget which is financed by a European tax imposed on coal and steel firms. The European Economic Community (EEC) and the European Atomic Energy Community (Euratom) were financed by national contributions, based on the GDP of the Member States. Today the Community is financed by its own resources.

At *The Hague Summit* in 1969, the Member States adopted a Budgetary Treaty which amended several budgetary provisions of the three Treaties: the increase in budgetary powers of the European Parliament was most significant. Since 1 January 1975, the European Parliament can even amend the non-compulsory part of a proposed budget. The Financial Provisions Treaty of 1975, which came into effect on 1 June 1977, was of great importance. New changes were:

* the European Parliament was given the exclusive right to adopt the annual budget and to give a discharge to the Commission in respect of its implementation;
* the "inverted majority rule", which is to be applied when modifications to the compulsory part of the budget have been proposed;
* the independent Court of Auditors was established, which replaced the Audit Board.

The 1980s were characterized by repeated conflict and crisis in budgetary matters not only between the European Parliament and the Council but also among the Member States. In the Inter-institutional Agreement of 1988 between the Commission, the Council and the Parliament, it was agreed to improve the budgetary discipline and procedure. The main elements of the budgetary reform were:

* The Community was given additional resources.
* The burden of financing the European Community was more fairly spread.

The TEU brought several amendments, too:

* Administrative expenditure relating to common foreign and security policy and to cooperation in the fields of justice and home affairs shall be charged to the budget.
* The budget shall be financed entirely from own resources.
* Before the European Parliament gives a discharge to the Commission, the European Parliament may ask to hear the Commission give evidence with regard to the execution of expenditure or the operation of financial control systems.

Budgetary Principles

The budgetary principles of all Member States have become part of the general budget of the Communities. They can be found either in the Treaties themselves or in the Financial Regulation of 21 December 1977. There is a controversy on how many principles exist.

The *Principle of Unity:* According to Article 199, "all items of revenue and expenditure ... shall be included ... in the budget". So the scope of the general budget includes the administrative expenditure of the ECSC, the revenue and expenditures of the EEC and of Euratom. However, there are some exceptions to this rule.

The *Principle of Annuality:* The budget shall be authorized for one financial year, which runs from 1 January to 31 December. Every year a new budget is adopted. However, there are also a number of exceptions to this principle.

The *Principle of Universality:* All revenue and expenditures being entered in the budget must be listed in full without any adjustments against each other. Additionally, the Principle of Universality includes the gross budget rule, meaning that netting in the accounts is only possible as far as Article 27 of Financial Regulation allows it.

The *Principle of Specification:* The budget is divided into sections and subsections. Expenditures entering the budget may not be classified as a lump sum but must be specified exactly.

The *Principle of Non-Assignment:* All revenue sources must always be available to cover all expenditures and may not be assigned to certain expenditures in advance.

The *Principle of Equilibrium:* The sum of revenue must correspond with the sum of expenditures. If the sum of revenue exceeds the sum of expenditures, the surplus must be transferred into the next budgetary year. If there are more expenditures than revenue, the budget may not be passed.

Structure of the Budget

The general budget is divided into five sections. Each section is dedicated to an institution: Parliament, Council, Commission, Court of Justice and Court of Auditors. (It should be noted that the section of the Commission is the largest because the Commission uses more than 95 per cent of the Community's revenues.) Usually, the Economic and Social Committee is attached as an annex to the Council's section. All items of revenue and expenditure of each section are classified as titles, chapters, articles and items. The title is the highest, and the item the lowest structural unit of a section.

Usually, the left page lists the different appropriations, while the right page includes explanations concerning the legal basis for the appropriations. In addition, the budget must show the revenue of the Communities for the preceding financial year and the estimated revenue of the financial year in question.

The Decision Making Process for Adopting the Budget according to Article 203

Before 1 July of the year preceding that in which the budget is to be implemented, each institution of the Community must draw up estimates of its expenditure. The Commission then consolidates these estimates in a preliminary draft budget, which also contains an estimate of revenue. The Commission must submit the preliminary draft budget to the Council no later than 1 September. The Council, acting by a qualified majority, establishes the draft budget and forwards it to the Parliament no later than 5 October. The Parliament has the right to amend the draft budget and to propose modifications of the draft budget to the Council. If, within 45 days of the draft budget being placed before it, the European Parliament gives its approval, the budget will be adopted. If, within this time period, the Parliament has neither amended the draft budget nor proposed any modifications thereto, the budget will also be adopted. If the Parliament has adopted amendments or proposed modifications, the draft budget together with the amendments or proposed modifications is then forwarded to the Council. The Council must discuss the draft budget with the Commission and, if necessary, with the other institutions concerned. The Council may modify any of the amendments adopted by the Parliament. As to the proposed modifications:

* A modification proposed by the Parliament which does not increase the total amount of the expenditure of an institution, may be rejected by the Council with qualified majority. If the proposed modification is not rejected, it is accepted.

* A modification proposed by the Parliament which does not increase the total amount of the expenditure of an institution may be accepted by the Council with qualified majority. Otherwise it is rejected.

The modified draft budget is then returned to the European Parliament, and the Council informs the Parliament of its deliberations. Within 15 days of the draft budget being placed before it, the Parliament may, acting by a majority of its members and three-fifths of the votes cast, amend or reject the modifications to its amendments made by the Council and shall adopt the budget accordingly. If the Parliament does not act within this time period, the budget will be adopted according to the modifications made by the Council.

If, within such 15 days of the draft being placed before it, the Council has not modified any of the amendments adopted by the European Parliament, and if the modifications proposed by the latter have been accepted, the budget will finally be adopted. When the budgetary procedure has been completed, the President of the European Parliament declares that the budget has been finally adopted.

Own Resources of the Communities

According to Article 2 of the Council Decision of 24 April 1988, the revenue for the Community's general budget includes:

* customs duties on products which enter the Community from a non Member State. There is a common customs tariff vis-à-vis third countries. Customs duties between the Member States have been abolished.

* levies on agricultural products, sugar and isoglucose coming from external countries. They are necessary to raise the prices of imported products to the Community level. This provision safeguards the existence and future of the Community's farmers.

* part of the value-added tax base, which is determined in a uniform manner for the Member States, and serves as a resource. However, a limit has been set: the VAT base should not be more than 55 per cent of GNP.

A forth resource was created in 1988 and is expressed as a percentage of the combined GNP of all Member States. Each year this rate is determined under the budgetary procedure.

CHAPTER 40: TAXATION

One of the first tasks of the Community was to remove the tax barriers between the Member States and establish a common customs tariff for goods originating in third countries in order to create a customs union. This aim is stipulated in Article 9:

> The Community shall be based on a customs union which shall cover all trade in goods and which shall involve the prohibition between Member States of customs duties on imports and exports and of all charges having equivalent effect, and the adoption of a common customs tariff in their relation with third countries.

To achieve the customs union the concept is based on Articles 9, 12, 13 and 95:

Article 12 prohibits the introduction of any new customs duties on imports or exports or any charges having equivalent effect.

Article 13 states that customs duties on imports in force between Member States shall be progressively abolished.

Article 95 prohibits any internal taxation which would indirectly protect national goods and discriminate against imports.

For the original Member States the customs union was achieved on 30 June 1968: the customs duties between the Member States were abolished and since then a common customs tariff has been applied on goods coming from non-EC countries. The removal of economic frontiers and legal obstacles to trade between the Member States made it possible to develop the next step of economic integration: the internal market.

The Commission's White Paper on completing the internal market devoted one of its three major chapters to taxation. The chapter on taxation relates solely to indirect taxes. As long as differences in VAT and other indirect taxes existed, Member States were permitted to carry out frontier checks to make sure that taxes had been paid.

Article 99 refers to the Community's power to harmonize indirect taxes. In its original version it was more general in scope but it was amended by the Single European Act to meet the needs of the internal market. Article 99 provides:

> The Council shall [...] adopt provisions for the harmonization of legislation concerning turnover taxes, excise duties and other forms of indirect taxation to the extent that such harmonization is necessary to ensure the establishment and the functioning of the internal market within the time limit laid down in Article 7a.

In 1991, the Member States were able to agree on a plan instituting the application of VAT in intra-Community trade from the beginning of 1993. Directive 91/680 provides a transitional plan which will be replaced in 1997 by a definitive agreement. In 1995, the Member States will review how the system will have operated and lay down arrangements for the permanent system.

According to the transitional plan there should be no more border controls. The VAT will not be administered anymore by the national officials at border posts, but by the firms themselves. A seller transporting his goods into another Member State does not invoice the VAT anymore. The purchase will be taxed in the state of importation. Every month, the buyer will then give account of all purchases from other Member States and pay the VAT. This is a very potential field for tax fraud. That is why the Member States issued Regulation 217/92 concerning the combat of fraud. The anti-fraud mechanisms introduced by this Regulation encompass, for instance, an information network between national tax authorities.

Furthermore, it was agreed that each Member State applies a standard rate of 15 per cent minimum, with no fixed upper limit. Additionally, the Member States have the possibility of using one or two reduced rates, not lower than 5 per cent. Existing rates lower than 5 per cent and zero-rates may be retained during the transitional period. On 1 January 1993, all the higher rates of VAT levied on cars, perfume and hi-fi equipment, etc. have been abolished.

Some changes for the definitive system will be introduced in 1997: VAT payments due to intra-Community trade will be made in the state of origin, the state of the seller and not anymore in the state of the purchaser.

The second form of indirect taxes are *excise duties,* which are imposed on alcohol, petrol and tobacco. Until 1 January 1993, the Member States had different structures and rates of these duties. Since then minimum rates for mineral oils, beer, wine and cigarettes have been harmonized. In addition, these goods were subject to border controls. Today they are moved between "bonded warehouses" without being checked at frontiers. The purchaser buying such goods from a warehouse must pay duty in the state of destination.

SECTION B

CASE SUMMARIES

FRANCOVICH

Francovich and Others v Italy - case 6/90, case 9/90

Facts

Directive 80/987 deals with the protection of employees in the event of the insolvency of their employer. Under Article 3 of the Directive an employee must be able to obtain payment of outstanding claims resulting from his contract of employment and arising prior to a date to be determined by the Member State, being either (a) the date of the occurrence of the employer's insolvency (b) the date of the notice of dismissal given to the employee on account of the insolvency or (c) a choice between (a) and (b). Payment could be limited to a certain time period by the Member State in order to put a ceiling on liability. The Member States were to set down detailed rules for the operation of the guarantee institutions which were to provide this protection to employees. They were required to comply with the Directive by 23rd August 1983. The Italian Government failed to do so and was successfully prosecuted by the Commission (Commission v Italy (1989) ECR 143).

Mr. Francovich worked for an Italian electronics company which only paid him sporadically. He brought an action against the company and was awarded damages. Bailiffs were unable to enforce judgement as the company had ceased trading. Mr. Bonifaci was owed money by the company he had worked for which had become insolvent. The receiver had told him there was little chance of his receiving any payment.

Both claimants argued that the Italian government should pay them damages, as they would have been awarded damages if the government had complied with its obligation to implement the Directive.

Issues

(1) Under EC law is an individual who is adversely affected by the failure of a Member State to implement a Directive entitled to require the Member State to give effect to those provisions of the Directive that are sufficiently precise and unconditional by directly invoking Community legislation against the Member State in default so as to obtain the guarantee which Member States should have provided or

can the individual claim damages in relation to provisions to which that right does not apply?

(2) Are the combined provisions of the Directive to be interpreted as meaning that when a Member State has not laid down limits as to time limits or levels of payment it is obliged to pay the claims of employees?

(3) If not, what is the minimum guarantee the State must provide pursuant to the Directive to an entitled employee so as to ensure the employee receives an amount sufficient to give effect to the Directive.

Judgement

The Directive was intended to guarantee an employee´s minimum level of protection under EC law in the event of the insolvency of the employer and without prejudice to the more favourable provisions which may exist in any Member State. In particular the Directive provides for specific guarantees of payment of unpaid wage claims. Member States were required to bring the Directive into effect by 23rd August 1983. The Italian Government had failed to do this and this default had been recorded in the judgement given against it.

The Court believed there were two issues:
(i) Did the provisions of the Directive have direct effect?
(ii) the existence and scope of the liability of a State for damage resulting from a breach of its obligations under EC law.

(i) Direct Effect

A Member State which has failed to adopt implementing measures required by a directive within the prescribed period may not plead its own failure to perform these obligations. Where the provisions of a directive appear unconditional and sufficiently precise they may, in the absence of implementing measures adopted within the prescribed period, be relied upon as against any national provision which is incompatible with the directive in so far as the provisions of the directive define rights which individuals can assert against the State.

Whether the directive was unconditional and sufficiently precise depended on three factors - the identity of the person entitled to the guarantee, the content of the guarantee and the identity of the person to provide the guarantee.

The Court ruled that the provision was sufficiently precise so as to enable a national court to determine whether or not a claimant was entitled to benefit. The question was whether the person was an employed person under national law.

On the question of the content of the guarantee, the Member State had some discretion in choosing the time limit to apply, either three months or eight weeks. The Court followed previous decisions by ruling that the right of the State to choose between several possible means of achieving a result did not preclude an individual from enforcing in a national court rights which could be determined precisely on the basis of the provisions of the Directive alone. The result required by the Directive is a guarantee that the outstanding claims of the employee will be paid in the event of the insolvency of the employer. The discretion given to Member States did not affect the precise and unconditional nature of the result required.

With regard to the identity of the person to provide the guarantee the Member States had been given a broad discretion as to how they organise an appropriate system. The Directive provided for the possibility that public authorities would entirely finance the guarantee institutions but this did not mean that the State was therefore identified as the person liable for unpaid claims.

The Court held that the identification of those entitled to the guarantee and the contents of the guarantee were not enough to enable the provisions to be relied upon by individuals before a national court. The provisions did not clearly identify the person liable to provide the guarantee and the Court would not make the State liable on the sole ground that it had failed to take transposition measures within the prescribed period.

(ii) Liability of the State for loss and damage resulting from the breach of an obligation under Community law.

This issue was to be considered in the light of the general system of the Treaty and fundamental principles.

The EEC Treaty had created its own legal system which was intergrated into the legal systems of Member States and which national courts were bound to apply. The subjects of EC law included both Member States and their nationals. It imposed burdens on individuals but also gave them rights. These arise not only where expressly granted by the Treaty but also through obligations which the Treaty imposes in a clearly defined manner on both individuals, Member States and Community institutions (the Court referred here to Costa v. ENEL and Van Gend en Loos). National courts must ensure these rules take full effect and must protect the rights they confer on individuals.

The effectiveness of Community law would be impaired and the protection of the rights of individuals weakened if individuals were unable to obtain redress when their rights were infringed by a breach of Community law for which the Member State could be held responsible.

The possibility of obtaining redress from a Member State was particularly indispensible where the full effectiveness of Community law was subject to prior action by the State and where in the absence of such action individuals could not enforce the rights conferred upon them by Community law in the national courts.

The principle that a State must be liable for loss and damage caused to an individual as a result of a breach of Community law for which the State can be held responsible is inherent in the system of the Treaty. It also has a basis in Article 5 of the Treaty which provides that a Member State is required to take all appropriate measures to ensure the fulfilment of its obligations under Community law.

The conditions under which liability of the State gives rise to the right to reparation depend on the nature of the breach of Community law which caused the loss and damage. Where, as in this case, a Member State fails to fulfil its obligations under Article 189 to take all measures necessary to achieve the result prescribed by a directive, the full effectiveness of that rule of Community law requires that there should be a right to reparation provided three conditions are fulfilled:

(i) The result prescribed by the Directive should entail the grant of rights to individuals.

(ii) It shall be possible to identify the content of those rights on the basis of the provisions of the directive.
(iii) There should be a causal link between the breach of the State´s obligation and the loss and damage suffered by the injured parties.

These conditions are sufficient to give rise to a right on the part of individuals to obtain reparation. This right is founded directly on Community law. It is the task of the national legal order to designate courts and lay down procedures to safeguard the rights of individuals which are derived from Community law. The substantive and procedural conditions for reparation must not be less favourable than those relating to similar domestic claims and must not be framed so as to make it excessively difficult to obtain reparation.

In this particular case the content of the individual right could be identified on the basis of the provisions of the directive. The national court must in accordance with national rules on liability uphold the right of the employee to obtain reparation for loss and damage caused as a result of the failure to transpose the Directive.

As a result of this decision the Court did not need to address itself to the second and third questions.

VAN GEND

Van Gend en Loos v Dutch Government - case 26/62

Facts

Article 12 of the EEC Treaty provides that "Member States shall refrain from introducing between themselves any new customs duties on imports or exports or any charges having equivalent effect and from increasing those which they already apply in their trade with each other". A Netherlands firm, Van Gend en Loos imported glue from Germany and paid customs duties of 3% before the EEC Treaty came into force. In 1959 a Dutch law ratified a Benelux customs agreement which put the duty up to 8%. The firm protested to the Dutch courts who referred two questions to the ECJ.

Issues

The two questions were:
(i) Did Article 12 have direct effect in that nationals of a state could claim individual rights which a national court must protect?
(ii) If so was the imposition of a duty of 8% unlawful under Article 12?

The governments which made submissions also questioned the jurisdiction of the ECJ to decide these two questions.

Judgement

(1) Direct effect of Article 12

(a) Jurisdiction

The court rejected the arguments of the Governments of the Netherlands and Belgium that the reference related not to the interpretation of the Treaty but to the application of the Treaty in the context of the constitutional law of the Netherlands and that the ECJ did not have jurisdiction to decide whether the provisions of the EEC Treaty prevailed over Netherlands legislation. The court did this on the basis that it was not asked to adjudicate upon the application of the Treaty according to the principles of the National law of the Netherlands but only to interpret Article 12 within the context of Community law and with reference to its effect on individuals.

(b) Substantive issues

The Court ruled that to decide whether Article 12 had direct effect in that it gave nationals of Member States rights which the national courts must protect it was necessary to consider the spirit, the general scheme and the wording of the provisions.

The object of the EEC Treaty, to establish a Common Market, meant that the Treaty did more than create mutual obligations between the contracting states. The Court found confirmation of this in the Preamble to the Treaty which referred not only to governments but to peoples and also in the establishment of institutions endowed with sovereign rights. The Court also considered its own role under Article 177, the aim of which was to secure uniform interpretation of the Treaty and said that this confirmed that the Member States had acknowledged that Community Law had an authority which could be invoked by their nationals before national courts. The ECJ stated that "the Community constitutes a new legal order of international law for the benefit of which the states have limited their sovereign rights, albeit within limited fields, and the subjects of which comprise not only Member States but also their nationals". Community law not only imposed obligations on individuals but also conferred rights upon them.

Article 12 was a clear and unconditional prohibition which was a negative prohibition. There was no qualification to this prohibition which would make its implementation conditional upon a positive measure enacted under national law. It was therefore ideally adapted to produce direct effects in the legal relationship between Member States and their subjects.

The Court rejected the Member States′ argument that individuals could not plead the obligations of Member States under the Treaty in national courts as to accept this argument would remove all direct protection of the individual rights of the nationals.

On the basis of the above considerations Article 12 had to be interpreted as producing direct effects and creating individual rights which the national courts must protect.

(2) Breach of Article 12

(a) Jurisdiction

The Court rejected arguments that the question was one of classification of the product for the purpose of customs duties. The question was whether a new classification of the product contravened Article 12. This was a question of interpretation of the Treaty and therefore the Court had jurisdiction to give a ruling.

(b) Substantive issues

The Court ruled that a breach of Article 12 could be caused by an actual increase in the rate of customs duty or by a rearrangement of customs tariffs resulting in a product being classified under a more highly taxed heading. The application of Article 12, in accordance with this interpretation, came within the jurisdiction of the national court.

DASSONVILLE

Procureur du Roi v Dassonville - case 8/74

Facts

Under Belgian law recognition of designation of origin of a product was subject to a declaration to the Belgian Government by the government concerned that the designation was officially adopted. Dassonville was a wholesaler in France and his son ran a branch of the business in Belgium. He imported Scotch whisky under the brand names "Johnny Walker" and "VAT 69" which he had purchased from French importers. When he imported them into Belgium he attached labels which gave details of the French excise bond. Under French law the excise bond was the document which had to accompany a product bearing a designation of origin. The Belgian authorities did not consider that these documents satisfied the requirements of Belgian law. They prosecuted Dassonville for contravening a decree which stated that it was an offence to import spirits bearing a designation of origin without them being supported by an official document certifying the right to such a designation. The Belgian companies brought action for damages. They were the exclusive importers and distributors of the two brands of whisky in Belgium.

Issues

Dassonville argued that Belgian law was incompatible with the prohibition on quantitative restrictions and measures having equivalent effect contained in Articles 30, 36 and 85 of the EEC Treaty. Belgian law prevented imports into Belgium from any country which did not have similar rules with regard to certificates of origin.

Two questions were referred to the Court:

(1) Must Articles 30-36 be interpreted as meaning that a national provision prohibiting the import of goods bearing a designation of origin, where the goods were not accompanied by an official document issued by the Government of the exporting country certifying the right to such designation, be considered as a quantitative restriction or as a measure having equivalent effect?

(2) Is an agreement void if its effect is to restrict competition and adversely affect trade between Member States only when taken in conjunction with national rules with regard to certificates of origin when the agreement only *authorises* and does not permit the exclusive importer from exploiting that role for the purpose of preventing parallel imports?

Judgement

Question 1

It was very difficult for a trader to obtain a certificate of origin from British customs for the purpose of importing whisky from France into Belgium. This was not so for the original importer. All trading rules enacted by Member States which are capable of hindering, directly or indirectly, trade within the Community are to be considered as measures having an effect equivalent to quantitative restrictions. In the absence of a Community system guaranteeing the authenticity of designation of origin of products to consumers, if a Member State takes measures to prevent unfair practices in this area, such measures must be reasonable. The means of proof required should not act as a hinderance to trade between Member States and should be accessible to all Community nationals. By virtue of Article 36 such measures must not constitute a means of arbitrary discrimination or a disguised restriction on trade between Member States. This may be the case where the formalities required by the Member State to prove the origin of the product are only obtainable without difficulties by direct importers.

Therefore the requirement by a Member State of a certificate of authenticity which was more difficult to obtain by importers of a product put into free circulation in another Member State than by direct importers of the product constituted a measure having an equivalent effect to a quantitative restriction as prohibited by the Treaty.

Question 2

An exclusive dealing agreement falls within the prohibition contained in Article 85 when it impedes in law or fact the import of the products in question from other Member States into the protected territory by persons other than the exclusive importer.

It may affect trade between Member States and affect competition if the combined effect of an agreement and national law was to prevent parallel imports from Member States into the territory covered by the exclusive import concession.

To decide whether this was the case the Court must take into account not only the rights and obligations flowing from the provisions of the agreement but also the legal and economic context in which it is situated. The Court must also consider the possible existence of similar agreements between the producer and importer established in other Member States.

The maintenance in a Member State of prices appreciably higher than those in another Member State may prompt an examination as to whether exclusive dealing arrangements were being used to prevent importers from obtaining the proof of authencity required by the rules in question. However, the fact that the agreement only authorised the exclusive importer to exploit such a national rule or did not prohibit it from doing so was not sufficient in itself to make the agreement null and void.

CASSIS DE DIJON

REWE Zentrale v Bundesmonopolverwaltung für Branntwein - case 120/78

Facts

A German firm wished to import a French liquor (Cassis de Dijon) whose strength was 15 - 20% alcohol by volume. However, German law forbade the marketing of fruit liquors with an alcohol content below 25%. The firm brought an action which led to a reference by the national court.

Issues

Article 30 forbids "measures having equivalent effect" to measures which impose quotas or otherwise prevent imports. France and Germany had different rules as to the minimum alcohol content of spirits. The effect of the stricter German rules was to keep French spirits out of the German market - i.e. it acted as a restriction on the free movement of goods between Member States. The German government argued that if its domestic laws did not apply to imports and the less strict French law applied then effectively Germany would be bound by the lowest standards in the Community. The Germans justified higher standards by referring to Article 36 which allowed national measures which could be justified on the grounds of public policy. The German government argued that their stricter measures were designed to protect their nationals from alcoholism.

Judgement

The court looked at the two arguments put forward by the German government. The first argument was that the purpose of the German regulations was to avoid the proliferation of alcoholic beverages in the German market as beverages with a low alcohol content could more easily encourage a tolerance towards alcohol than those beverages with a high alcohol content. This argument did not satisfy the court as German consumers were able to purchase beverages with a wide range of alcoholic strength and those of higher strength were generally consumed in a diluted form.

The second argument was that the regulations were designed to protect consumers from unfair practices. The basis of this argument was that there was a relationship between the alcohol content of a product and the cost of the product, as those beverages with higher alcohol contents were subject to higher taxes. The German government also argued that to allow beverages into circulation provided they complied with the rules in their state of production would have the effect that the common standard in the Community would be the lowest standard permitted in any of the Member States. The Court regarded it as being a simple matter to ensure that the purchaser was aware of the contents of the beverage by requiring that the packaging show an indication of where the beverage was produced and its alcohol content. Requirement of minimal alcohol content did not therefore serve a purpose in the general interest which took precedence over the requirement of the free movement of goods. Such requirements constituted an obstacle to trade which was incompatible with Article 30

COSTA

Costa v ENEL - case 6/64

Facts

Italian private electricity companies were nationalised in 1962 and their assets were transferred to ENEL, the National Electricity Board. Mr. Costa was a shareholder in one of the private electricity firms and refused to pay an electricity bill sent to him by ENEL as he objected to the nationalisation of the electricity industry. ENEL sued him and in his defence he pleaded that the nationalisation was both unconstitutional under Italian law and in breach of community law. The Articles of the Treaty alleged to have been breached were Article 102 (Member States must consult the Commission before executing provisions which might distort the Common Market), Article 93 (Member States must inform the Commission if they intend to grant aid), Article 53 (Member States cannot introduce new restrictions on freedom of establishment of nationals of other Member States), Article 37 (providing for diminution of discriminatory provisions protecting State commercial monopolies).

Issues

(i) The reference from the Italian Court appeared only to ask the ECJ to look at whether the Italian laws infringed the Treaty. This was not a question the Court could address. Instead the Court considered whether the Articles were of direct effect and created individual rights which the national court must protect.

(ii) The need for a reference. The Italian government argued that the Italian court did not need to look at the Treaty in order to reach a decision.

(iii) The admissibility of the reference. The Italian government argued that its court should apply national laws and that if those laws were incompatible with the Treaty that was a matter of international law to be decided under Articles 169 and 170.

(iv) Where two sets of rules, national and Community, can apply to a situation one must take precedence. The question was which one prevailed and who decided.

(v) The problem also arose of the effect of national laws which came into effect after the Treaty and which conflicted with it.

Judgement

(1) Wording of the reference

The court ruled that it had the power to extract those questions which pertained to the interpretation of the Treaty from a question imperfectly formulated by a national court.

(2) Was interpretation necessary?

The court dealt with the objection that the reference was not needed by saying that it would not investigate the facts of the case or criticise the grounds and purpose of the request for interpretation.

(3) Was a national court obliged to apply national law?

The court stated that the EEC Treaty had created its own legal system which became an integral part of the legal system of Member States when the Treaty came into force. The national courts were bound to enforce this legal system - "By creating a Community of unlimited duration, having its own institutions, its own personality, its own legal capacity and capacity of representation on the international plane, and, more particularly, real power stemming from a limitation of sovereignty or a transfer of powers from the States to the Community, the Member States have limited their sovereign rights, albeit within limited fields, and have thus created a body of law which binds both their nationals and themselves."

The integration of Community provisions into the laws of Member States together with the general terms and spirit of the Treaty did not allow a Member State to give precedence to a subsequent unilateral measure over a legal system which had been accepted by the Member States on the basis of reciprocity. The effect of Community law should not vary between Member States as a result of domestic legislation.

The Treaty obligations would be merely contingent if they were subject to later national legislation. If Member States could avoid obligations there would be no need for the special procedures for derogation set out in the Treaty. The Court ruled that the Treaty was an independent source of law which because of its unique nature could not be overridden by domestic laws. To do this would be to deprive Community law of its character and call into question the legal functions of the Community. Article 177 was to be applied regardless of any domestic law.

(4) Direct applicability

Article 102: The effect of this Article was that Member States bound themselves to consult the Commission in all cases where the proposed legislation might cause a "distortion". This obligation bound the State but did not create individual rights which national courts must protect.

Article 93: The aim of this provision was the gradual elimination of existing aids and the prevention of the introduction of new aids likely to favour certain products or undertakings in an appreciable way or distort competition. This obligation bound the State but did not create individual rights.

Article 53: This Article prevented Member States from introducing new restrictions on the right of establishment of nationals of other Member States in their territories. This was a legal duty not to act in a specific manner which did not require implementing legislation by the Member States. It was therefore legally complete and produced direct effects on the relations between Member States and individuals. The prohibition came into force when the Treaty came into force and from that moment formed part of the legal system of Member States. The provision created individual rights which national courts must protect. Article 53 is satisfied if no new measure subjects the establishment of nationals of other Member States to rules which are more severe than those applicable to nationals of the state of establishment.

Article 37: This Article provided for Member States to adjust state monopolies of a commercial character to ensure that there was no discrimination between nationals of Member States in the way in which goods were procured and marketed. This imposed a direct obligation on Member States, to adjust state monopolies and to avoid new measures. It was the second of these which the Court had to interpret. This was an absolute prohibition which did not require implementing legislation by Member States and was therefore capable of producing direct effects on the legal relations between Member States and their nationals. Again, this prohibition came into force with the Treaty and became part of the law of the Member States. The entities affected by Article 37(1) were monopolies which firstly had as their object transactions affecting commercial products capable of being the subject of competition and trade between Member States and secondly which played an effective part in such trade.

BONSIGNORE

Bonsignore - case 67/74

Facts

Mr. Bonsignore was an Italian national who had moved to Germany to take up employment as a chemical worker. While in Germany he purchased a pistol without having a firearms permit. While handling the weapon he accidentally shot and killed his brother. A German court fined Mr. Bonsignore for his offence under firearms laws and although it found him guilty of negligent homicide imposed no punishment on this count. Following Mr. Bonsignore´s conviction the German authorities decided to deport him. He appealed against the order and in considering his appeal the national court looked at the Treaty provisions dealing with freedom of movement and Directive 64/221. This provided that deportation or expulsion could only be ordered for reasons of public security or if the presence of the party concerned was such as to prejudice certain other important interests of the Member State. The decision or measure leading to deportation or expulsion could only be adopted if it was justified on the grounds of the personal conduct of the foreigner in question. It was further provided that the existence of a criminal conviction could not in itself constitute grounds for taking such decisions or measures.

Issues

Two questions were put to the Court

(1) Was Directive 64/221 to be interpreted as excluding the deportation of a national of a Member State by the authorities of another Member State for the purpose of deterring other foreign nationals from committing such criminal offences as those with which the person deported was charged or similar offences or other infringements of public security or public policy, that is, for reasons of a general preventive nature?

(2) Does the provision mean that the expulsion of a national of a Member State is only possible where there are clear indications that the person who has been convicted of an offence will commit further offences or

will in some other way disregard public security or public policy of a Member State, that is for reasons of a special preventive nature?

Arguments

The German authorities argued that the distinction between reasons of a "special preventive nature" and those of a "general preventive nature" was irrelevant. Both reasons referred to personal conduct and public policy and public security grounds. The personal conduct of someone convicted of an offence was in itself a reason for deportation. German law considered firearms offences as a particular danger to the peaceful coexistence of Germans and foreigners. The authorities considered that they were justified in taking account of the general danger from foreign nationals convicted of acts of particular danger to the population. The deportation would also have the subsidiary consequence of having a deterrent effect.

The Italian government argued that the Directive was aimed at setting strict limits on the concepts of public policy and public security. The special measures which were exempt from the general rules could only be adopted for reasons of a special preventive nature and not those of a general preventive nature. There had to be a close connection between the expected threat to public policy and the conduct of the worker concerned. In the case of Mr. Bonsignore his conduct was not the cause of the expected threat to public policy. To allow a restrictive measure to be adopted on the basis of a general danger to order in the absence of any expectation of future misconduct by the worker concerned amounted to penalizing a non-national worker by reasons of specific conduct of other persons. The Article expressly excluded the adoption of special measures based solely on the existence of a criminal conviction. General preventive measures were not based on an assessment of the conduct of particular workers but on an abstract assessment of factors which were less objective and less easily verified than the existence of a criminal conviction.

The Commission argued that exceptions to general rules must be interpreted restrictively. Measures "shall be based exclusively on the personal conduct of the individual concerned". This meant that each case must be examined individually. The discretionary power of the state was limited by the Directive to exclude references to previous criminal convictions which did not justify such measures in themselves. The deterrent effect was irrelevant.

If measures of general preventive nature were sufficient to allow the deportation of EC nationals then such nationals would be no better protected than other nationals, which was not the intention of the Treaty.

Judgement

The Court ruled that the provision must be interpreted in the light of the objectives of the Directive which sought to coordinate measures justified on grounds of public policy and maintenance of public security with the basic principle of free movement of persons and the elimination of discrimination in the application of the Treaty between the nationals of the state in question and those of the other Member States.

The Directive provided that measures on the grounds of public policy and the maintenance of public security against nationals of Member States cannot be justified on grounds outside the individual case. Departures from the rule on the freedeom of movement must be strictly construed. "Personal conduct" required that the deportation was ordered only in respect of breach of the peace and public security which might be committed by the individual affected.

The Directive prevented the deportation of a national of a Member State if such deportation was ordered for the purpose of deterring other aliens, i.e.if it was based on reasons of a "general preventive nature".

GEIGY

J.R. Geigy AG v Commission of the European Communities - case 52/69

Facts

The Commission set up an investigation into whether price increases in the dyestuff industry were made by mutual agreement between the undertakings concerned. It found that three uniform price increases had taken place. The Commission began proceedings for infringement of Article 85. A letter was sent to the companies concerned informing them of the decision to take proceedings and giving notice of the objections made by the Commission against the undertakings which had participated.

The Geigy company returned the letter and denied that it could be served by post in Switzerland. The Director General for competition wrote back saying that the notice was only for the purpose of allowing the Company to defend its rights. Silence on the part of the Company would not affect the procedure. The Commission fined the Company without the company making known its point of view. A copy of this decision was sent to the company via a subsidiary in Frankfurt.

Judgement

(1) The Company complained that the letter was signed by the Director General and not a Commissioner and that this was an irregularity which annulled the decision. The Court ruled that this argument was not founded and that as the Commission had approved the letter and delegated the signing of it to the Director General there was no irregularity.
(2) The Company also objected to disparities between the notice of objections and the decision to commence the administrative procedure. The Court ruled that it was the notice of objections and not the decision to commence proceedings which was the measure which stated the final attitude of the Commission concerning undertakings against which proceedings for infringement of the rules on competition had been commenced.
(3) The Company argued that the notice of objections was not served in accordance with Swiss Law (the registered office was in Switzerland) and was therefore null and void. The Court held that the purpose of the notice was to allow those concerned to put forward arguments in the context of

proceedings initiated against them by the Commission. There were no convention between the Community and Switzerland. Therefore the service procedure depended on international practice. The Swiss authorities did not envisage any practice of service on the territory of Switzerland which would be valid under international law. International law could not therefore be invoked to deny the Community the power to ensure the effectiveness of measures aimed at curtailing conduct adversely affecting competition in the Common Market even if the registered office of the undertaking was situated in a third country.

The main purpose of the notice was to allow the undertaking to exercise the rights it enjoys under Community legislation. It achieved this purpose by allowing the recipient to know of the objections and this service would not be held to invalidate the administrative procedure.

(4) The Company also complained that the Commission continued its enquiries after the notice of objection had been served. The Court ruled that the Commission could start fresh inquiries during the administrative procedure if they appeared necessary. The Commission would only need to send an additional notice of objection if the investigations resulted in the discovery of new facts which would be taken into account against the undertaking. This was not the case in those proceedings. The notice sent to the company contained all the information needed to determine the objections made against it.

(5) There was a further complaint by the Company that notification to the subsidiary was ineffective. The Court ruled that irregularities in the procedure for notification of the decision were extraneous to the measure and could not invalidate it.

(6) Finally on the procedural points, the Company argued that by May 1967 it was too late to institute proceedings against it for price increases in January 1964. The court noted that the provisions governing the Commission´s power to fine undertakings for infringement of the competition rules were not subject to a period of limitation. The Court held that the fundamental requirement of legal certainty had the effect that the Commission could not delay the exercise of the power to impose fines indefinitely. However, its conduct in the present case could not be regarded as constituting a bar to the exercise of that power.

Concerted Practices

The Commission produced evidence to show that price increases had been the same, that with rare exceptions the same dyestuffs were involved and the increases were put into effect over a very short period if not on the same date. The Commission argued that it was unrealistic to believe that producers could increase prices by identical percentages at practically the same moment for the same range of products in a number of countries where the conditions on the market were different without previous concertation. The Company argued that the Commission had undertaken an inadequate analysis of the market. The conduct of the business concerned was due to independent business decisions determined by objective business needs especially the need to increase the low rate of profit on the production of dyestuffs. The similarity of rates was the result of "price leadership" by one undertaking.

The Court examined the structure of the dyestuff market, where 80% of dyestuffs were produced by ten undertakings. Except for some special dyes most of these products could be replaced by others quite easily . In the Community there were five separate national markets. Each had different price levels which could not be explained by differences in the cost of producing dyestuffs in those countries. The data showed that even where a producer in one Member State supplied goods to a consumer in another Member State the price was usually fixed in relation to the place where the user was established and prices therefore followed the level in the national market. The resulting division of the market prevented competition.

Advance announcements from the undertakings to each other eliminated uncertainty as to their future conduct. By removing the risk of independent changes of conduct undertakings temporarily eliminated some of the preconditions for competition on the market.

Producers liaised enough not to have to follow each other. The division of the market into five national markets should have made equal price increases on all national markets unlikely. Even if there was a price increase it would be expected to vary according to the particular characteristics of the different national markets. It was also unlikely that those increases could have been brought into effect within a period of two or three days without prior concertation.

The Court stated that it was the function of price competition to keep prices down to the lowest possible level and encourage the movement of goods between Member States. This would allow the most efficient distribution of activities in the matter of productivity and the capacity of undertakings to adapt themselves to change. It was contrary to the rules on competition contained in the Treaty for a producer to cooperate with its competitors, in any way whatsoever, in order to determine a coordinated course of action relating to price increases and ensure their success by the prior elimination of uncertainty regarding each others conduct as to the amount, subject-matter, date and place of the increases. In the circumstances and taking into account the nature of the market, the conduct of the applicant Company and the other undertakings in replacing the risks of competition and hazards of competitors spontaneous reactions by cooperation constituted a concerted practice under Article 85(1).

The Court also addressed two further arguments put forward by the Geigy Company. The first was that as consumers did not usually buy the products outside their own country the actions of the undertakings had not affected trade *between* Member States. The Court held that concerted practices affected the circumstances in which trade between Member States took place. The parties sought to minimize the risk of changing the conditions of competition and as such the applicant's arguments were unfounded.

The second argument was that the Geigy Company was based outside the Community and was therefore not subject to its jurisdiction. The Court held that the conduct of the Company had an effect inside the Community. It had used its power to control subsidiaries in the Community to implement its decisions. The fact that the subsidiaries had separate personalities was not sufficient to exclude the possibility of imputing their conduct to the parent Company. This was particularly so where the subsidiariy did not decide independently on its own conduct. Therefore in certain circumstances the actions of the subsidiary could be attributed to the parent Company. The subsidiary was entirely under the applicants control especially in regard to selling prices. The formal separation of the companies could not outweigh their unity of conduct on the market for the purpose of applying the rules on competition.

CONTINENTAL CAN

Europemballage Corporation and Continental Can Company Inc. v Commission of the European Communities - case 6/72

Facts

The Continental Can Co Inc of New York held a majority stake in a German company and later formed another company which acquired over 90% of the shares in a Dutch company. The Commission instituted proceedings against the American companies for a breach of Article 86 EEC and ordered that a scheme of divestiture be submitted to it.

Issues

The companies argued that the proceedings were irregular, the Commission did not have jurisdiction to take action against undertakings outside the Community and that their actions did not constitute abuse of a dominant position under Article 86.

Judgement

(1) Irregularity of administrative proceedings

Continental Can maintained that it had not had the opportunity to submit its views and the decision did not observe due legal process. The Court disapproved, as a director of both companies had been present at the hearings. The Court further ruled that the notification sent to the company described the essential facts upon which the Commission relied and was therefore sufficient. The Commission had to give reasons for its decisions but was not bound to refute all arguments submitted in the course of the administrative proceedings. The company also complained about the method of service of the decision. The Court ruled that a decision was duly served within the meaning of the Treaty if it was communicated to its addressee and the addressee was enabled to take notice of it.

(2) Jurisdiction of the Commission

Continental Can argued that because it was based outside the Community it was not subject to the jurisdiction of the Commission or the Court of Justice.

It further argued that the conduct in respect of which the Commission had taken proceedings was attributable to the Company's subsidiary. The Court ruled that the fact that the subsidiary had its own legal personality could not rule out the possibility that its conduct could be imputed to its parent company. This was particularly the case where the subsidiary did not autonomously decide its behaviour in the market but generally followed the instructions of its parent company. Continental Can caused its subsidiary to purchase the shares in the Dutch company and provided the necessary funds. As a result the transaction could be attributed to Continental Can. Community law applied to an acquisition which affected market conditions within the Community. The fact that Continental Can did not have a seat in the territory of a Member State was not sufficient to remove it from the jurisdiction of Community law. The plea of lack of jurisdiction was therefore rejected.

(3) Article 86 of the Treaty and the concept of abusive exploitation of a dominant position.

Continental Can was accused of abusing a dominant position in the market of light containers for goods. By the acquisition of the Dutch company it was alleged that the market for these products was almost eliminated in a substantial part of the Common Market. The Company argued that the Commission was attempting to control mergers of undertakings through its erroneous interpretation of Article 86. It also argued that structural measures adopted by undertakings such as the strengthening of a dominant position by means of a merger did not constitute an abusive exploitation of this position.

Article 86 prohibited the abusive exploitation of a "dominant position within the Common Market or in a substantial part of it" by "one or more undertakings [...] in so far as trade between Member States may be affected by it." The Court had to consider whether this was intended only to cover behaviour by undertakings which had a direct effect on the market or whether it also referred to alterations in the structure of an undertaking which led to serious impairment of competition in a substantial part of the Common Market. The Court stated that the rules on competition derived from Article 3 of the Treaty whereby the activity of the Community included the establishment of a system to protect competition within the Common Market from distortion.

The pursuit of this aim was indispensable for the achievement of the tasks of the Community. The general provisions contained in Articles 85 to 90 were aimed at achieving the aims of Articles 2 and 3, in particular, to maintain effective competition in the Common Market. The Court held that in the absence of express provisions it could not be supposed that the Treaty intended in Article 86 to permit undertakings, by merging into an organic unit, to obtain such a dominant position that any serious possibility of competition is almost eliminated. If it were possible to form connections between undertakings so that they escaped Article 85 and Article 86 the partitioning of a substantial part of the Common Market would be permitted contrary to its fundamental principles. Article 86 listed a number of abusive practices which it prohibited. These were examples only and not an exhaustive list of types of abusive exploitations. The provisions applied not only to practices that may cause a direct prejudice to consumers but also to those that cause a prejudice to consumers through interference in the structure of actual competition.

(4) The facts relied on in the decision

The Court ruled that it may be regarded as abusive if an undertaking has such a dominant position that the objectives of the Treaty are frustrated by a substantial change in the supply structure which seriously jeopardizes the consumer´s freedom of action in the market. This is necessarily the case if competition is almost eliminated. If the Commission bases its decision on such an elimination of competition it must give reasons that are sufficient in law to justify it or prove that competition was so substantially impaired that the remaining competitors could not constitute an adequate balance. The Court stated that four essential criteria must be distinguished in the motivation of the decision: (a) the share of the market for the products in question held at the relevant time by the merged enterprises (b) the size of the new unit created by the merger in relation to the size of any competitors in this market (c) the economic strength of customers in relation to the new unit and (d) potential competition either from manufacturers of the same products situated in other geographical markets or from manufacturers of other products situated in the Common Market.

In this case the Commission based its decision on the large share of the market held by the German company, the weak competitive position of the other undertakings in the market, the economic weakness of most consumers in relation to the new unit, the numerous connections between Continental

Can and its competitors and the difficulties (both financial and technical) involved in any other undertaking entering such a market.

The problem was whether or not the German Company dominated the market for light metal containers. It had 70 - 80% of the market share for meat product cans and 80 - 90% of the market for fish cans according to the Commission. The German Company disputed these figures and argued that the Commission had ignored the possibility of competition from substitute products such as glass and plastic containers. The Court accepted that in deciding if there was a dominant position the delimitation of the market concerned was of crucial importance. The Commission had not stated in detail the factors which distinguished the markets for meat containers, fish containers and metal closures from one another or from the general market for light metal containers. A special market could only exist if the product could be individualised not only because it was used to package certain products but also because it had special production characteristics which gave it a specific suitability for that purpose. Therefore a dominant position in the market for light metal containers could not be decisive if it had not been proved that other undertakings could not adapt their products and enter this market. The Court ruled that the Commission had not defined the market sufficiently accurately and that as a consequence its decision was tainted by uncertainty. This uncertainty affected the basis of the decision as to the absence of competition in the relevant market. It followed that the decision had not sufficiently explained the facts and appraisals on which it was based. It was therefore annulled.

CHIQUITA BANANAS

United Brands v Commission - case 27/76

Facts

United Brands Company (UBC) was the largest group in the world banana market, holding 35% of the world market in 1974. The Commission instituted proceedings for infringement of Article 86 after complaints from Danish and Irish companies. It then notified the Company that in its opinion there had been an abuse of a dominant position on the following grounds

- UBC required distributors/ripeners not to sell their bananas while they were green
- distributors/ripeners were charged differing amounts for bananas of the same quality in different Member States without any objective justification
- UBC had refused to supply a Danish Company with Chiquita bananas as it had taken part in an advertising campaign for bananas of a competing brand.

Issues

UBC was fined and ordered to end the infringement. It challenged the Commission's analysis, denied having a dominant position, stated that the requirement relating to green bananas was to safeguard the quality of the product and argued that the refusal to supply to the Danish company was justified. UBC further maintained that its pricing was not discriminatory.

Judgement

(i) The relevant market

In order to decide whether UBC had a dominant position it was necessary to define the market from the standpoint of the product and from a geographical point of view.

(a) The product market

It was first necessary to ascertain whether bananas were part of the fresh fruit market because they were interchangeable with other kinds of fruit such as apples and oranges or whether there was a separate market for bananas. If there was a specific banana market the question was whether it included branded and unlabelled bananas. UBC argued that bananas were part of the general fruit market. The Commission argued that there was a separate market for bananas, which formed an important part of the diet of some sections of the Community. Bananas had special features which distinguished them from other fruits - ripening took place throughout the whole year so there was no season, production exceeded demand throughout the year and marketing could be adapted to other fruit seasons. The fruit had a special appearance, taste and softness. It was also seedless and easy to handle. This made it attractive to the young, elderly and sick. The Court concluded that consumers had a constant need for bananas and were not enticed away by other fruit. The banana market was therefore distinct.

(b) The geographical market

The Commission looked at Germany, Denmark, Ireland, the Netherlands and BLEU (Belgo-Luxembourg Economic Union) and excluded the other Member States because of special import arrangements and conditions which they had. UBC argued that the area selected by the Commission contained Member States with different customs duties and consumer habits. The Court accepted the Commission's submissions.

(2) UBC position on the relevant market

The Court held that Article 86 represents the institution of a system to ensure that competition in the Common Market was not distorted. It prohibits the abuse of a dominant position in a substantial part of the Common Market in so far as it may affect trade between Member States. A dominant position was a "position of economic strength enjoyed by an undertaking which enabled it to prevent effective competition being maintained on the relevant market by giving it the power to behave to an appreciable extent independently of its competitors, customers and ultimately of its consumers". Such a position generally resulted from a combination of factors which were not decisive in themselves. It was necessary to examine the structure of UBC and then the situation in the market as far as competition was concerned.

(a) The structure of UBC

The Court looked at the methods of producing, packaging, transporting, selling and displaying the product.

UBC was vertically integrated to a high degree, from plantation to retailing. It owned large plantations and could purchase from independent producers if necessary. Several independent producers had contractual links with UBC. The Company also had its own factories, machinery and manpower together with its own fleet of ships which could carry two-thirds of its capacity. Research and technical developments allowed UBC to increase productivity and other firms were unable to develop at a comparable level. Large scale advertising had persuaded consumers to show a preference for UBC bananas. Chiquita was a premier brand name and distributors could not afford not to stock it.

(b) Competition on the market

The Court ruled that a trader could only be in a dominant position on the market if he had succeeded in winning a large part of this market. UBC had a 40-45% share of the relevant market. The size of the share did not permit the conclusion that UBC automatically controlled the market. It was necessary to look at the size and strength of the competitors. UBC had a market share several times larger than that of its nearest rival. Although there had been some competitive struggles, UBC competitors had not succeeded in enlarging their market share. In each of the national markets concerned UBC sold almost twice as many bananas as the next placed competitor.

It was also difficult for new competitors to enter the market. A large capital investment was needed to run plantations. Special logistical systems were needed to deal with a perishable product. There were also general expenses which were incurred in penetrating a new market. This was another factor peculiar to a dominant position.

UBC had argued that it lost money in some regions. The Court said that reduced profit margins, or even losses, were not incompatible with a dominant position and must be considered in the light of the whole of the Company's operations. The finding that customers of UBC continued to buy more goods from UBC, which was the most expensive seller, was more significant. Such a finding was a particular feature of a dominant position. The verification of this finding was decisive in this case.

The cumulative effect of all the advantages enjoyed by UBC ensured that it had a dominant position in the relevant market.

(3) Abuse of a dominant position

Regarding UBC's conduct in respect of the ripeners there were two clauses in the agreement which it was alleged caused trade to be impeded. One clause prohibited the resale of bananas while they were green and the other prohibited the ripeners from selling bananas to dealers from other countries.

The UBC clause forbidding resale state that UBC "would not hesitate to take such steps as it deems to be necessary if the foregoing is not complied with in one way or another". The Court regarded this as a threat to impose sanctions if ripeners/distributors did not comply with its directions. The Danish company had experienced the effect of this clause when UBC refused to supply it. The Court ruled that to impose on the ripeners the obligation not to resell bananas so long as they had not been ripened and to cut down the operations of such a ripener to contacts only with retailers was a restriction of competition. UBC claimed the clause was part of their quality policy. This argument could only be justified if the policy did not raise obstacles, the effect of which went beyond the objective to be attained. In this case the prohibitions were an abuse of the dominant position since they limited the market to the prejudice of consumers, in particular by partitioning national markets. The clause prohibiting the sale of green bananas infringed Article 86 of the Treaty.

UBC maintained that it had stopped supplying the Danish Company because it had taken part in an advertising campaign for another supplier. The Commission argued that UBC had taken this action as a deterrent to its other distributors. The Court said that an undertaking in a dominant position for the purpose of marketing a product which was a brand name known to and valued by consumers could not stop supplying a longstanding customer who abides by regular practice. To do so would be to limit the market to the prejudice of consumers. An undertaking in a dominant position could protect its reasonable interests but not if its actual purpose was to strengthen its dominant position and abuse it. A counter attack to competition must be proportionate to the threat, taking into account the economic strength of the undertakings confronting each other. The refusal to supply was an excessive sanction. UBC must have known of the deterrent effect of its actions and its conduct was a serious interference with the independence of small and medium sized firms.

UBC had also argued that its actions did not affect trade within the Community as bananas were imported from third countries. The Court said that if this argument was valid Community law would not apply to UBC in this case. The Court ruled that if an undertaking in a dominant position aimed to eliminate a competitor and it was shown that this elimination would have repercussions on patterns of competition in the Common Market it was immaterial whether or not this behaviour related to trade between Member States. The refusal to supply the Danish company affected the normal movement of trade and the Commission was therefore justified in its decision.

(4) Pricing practice

The cost of importing bananas to the EC was the same for all shipments but the price in the EC varied according to the Member State in which the customer was established. The Commission said that this was an abuse of a dominant position as it put some purchasers at a competitive disadvantage against others. The Court stated that UBC was able to impose a selling price on intermediate purchasers because of its dominant position. Discriminatory prices were an obstacle to the free movement of goods. Together with the clauses in the agreements this created rigid partitioning of national markets. The Court held that the policy of differing prices which enabled UBC to apply dissimilar conditions to equivalent transactions with other trading parties, thereby placing them at a competitive disadvantage, was an abuse of a dominant position.

Unfair Prices

The Commission had ordered UBC to reduce some of its prices because of the partitioning of the market which had sheltered UBC's products from effective competition. The Court ruled that the imposition of an unfair price by an undertaking in a dominant position was an abuse under Article 86 of the Treaty. An excessive price could be ascertained by comparing the sale price and the cost of production. In this case the Commission had failed to prove that UBC had charged unfair prices and its decision was annulled.

<u>Sanctions</u>

UBC had been given a one million units fine by the Commission. The Court ruled that the fine should be related to the gravity of the infringement, their duration and the size of the undertaking. In this case the gravity of the infringement was serious because the product was widely consumed and the consequences of the actions were manifestly inconsistent with the objectives of the Treaty. The infringements had lasted for several years and UBC was a major undertaking. As a result, and considering that UBC had succeeded in its application on one issue, the fine would be 850,000 units of account.

REYNERS

Jean Reyners v Belgian State - case 2/74

Facts

Reyners was a Dutch citizen who was born in Belgium and had been brought up there. He wished to work as a lawyer in Belgium and had completed the normal Belgian legal education. Under domestic law only Belgian nationals can practise in Belgium. A decree of 24 August 1972 made an exception to this rule for nationals of states which allowed Belgians to practise. This did not apply to Reyners, as the Netherlands Bar was not open to Belgian citizens. Reyners brought an action in the Conseil d'Etat, the highest public court in Belgium, to have this decree quashed on the grounds that it was incompatible with Article 52 of the EC Treaty.

Issues

1. The Court referred the question of whether Article 52 became directly applicable when the transitional period given to Member States to implement it ended.

2. The Court also requested a definition of the first paragraph of Article 55, which dealt with activities of the state which related "even occasionally with the exercise of official authority".

Arguments

Article 52

The Belgian, Irish, British and Luxembourg Governments together with the Belgian Bar argued that the Article constituted the expression of a simple provision which could only be implemented through Articles 54 and 57. These Articles provided for a general programme put into effect through directives and the existence of this programme suggested that the Article was not to have direct effect.

The Plaintiff argued that he was the victim of simple discrimination based on nationality and that Article 52 was clear and complete and was capable of producing direct effect. The German and Belgian Governments considered that provisions which obliged member states to fulfill certain obligations within a set period of time should have direct effect when this period had elapsed. Article 54 was only of significance during the transitional period, since freedom of establishment should have been attained at the end of the period.

Article 55

The Article provides an exception to the principle of freedom of establishment where the activities concerned are connected to the exercise of official authority. The Belgian Bar and Luxembourg Government argued that the role of the avocat in judicial procedure and administration of justice meant that the whole profession should be excluded from Article 52. The Plaintiff argued that only certain activities of the avocat where connected with the exercise of official authority and only these came within the exception.

Judgement

Article 52

The Court ruled that the Articles were intended to fulfill two functions:

(i) to eliminate obstacles to the attaining of freedom of establishment during the transitional period, and
(ii) to introduce into the law of member states a set of provisions intended to facilitate the effective exercise of this freedom.

Parts of Article 54 (3) and Article 57 related to the second objective. Article 52 was to be considered within the framework of this system. The rule on equal treatment with nationals was a fundamental legal provision of the Community. Because the rule acted as a reference for national provisions applied by a state to its own nationals it was capable of being directly invoked by nationals of other Member States. Article 52 imposed an obligation to reach a precise result - that freedom of establishment be attained by the end of the transitional period. The achievement of this result was facilitated by a programme of progressive measures. However, it was not dependent on this programme. The obligation continued even if the programme was not fully implemented. This interpretation was in accordance with Article 8 (7) which provided that the end of the transitional period marked the last date by which all the rules and measures to establish the Common Market must be implemented. Once the transitional period was over the programme of directives was superfluous, as the Article then had direct effect. However, these directives did retain a role as measures to make the effective exercise of freedom of establishment more easy.

Article 55

Article 55 could not be given a scope which would exceed the objective for which this exemption provision was inserted. The need to exclude non-nationals from functions involving the exercise of official authority was fully satisfied when the exclusion was limited to those activities which taken on their own constituted a direct and specific connection with the exercise of official authority. The exception could only extend to an entire profession where the imposition of freedom of establishment would result in obliging the Member State concerned to allow the exercise - even occasionally - by non-nationals of functions appertaining to official authority. Where the activities were separable this exception would not be granted.

Professional activities involving contacts, even regular and organic with the courts, including even compulsory cooperation in their functioning do not constitute as such connection with the exercise of official authority. The exercise of activities of an avocat left the discretion of judicial authority and the free exercise of judicial power intact. Official activities did not include activities such as consultation and legal assistance or the representation and defence of parties in court.

VAN BINSBERGEN

Van Binsbergen v Besturr van de Bedrijsverenging voor de Metaalnijverheid - case 33/74

Facts

During proceedings before a social security court in the Netherlands the capacity of one of the legal representatives was questioned. The representative was a national of the Netherlands who had moved his residence to Belgium. Under Netherlands law only persons established in the Netherlands could act as legal representatives before the court.

Issue

The question before the court was whether, once the transitional period had expired, Articles 59 and 60 were directly applicable.

Judgement

(1) Scope of Articles 59 and 60

The restrictions abolished by Articles 59 and 60 included all restrictions which were not applicable to somebody established in the national territory and which were imposed on the person providing the service by reason of his nationality or place of residence and which prevented or interfered with the activities of the person providing the service.

A requirement that the person providing the service be habitually resident in the territory of the state deprived Article 59 of all useful effect as the entire aim of the Article was to abolish such restrictions. However, where such requirements had as their purpose the application of professional rules, especially those relating to organisation, qualifications, professional ethics, supervision and liability which were justified by the general good they would not be considered incompatible with the Treaty where such rules could otherwise be evaded by someone who provided the service in another Member State. Member States would not be prevented from regulating the services of people whose activities were directed towards their territories where these people were established in another Member State for the purpose of avoiding the professional rules of conduct which would apply to them if they were established within that Member State. Situations such as this would be regulated by the Court under the provisions relating to the right of establishment and not those on the provision of services.

On this basis, a requirement that a person who provided services in connection with the administration of justice be permanently established within the jurisdiction of certain courts or tribunals would not be considered incompatible with the provisions of Articles 59 and 60 where such a requirement was objectively justified in order to ensure that professional rules of conduct, especially those concerned with the administration of justice and professional ethics, were observed. However, this was not the case where the provision of a service was not subject to any sort of qualification or professional regulation and where the requirement of establishment was fixed by reference to the territory of the Member State in question. Where the exercise of an activity within the territory of a Member State is unrestricted the requirement of residence within the state constitutes a restriction which is incompatible with Articles 59 and 60 if the administration of justice can be ensured by less restrictive measures.

Articles 59 and 60 must be interpreted as meaning that the national law of a Member State cannot deny persons established in another Member State the right to provide services by way of imposing a requirement of residence within the territory of the Member State where the provision of services is not subject to any special condition under the applicable national law.

(2) Direct Applicability of Articles 59 and 60

The question of direct applicability was to be determined in the light of the whole of the chapter on services contained in the EEC Treaty. During the transitional period restrictions were to be progressively abolished by a series of directives. These directives had several functions:

(i) To abolish restrictions on freedom to provide services during the transitional period.
(ii) To introduce provisions into the law of Member States to facilitate the exercise of this freedom.

(iii) To resolve problems arising from the situation where the person providing the service is not established in the Member State where the service is performed and is therefore not fully subject to the professional rules of conduct in force in that state.

In accordance with Article 8(7) the aim of Article 59 was to abolish restrictions on freedom to provide services by the end of the transitional period. The provisions of Article 59 therefore became unconditional on the expiry of that period. The obligations under Article 59 and 60 cannot be delayed or jeopardised by the absence of provisions which were to be adopted under powers conferred by Article 166. Paragraph 1 of Article 59 and paragraph 3 of Article 60 have direct effect in so far as they seek to abolish any discrimination against somebody providing a service by reason of his nationality or the fact that he resides in a Member State other than that in which the service is to be provided.

COMMISSION v GERMANY - case 427/85

Facts

The German government enacted a statute to put into effect Directive 77/249. The German statute contained the following requirements:
- That a lawyer providing services in Germany had to act in conjunction with a lawyer established on German territory, even where under German law there was no requirement of representation by a lawyer.
- That the German lawyer, in conjunction with whom he must act, be the authorised representative or defending counsel in the case.

It also did not allow the lawyer providing services to appear in oral proceedings unless accompanied by the German lawyer and imposed requirements regarding proof of the co-involvement of the two lawyers. The statute further provided that the lawyer providing services was to be accompanied by a German lawyer if he visited a person in custody and was not to correspond with that person except through the German lawyer. The lawyer providing services was also made subject to the rule of territorial exclusivity laid down in the Bundesrechtsanwaltordnung.

The Commission brought an action under Article 169 for a declaration that the Federal Republic of Germany had failed in its obligations to facilitate the effective exercise by lawyers of freedom to provide services.

Issues

The Court identified three problems

(i) the scope of the work which must be done in conjunction with a German lawyer
(ii) the detailed rules governing work in conjunction
(iii) the restriction of the right to plead to a specific geographical area.

Judgement

(i) The scope of the work in conjunction

The German statute obliged the lawyer providing services to work in conjunction with a lawyer established in Germany whenever he proposed to act "as the representative or defending Counsel of a client" in legal proceedings and some administrative proceedings. The Commission argued that this obligation was too broad and identified three specific areas (i) practising before courts of law (ii) practising before administrative authorities (iii) contacts with persons held in custody.

The Commission argued that in relation to practising before courts of law the obligation to work in conjunction with a national lawyer should only apply where the domestic law of the Member State laid down that a party could only be represented by a lawyer acting as representative of defending Counsel. Where this was not a mandatory requirement and where a party could defend his own interests or allow a non-lawyer to do so, a lawyer providing services should be allowed to represent or defend a client without working in conjunction with a German lawyer.

The Court took the approach that the Treaty had prohibited any restriction on the provision of services and the Directive only contained measures intended to facilitate this objective. The prohibition requires the abolition of all discrimination against the person providing the service by reason of his nationality or the fact that he is established in a Member State other than that in which the service is to be provided. Article 60 of the EEC Treaty provided that a person could temporarily pursue his activity in the State where the service is provided "under the same conditions as are imposed by that State on its own nationals". Freedom to provide services was a fundamental principle of the Treaty. It could only be restricted by rules which were justified in the general good and which were imposed on all persons pursuing activities in the Member States and only if that interest was not protected by the rules to which the provider of the service was subject in the Member State in which he was established.

As German law allowed parties to conduct their cases themselves or to entrust them to someone who was not a lawyer (provided that person did not act in a professional capacity) there was no consideration relating to the public interest which could justify the obligation for a lawyer established in another Member State who is providing his services in a professional capacity, to work in conjunction with a German lawyer. A lawyer providing services had to comply with all the professional rules applicable in Germany. The requirement to work in conjunction set out in the German Statute therefore infringed the Directive.

The same criteria applied to the activities of lawyers providing services before administrative authorities.

(2) The detailed rules concerning work in conjunction

The Commission criticised the approach of the German Government to determining the meaning of "work in conjunction" and especially the requirements of proof of work in conjunction, the role of the German lawyer and contacts with persons in custody. The German government argued that it was necessary for a German lawyer to be involved at all stages of proceedings and that the freedom to provide services should not interfere with the administration of justice.

The Court ruled that the meaning of "work in conjunction" in Article 5 of the Directive had to be interpreted in the light of the purpose of the Directive which was "to facilitate the effective exercise by lawyers of freedom to provide services". As a consequence, whilst the Directive allowed national legislation to provide that a lawyer providing services must work in conjunction with a local lawyer it was the intention of the Directive to allow lawyers providing services to carry out the tasks entrusted to him by his client. The requirement to act in conjunction was intended to give the lawyer providing services the support necessary to enable him to act within a judicial system different to his own. The two lawyers should be able to agree upon the appropriate form of their cooperation. This did not mean that Member States could not lay down a general framework for cooperation but the obligation imposed by such a framework for cooperation should not be disproportionate in relation to the objectives of the duty to work in cooperation.

The Court held that the requirements laid down by the German statute imposed obligations which went further than was necessary for the attainment of these objectives. There was one exception, which related to the rules governing contacts between lawyers and persons in custody, where there were public security considerations the appraisal of which was a matter for the Member State concerned.

(3) Restriction to a specific geographical area of the right to plead

The German Code of Civil Procedure laid down that representation by a lawyer was compulsory before some courts. Where this was the case the lawyer had to be admitted before the court in which the case was brought. The Commission did not believe this rule should apply to lawyers providing services as they did not have establishment in Member States other than their own and would not be admitted to practise before other judicial authorities. The German government argued that a German lawyer not admitted before the judicial authority in question would be in the same position as the lawyer providing services who was based in another Member State. The restriction of the right to plead to a specific geographical area was introduced to aid the administration of justice and improve communications between lawyers and judicial authorities.

The Court stated that the aim of Articles 59 and 60 was to enable the provider of a service to pursue his activities in Member States where he was not established without suffering discrimination in favour of the nationals of that State. This did not mean that all national legislation was to be applied in its entirety to the temporary activities of persons who were established in other Member States. The Court concluded that the rule of territorial exclusivity could not be applied to the activities of a temporary nature pursued by lawyers established in other Member States. This finding applied subject to the obligation of the lawyer providing services to work in conjunction (within the limits set out in the rest of the judgement) with a lawyer admitted to practice before the judicial authority in question. There was an exception in the case of the Bundesgerichtshof. Admission to this court was granted on the basis of selective admission to a specialised group of lawyers who had special knowledge or experience. Admission was not restricted on the basis of territorial exclusivity.

SECTION C

LANGUAGE PRACTICE

Chapters 1-3

A. Comprehension

Please answer the following questions:

1. **What does the phrase "sectoral integration" mean?**
2. **When was the term "European Community" officially approved?**
3. **What are the requirements for becoming a member of the Community?**
4. **What do the abbreviations EMS, ERM, and ECU stand for?**
5. **What was the major effect of the Cecchini Report?**
6. **What does the Schengen Agreement provide for?**
7. **What is the WEU?**
8. **Which Member States had the Maastricht Treaty approved by a popular referendum?**

B. Vocabulary

Please explain the following terms in English:

1. **to approximate**
2. **to distort**
3. **to comprise**
4. **transitional**
5. **accession**
6. **acquis communautaire**
7. **Single European Act**
8. **dissenting**
9. **to attain**
10. **Director-general**

C. Language Practice

C.1. Please pronounce the following words or describe them using phonetic transcription:

1. **inevitably**
2. **sovereignty**
3. **irrevocable**
4. **unanimously**
5. **assent**
6. **plebiscite**
7. **suffrage**
8. **noticeable**

C.2 Please match the following:

(a) One treaty lists restrictions...	1. of economic convergence.
(b) The United Kingdom showed divided interest...	2. for economic convergence.
(c) The two oil crises helped cause the need.	3. on imports and exports.
(d) They were in need...	4. in joining the Community.

C.3 Please fill in the missing prepositions:

(a) Free movement of goods, persons, services, and capital is ensured ___ accordance ___ the provisions of Article 7a EC Treaty.

(b) The Council and the Commission were to be assisted ___ an Economic and Social Committee.

C.4 Please list the past tense forms of the following verbs:

(a) to seek (b) to mean

C.5 The following sentences are grammatically incorrect. Please correct them.

(a) Italy is a Member State since 1990.

(b) As regarding the functional approach to achieving the European Community, the foreign ministers of the ECSC countries decided to take further steps towards economic integration at the Conference of Messina in June 1955.

(c) The fact that Eastern Europe was controlled by the Soviet Union in the late 1940's changed the idea of how a united Europe would look like.

D. Translation

Please translate the following excerpt:

After World War II the idea of a united Europe intensified. Sir Winston Churchill was the first to express the idea of a united Europe by calling upon

reconciliation between France and Germany in his speech in Zurich in 1946. One year later, on 14 March 1947, Belgium, Luxembourg and the Netherlands signed a treaty setting up the *"Benelux Economic Union"*. This was the first economic supranational organization in Western Europe. It became clear that plans for European integration would only extend to Western Europe, because the eastern part was controlled by the Soviet Union at that time. The destroyed continent was in bitter need of financial support, which was offered by the US through the Marshall Plan. This plan demanded an international organization to distribute and use the funds in an effective way: the Organization for European Economic Cooperation (OEEC) was established in Paris in 1948. This European Recovery Programme (ERP) was directed to the Eastern European countries, too, but they refused to accept, fearing exposure to American economic domination. [Having fulfilled its post-war purposes the OEEC changed into the Organization for Economic Cooperation and Development (OECD) in 1961. It proved to be an essential contribution towards the recovery of the European national economies.

E. Composition

Please write an essay or conduct a discussion on the following:

> How did the federalist and functional approaches to a European community differ? Compare the arguments pro and con for each view.

Chapters 4-5

A. Comprehension

Please answer the following questions:

1. What are the four most important institutions of the EC, and by which treaties were they established?
2. What is the name of the Community's financial institution?
3. In a "separation of powers" system, what are the three branches of power?
4. What does the principle of subsidiarity allow for?
5. Which institution of the Community initiates Community policy,

serves as the executive branch, defends the Community interest in the Council, and acts as the guardian of the Treaties?

6. How many Commissioners does the Commission have, including the President?
7. Describe the ratio of Commissioners to Member States. (How many may each Member State appoint?) What is the method based on?
8. What are the requirements of becoming a Commissioner?
9. Which institution supervises Commissioners?
10. How long is a Commissioner's term, and is it renewable?
11. What occupational stipulation is put on the Commissioners?
12. How are the President and Vice President(s) of the Commission chosen?
13. What are some of the President's main tasks?
14. How long may a President serve, and who has proved to be an exception to this rule?
15. Which institution may apply for the dismissal of a Commissioner and which institution may execute the dismissal?
16. What is the unwritten rule which is understood by Commissioners in regards to the Commission's decisions?
17. What is the Commission's main legislative role?
18. What is the three stage plan of action used by the Commission if a Member State is not fulfilling its obligations?

B. Vocabulary

Please explain the following terms in English and provide a translation into German:

1. autonomous
2. competence
3. allocation
4. consensus
5. deadlock
6. to implement
7. co-operation and co-ordination
8. principle of subsidiarity

C. Language Practice

Please fill in the missing prepositions:

1. Contrary ___ most other international organizations, the EC is based on a set of institutions that share the tasks of the Community.
2. Co-ordination is the commitment ___ mutual exchange of information and to match certain actions.
3. The President is appointed ___ common accord.
4. The Commission is subject ___ supervision of the EP.
5. Decisions must be taken ___ majority vote.
6. Some Commissioners are responsible ___ one area.

D. Composition

Please write an essay on the following:

Explain the interacting powers of the EP, Commission, Council, and Court of Justice. Include legislative, executive, and judiciary roles.

Chapter 6

A. Comprehension

Please answer the following questions:

1. What form of electing members to the European Parliament took 20 years to accomplish?
2. Which electoral procedure do the Member States use when electing a member to the EP?
3. How often are EP elections held?
4. Which members of the Bureau of the EP are not allowed voting rights?
5. How many standing committees are there in the EP?
6. What do these committees do?
7. What is the most drastic power the EP can use against the Commission?
8. The Parliament's role was a purely consultative one before which two treaties?
9. What are the two types of expenditure in the Community's budget, and who has authorisation over which part?
10. Which procedure was introduced by the Single European Act?

B. Vocabulary

Please explain the following terms in English:

1. to envisage
2. suffrage
3. plenary session
4. ombudsman
5. co-operation procedure
6. non-compulsory expenditure
7. petition

C. Translation

Please translate the following excerpt:

A draft budget for the following calendar year must be submitted to the EP by the Council for its first reading no later than 5 October - Article 203 (4) EC. The Parliament has the right to amend the draft budget, acting by an absolute majority of the votes cast; however, it can only amend the NCE parts of the budget. It can only propose modifications to the compulsory expenditure parts of the budget. If the Parliament makes amendments and proposes modifications - which is usually the case - the draft budget is forwarded to the Council. After discussing the draft budget with the Commission, the Council may modify any of the amendments adopted by the EP and modify the other parts of the draft budget on the basis of the proposed modifications. Then the modified draft budget must be presented to the EP for a second reading. In this respect, the Parliament has no power to alter the parts of the budget relating to compulsory expenditure. It has, however, 15 days within which to amend or reject the modifications made by the Council to the Parliament's first reading amendments on NCE.

D. Composition

Please compose an essay in answer to the following:

> Which treaties and/or institutions give power to the EP and which subject matters fall under its jurisdiction?

Chapter 7

A. Comprehension

Please answer the following questions:

1. **Which institution of the Community has the greatest legislative power?**
2. **Who are its members?**
3. **Who is regarded as the main representative of a country?**
4. **Please describe the rotation of the presidency in the Council.**
5. **How are the councils meetings held? (Who attends the meetings?)**
6. **What are the three voting methods recognised by the EC Treaty?**
7. **Which procedural decisions of the Council require unanimity?**
8. **Which country did not approve of the qualified majority voting procedure and consequently did not attend the Council's meetings for six months?**
9. **What does the abbreviation COREPER stand for?**

B. Vocabulary

Please explain the following terms in English and provide a translation into German:

1. **unanimity**
2. **qualified majority**
3. **simple majority**

C. Language Practice

C.1 Please fill in the missing words:

The d____n of votes in the q_______d m_______y voting system does not depend on the p______n of a state. It is said the votes are w_______d.

C.2 Please match the following terms to the words that best describe them:

1. impetus	**(a) to establish**
2. accession	**(b) joining**
3. to block	**(c) driving force**
4. to institute	**(d) to obstruct**

C.3 Please list the noun forms of the following terms:

1. the office held by the president
2. competent
3. autonomous
4. to implement
5. according
6. unanimous

D. Composition

Please discuss the weighting of votes in the qualified majority system and how the voting system works.

Chapter 8

A. Comprehension

A.1 Please fill in the missing words:

The judges of the Court of Justice are a_____d by c_____n a______d of the governments of the Member States. They serve a t___m of six years.

Due to the r_______n system of the judge's seat, it is impossible to be r__________d for another term.

A.2 Please answer the following questions:

1. Which position in the Court of Justice best prepares one to become a judge?
2. What number of judges is needed to take a decision?
3. How are discussions for decision-taking held?
4. The Court of Justice was relieved of some of its work with the establishment of which institution?
5. Which court has higher requirements and is considered the high court?
6. What are the four methods of interpretation?
7. Which interpretation method does the Court prefer?
8. What are the four grounds of review stipulated by Article 173?
9. How long is the average waiting period for a decision from the Court of Justice in a preliminary ruling?

10. **What are the three requirements for the Court to grant liability in a case brought before it?**

B. Vocabulary

Please explain the following terms in English and provide a translation into German:

1. literal interpretation
2. historical interpretation
3. contextual interpretation
4. purposive interpretation
5. locus standi

C. Language Practice

Please match the following terms with the words that best describe them:

1. attribute	(a) to officially hand down
2. annulment	(b) following
3. subsequent	(c) awaiting decision
4. infringement	(d) invalidation
5. to render	(e) characteristic
6. pending	(f) to put right
7. to remedy	(g) violation

D. Translation

Please translate following excerpt:

Secondly, the Court was relieved of a part of its work with the Single European Act by the establishment of the *Court of First Instance*. It took up its work in 1989. It has its seat in Luxembourg next to the European Court. There are twelve judges, one nominated by each Member State. The Council decision setting up the Court of First Instance did not plan any associated advocates-general, although the Court may ask any member to perform the task of an advocate-general. In such a case he does not take part in the decision of the case and has the same tasks as an advocate-general of the Court of Justice. The member who acts as an advocate-general in a special case is nominated by the President of the Court. There are three chambers which deal with staff cases, each with three judges deliberating, and two chambers dealing with competition cases where five judges deliberate.

Sometimes the Court meets in plenary session. This is only the case when the assigned chamber requests that the case be heard in a plenary session. The decisions are taken in secret on the basis of a majority vote at the Court of Justice. The judges of the Court of First Instance were usually holders of national judicial office, academics, or legal civil servants. The requirements are not as high as those for appointment to the European Court.

E. Composition

Please explain the interactive system of the different institutions when dealing with a Member State which has failed to fulfil an obligation.

Chapters 9-12

A. Comprehension

Please provide answers to the following by first formulating a question and then answering the same:

> Ex.: The effect of *this* Treaty was to introduce the cooperation procedure.
> (*Quest: Which was the treaty that introduced .....? or*
> *What was the name of the treaty that introduced .....?)*
> *Answer: (Which was) the Single European Act*

1. Manufacturers, farmers, carriers, workers, dealers, craftsmen, and other groups are represented by *this* Committee of the Community.
2. *This* bank is a non-profit organization which grants loans and gives guarantees for financing in all sectors of the economy.
3. *This* group draws up an annual report at the end of each financial year and also assists the EP and the Council in implementing the budget.
4. *This* Committee consists of 189 representatives of regional and local bodies with advisory function. It advises the Council and Commission in cases of educational, cultural, and health protecting measures.

B. Vocabulary

Please match the word to its corresponding sentence:

a. convenes
b. cohesion
c. contributes
d. facilitate
e. implementation

1. The president of the committee ______ the meetings.
2. The European Investment Bank ______ to the balanced and steady development of the common market.
3. The loans and guarantees of the European Investment Bank _________ the financing of projects.
4. The Economic and Social Committee must be consulted in the field of economic and social ______.
5. The Court of Auditors assists the EP and Council in ________ of the budget.

C. Language Practice

Please fill in the missing prepositions:

1. in conjunction ____
2. at a rate __
3. critical __
4. succeed __ (doing something)
5. supply someone ____ something
6. increase __ number
7. entitled __

D. Translation

Please translate the following excerpt:

The Bank can borrow money on the capital markets and lend it to private and public undertakings. Most of the loans are granted for projects within the Community, but some are meant to provide aid to other countries all over the world. The loans are used to finance infrastructure and industrial and agricultural projects in the Mediterranean countries, the countries of Africa, the Caribbean and the Pacific. The Bank's financial aid to the countries of Central and Eastern Europe, especially Hungary and Poland but also the Czech Republic, Bulgaria and Romania is of great importance.

E. Composition

Imagine that you are a representative of the Economic and Social Committee. Describe your duties and some of the interest groups you deal with. Include some of the matters you represent them in.

Chapters 13-15

A. Comprehension

A.1 Please answer the following questions:

1. How can the Community's legislation be compared to the legal structure of a democratic country?
2. With which organization does the EC team up to form the European Economic Area?
3. What are the four freedoms established by the Treaty?
4. Please describe, in short, the principle of proportionality.
5. What is the relationship between Community law and the laws of the Member States?
6. Which document is considered the most important constitutional document?

A.2 Please fill in the missing words:

The principle of subsidiarity:

"In areas which do not fall w____n its exclusive c_______e, the Community shall take actions, in a_______e with the p_______e of subsidiarity, only if and in so far as the objectives of the proposed action cannot be s_______y achieved by the Member States and can therefore, ... , be better a_______d by the Community."

B. Vocabulary

Please describe the following terms in English:

1. free movement of goods
2. free movement of persons
3. free movement of services
4. free movement of capital

C. Language Practice

C.1 Please restructure the following sentences according to the example:

Ex. : Which organization does the EC team up with?
With which organization does the EC team up?

1. Where is the President of the Court appointed from?
2. An absolute ban on importation is established by what?
3. Which territory may workers move freely in?

C.2 Please match the following terms with the words that best describe them:

1. exclusive	(a) capable of being measured
2. quantitative	(b) limited
3. vigorous	(c) adequate
4. sufficient	(d) to be in accordance
5. conforming	(e) powerful, strong

C.3 Now, please list the noun forms of the above listed adjectives 1-5.

D. Translation

The Community's legislation can be compared to the legal structure of a democratic country: a constitution establishing the legal foundation and a system of laws based thereupon. The constitutional documents of the Community are the Treaty that established the European Community and all of its amendments, the Treaty that established the European Coal and Steel Community, and the Treaty on the European Atomic Energy Community. According to these Treaties, the Council and the Commission are supposed to make regulations, issue directives, take decisions, make recommendations, or deliver opinions (Article 189 EEC Treaty, Article 161 Euratom Treaty, and Article 14 Treaty on Coal and Steel Community). Regulations, directives, decisions, recommendations, and opinions are considered as secondary legislation.

Chapters 16-18

A. Comprehension

Please answer the following questions:

1. **How do other states take up relations with the EC?**
2. **What does the abbreviation GATT stand for?**
3. **What has happened to the GATT memberships of the twelve Member States?**
4. **What name is used for the system of stabilising the export proceeds of agricultural products?**
5. **What name is used for the balance and aid system for mining products?**
6. **From which fund is most financial aid granted?**
7. **Which financial institution gives credits to ACP countries?**
8. **What does the abbreviation ACP stand for?**
9. **What does the abbreviation EFTA stand for?**
10. **Which countries established the EFTA?**
11. **The European Economic Area established improved association between what two entities?**
12. **When was the EEA Treaty finally signed?**
13. **What percentage of the world's trade takes place in the European Economic Area?**
14. **Please describe the Cassis de Dijon principle.**

B. Vocabulary

Please match each term to the corresponding sentence:

(a) plebiscite	**(d) pursuant**
(b) accredited	**(e) reciprocal**
(c) scrupulous	

1. **Unfortunately, the doctor could not practice medicine because he had not attended a(n) _______ university.**
2. **The law is described in ________ detail.**
3. **These countries allow each other _______ privileges.**
4. **To accept or reject the plan, a _______ was held.**

5. Because of strict regulations, this must be done ________to instructions.

C. Language Practice

Please fill in the missing prepositions:

1. All trade agreements must comply ____ EC law.
2. Some regulations are not permanent, but are only __ use for the time being.
3. The Member States must carry out their obligations _____ the Treaty.
4. The customs union and the common trade policy of the EC must be carried out__ compliance ____GATT.

D. Translation

Please translate the following excerpt:

In the late 1980s, it became clear that the European Community would complete the common market by 1993. The EFTA countries feared serious disadvantages in trade with the Community, its most important trade partner. For this reason solutions were searched for. In 1984, the ministers of the then 16 EEC and EFTA states suggested the creation of a European Economic Area. Jacques Delors, President of the Commission, again brought this idea up in a speech before the European Parliament in 1989. From the point of view of the EEC this improved form of association might prevent potential candidates from applying for accession. Some EFTA countries considered this offer as the golden mean between isolation and full membership, allowing them to participate in the internal market.

Chapters 19-23

A. Comprehension

Please answer the following questions:

1. What does the form of legislation (regulation, directive) mainly depend on?

2. Please explain, in short, the difference between a regulation and a directive.
3. What is the nature of recommendations and opinions?
4. The opinion of which institution is binding?
5. Which form of legislation is binding in its entirety, and is commonly issued to only one Member State or company?

B. Vocabulary

Please match the following terms with the words that best describe them:

1. derogation	(a) partial repeal or abolishing of a law
2. approximation	(b) to examine
3. to embody	(c) to list
4. to scrutinise	(d) the act of drawing together
5. to enumerate	(e) to comprise or give form to

C. Language Practice

Please list the adjective forms of the following terms:

1. residence
2. initially
3. stipulate
4. favour
5. advice

D. Translation

Please translate the following excerpt:

The different types of legislation are used for different purposes depending on what the institution wants to regulate, how important the matter is and to whom it is directed. In important matters, for instance, the Commission would issue a regulation to bind all Member States. In other cases a directive may be sufficient if only one Member State or even only one or more undertakings are concerned. Thus, the form of legislation depends entirely on the subject matter. Most of the provisions in the Treaty stipulate which form is to be used. In some cases the institution may even have a choice. The effect of the Court's decisions on Community legislation is very interesting and important. In several judgements, the Court has explained how a certain provision of the Treaty is to be understood.

E. Composition

Please briefly list some occasions which require each of the forms of legislation (regulation, directive, decision, opinion, and recommendation.)

Chapters 24-26

A. Comprehension

Please answer the following questions:

1. What are two important procedures for the making of Community law?
2. What happens in the event of a clashing of laws between the EC and the legal system of one of the Member States?
3. Several countries reject the supremacy of EC law when these laws violate what?
4. What did the Dassonville formula explain?
5. Which principle allowed regulations restricting the movement of goods in the Community?

B. Vocabulary

Please match the following terms with the words that best describe them:

1. conciliation	(a) study of the law and legal system
2. primacy	(b) supreme
3. sovereign	(c) supremacy
4. corollary	(d) agreement based on compromise
5. jurisprudence	(e) secondary consequence

C. Language Practice

Please fill in the missing prepositions:

1. voting ____ absolute majority

2. take all of the facts ____ consideration
3. the amendment was accepted __ the EP
4. gaining access __ the Community
5. the procedures differ __ format

D. Translation

Please translate the following excerpt:

> By creating a Community of unlimited duration, having its own institutions, its own personality, its own legal capacity and capacity of representation on the international plane and, more particularly, real powers stemming from a limitation of sovereignty or a transfer of powers from the States to the Community, the Member States have limited their sovereign rights, albeit within limited fields, and have thus created a body of law which bonds both their nationals and themselves. The integration into the laws of each Member States of provisions which derive from the Community, and more generally the terms and spirit of the Treaty, make it impossible for the States, as a corollary, to accord precedence to a unilateral and subsequent measure over a legal system accepted by them on a basis of reciprocity.

Chapters 27-29

A. Comprehension

Please answer the following questions:

1. Please describe, briefly, how the free movement of capital differs from the other three freedoms.
2. What was the hardest part of setting up a financial common market in the Community?
3. What happened in the late 1960's and in the 1970's that caused many Member States to reintroduce controls on the movement of capital?
4. What does the abbreviation EMS stand for, and what was it expected to change?
5. Please describe, briefly, the ERM.
6. What is the EMCF and who are its members?
7. Please describe the success of the EMS.

8. What did the White Paper aim to accomplish?
9. What advantages would a single European currency bring to the EC?
10. When were the four freedoms implemented?

B. Vocabulary

Please match the following terms to the words that best describe them:

1. divergence	(a) deviation, difference
2. logistical	(b) unalterable
3. irrevocable	(c) planned in detail
4. commencement	(d) beginning

C. Language Practice

Please use the correct form of the given words in the following sentences:

1. established:	A three stage plan provides for the ________ of a single currency.
2. fluctuate:	Some countries are allowed special rates of ________.
3. generation:	A single currency could ________ stability.
4. symbolise:	Some benefits would be purely ________.
5. remove:	One goal is the ________ of physical, technical and fiscal barriers.

D. Composition

Please explain, in your own words, the three stage plan for the establishment of an economic and monetary union consisting of a single currency.

Chapter 30

A. Comprehension

1. Please describe some advantages provided by competition.
2. What is the term used to describe the produced amount of a product and the need for it from the consumer?
3. What are the four conditions to be fulfilled for an exemption to the competition policy?

4. Of the four conditions, which one is better known as the economic benefit criterion?
5. How is the workload of the Commission minimised in dealing with exemptions?
6. What is sometimes the practice of large firms, which is incompatible with EC laws on competition policy?
7. What provision forbids this practice? (It is another name for Article 86.)

B. Vocabulary

Please match the following terms with the words that best describe them:

1. cartel	(a) discovery
2. exemption	(b) property
3. prohibition	(c) syndicate
4. detection	(d) immunity
5. premises	(e) forbiddance

C. Language Practice

Please change the following words into antonyms by adding the appropriate prefix:

Ex. : conformity - nonconformity

1. fair	4. dependent
2. compatible	5. discriminatory
3. competitive	6. explicit

D. Composition

Please set up and describe an imaginary company which abuses its dominant position on the market. Describe its product(s) and its effect on competition.

Chapters 31-33

A. Comprehension

1. In the beginning, the Community's social policy focused only on employment. How has it expanded?
2. How does Directive 76/207 go beyond Article 119's demand for equal pay regardless of the employee's sex?
3. What employment benefit does Directive 79/7 regulate?
4. Why did the United Kingdom reject the Community Charter of the Fundamental Social Rights?
5. What is the term given to the attainment of goods or services for public use?
6. There are several directives concerning the opening up of government procurement and the stipulation that contracts must be advertised in the Official Journal. Which interest group is protected from discrimination by these directives?
7. What is the basic function of the European Economic Interest Grouping?

B. Vocabulary

Please match the following terms with the words that best describe them:

1. acquisition	(a) addition
2. procurement	(b) discriminating
3. vocational	(c) limit
4. biased	(d) occupational
5. threshold	(e) attainment

C. Language Practice

Please fill in the missing prepositions:

1. in respect __	5. in addition __
2. focus __ a topic	6. to have effect __
3. used __ one's advantage	7. __ so far __
4. calculated __ the basis of time	

D. Composition

Please explain, in your own words, the three types of procurement procedures set up by Directive 88/295. (open, restricted, and negotiated)

Chapters 34-36

A. Comprehension

A.1 Please answer the following questions:

1. What does the abbreviation CAP stand for and which interest groups should benefit from it?
2. How are agricultural products of the Member States able to compete on the market with prices higher than world market prices?
3. What are the types of prices in the price system of agricultural products? Please describe them briefly.
4. What is the MGQ and what does it regulate?

A.2 Please answer the following by first formulating a question and then answering the same: (*for an example see language practice section A of Chapters 9-12)*

1. The provisions of the EC provide for equal treatment of professions practised in Member States when the educational background comes from a different Member State. There is, however, no directly applicable provision in the EC Treaty to provide for this practice.

2. The EC tried to regulate professions using this method, which ended up being too difficult.

3. This general directive was adopted by the EC to regulate all professions.

4. These types of courses are not included in the EC's definition of vocational training.

B. Vocabulary

Please choose the word that fits in each sentence.

(a) subsidy
(b) exodus
(c) intervention
(d) regime

1. Because of its economic downfall, the country was provided with a(n) ________ from another government.
2. Countries which are neutral do not practice _________ in affairs of other countries.
3. The old system of governing is no longer applied; a new ______ was established.
4. Every summer there is a(n) ____________ out of the Country.

C. Language Practice

Please list the past tense forms of the following verbs:

1. deal
2. forbid
3. lend
4. wake

D. Translation

Please translate the following excerpt:

Soon after this First Programme was published (Annex to Council Resolution of 14 April 1975), about 80 directives were issued on the protection of consumers' health and safety. These directives covered provisions on food stuffs, fruit, vegetables, animal health, motor vehicles, chemical substances, household goods and cosmetics. The right to protection of legal and economic interests aims at fighting "against the abuse of power by the seller, in particular against one-sided standard contracts, the unfair exclusion of essential rights in contracts, harsh conditions of credit, demands for payment for unsolicited goods and against high-pressure selling methods" (OJ 1975, C92, Article 19). Furthermore, the consumer must have the right to complain about defective products or unsatisfactory services and be awarded redress for injury or damage deriving from them. The right to information should enable the purchase of goods or services to recognize differences between competing products and services and to make a rational choice. The consumer should have access to information about the safe use of dangerous products. Organization representing the consumer's interests have been established, e.g. the Consumers Consultative Committee in 1973.

E. Composition

Please construct an imaginary consumer and create a story explaining how one provision in each of the four programmes of consumer protection has defended his interests or helped him in some way.

Chapters 37-38

A. Comprehension

Please answer the following questions:

1. When were frontier checks and quota restrictions on goods crossing from one Member State to another lifted?
2. What does the abbreviation TEN stand for?
3. What activities will TEN facilitate?
4. What is the name given to the directive which allows the free movement of television broadcasting within the Community?
5. What are some restrictions placed on advertising under the "television without frontiers" directive?
6. How does this directive provide for the protection of minors?

B. Vocabulary

Please match the following terms to the words that best describe them:

1. mode	(a) pertaining to the sea
2. sanctions	(b) type, method, or way
3. cabotage	(c) provision of law enacting a penalty
4. maritime	(d) coastal navigation or trade
5. compulsory	(e) mandatory

C. Language Practice

Please list the noun forms of the following terms:

1. efficient	5. characterising
2. eliminating	6. recognise

3. acknowledge
4. introduce
7. improving
8. integrated

D. Translation

Please translate the following excerpt:
The Community has established a policy to try to attain certain cultural objectives in the European audio-visual industry. For this reason, the Council adopted a five years programme (1991-1995) with a financial support of ECU 200 million. This cultural media programme is also open to the EFTA countries, since European culture cannot be bound by frontiers. The programme may even be extended to East European countries. The measures of the programme pay attention to national differences and try to maintain them, avoiding cultural uniformity. Presently more than 20 projects are being supported:

Chapters 39-40

A. Comprehension

Please answer the following questions:

1. How is the budget of the European Coal and Steel Community financed?
2. What was the most significant amendment made to budgetary provisions at the Hague Summit?
3. What changes were brought about by the Financial Provisions Treaty of 1975?
4. What agreement provided for the improvement of budgetary discipline and procedure?
5. What was replaced by the Court of Auditors?
6. When was the customs union achieved for the original Member States?
7. How was this accomplished?

B. Vocabulary

Please describe the following principles:

1. Principle of Unity
2. Principle of Annuality
3. Principle of Universality
4. Principle of Specification
5. Principle of Non-Assignment
6. Principle of Equilibrium

C. Language Practice

Please change the following sentences from informal to formal:

> Ex. : The store I work for is going out of business.
> The store *for which I work* is going out of business.

1. The land the house was built on belongs to her.
2. The pet store we bought our dog from is right across the street.
3. The price we agreed on was fair.
4. The man you were speaking to was Mr. Miller.
5. The door we just came through is made of cedar.
6. The theatre piece you read about is playing tonight.

D. Translation

Please translate the following excerpt:

> The Community shall be based on a customs union which shall cover all trade in goods and which shall involve the prohibition between Member States of customs duties on imports and exports and of all charges having equivalent effect, and the adoption of a common customs tariff in their relation with third countries.

E. Composition

Please explain the decision-making process for adopting a budget.

Key to the language practice section

Chapters 1-3

A. Comprehension

1. the unification of Europe sector by sector 2. in 1977 3. Any European country may apply but must be accepted. 4. European Monetary System, Exchange Rate Mechanism, European Currency Unit 5. It gained approval from business, industry, and trade unions for a barrier-free market. 6. a frontier-free market 7. Western European Union, formerly the West Union 8. only Denmark and France

B. Vocabulary

1. to estimate, simulate, or approach closely to 2. to alter, misrepresent, or twist 3. to include, contain, or consist of 4. undergoing change 5. addition 6. the totality of EC law 7. Treaty of 18 February 1986 introducing inter alia the internal market concept 8. differing, rejecting, or disagreeing 9. to achieve, reach or succeed in 10. head of an administrative department of the Commission

C. Language Practice

C.1 Pronunciation: 1. in ev′ i te blee 2. sov′ rin tee 3. i rev′e ke bel 4. yoo nan′e mes lee 5. e sent′ 6. pleb′e site or pleb′e sit 7. suf′rij 8. no′ti se bel

C.2 Prepositional phrases: A. 3,B. 4,C. 2,D. 1.

C.3 Fill in: A. in accordance with, B. assisted by.

C.4 Verb tenses: A. sought, B. meant

C.5 Syntax

A. Italy has been a Member State since 1990. ("has been" because of "since")

B. As regards the functional approach...or Regarding the functional approach...

C. ...changed the idea of how a united Europe would look. or ...changed the idea of what a united Europe would look like.

Chapters 4-5

A. Comprehension

1.a. the Council, the Commission, the European Parliament, the Court of Justice;
b. They were established by the Treaty of Paris and the Treaty of Rome. 2. the European Investment Bank 3. legislative, executive, and judiciary 4. It allows Member States to act on their own, unless they need or wish to refer the responsibility to the Community level. 5. the Commission 6. 17; 7. France, Germany, Italy, Spain, and the United Kingdom may appoint two Commissioners each, because they are the largest countries. The other countries may appoint only one each. 8. One must have general competence, may not receive instructions from any national government, and must be a national of a Member State. 9. The European Parliament 10. A term lasts 5 years and is renewable. 11. The Commissioners may not engage in any other occupation, whether gainful or not. 12. The President is nominated by the governments of the Member States by common accord after having consulted the EP. The Vice President(s) is/are appointed by the Commission from among its members. 13. Chairing the Commission's meetings, proposing the allocation of portfolios to individual Commissioners, presenting the Commission's legislative programs to the EP yearly. 14. The President's term lasts two or at most four years. Jacques Delors served a ten year term. 15. The Council may apply, and the Court may dismiss. 16. The

Commission's decision must be supported in public by all Commissioners, even by those who voted against it. 17. to initiate proposals 18. A. The Commission sends a letter of formal notice to that Member State. B. The Commission delivers a reasoned opinion on the matter. C. The Commission may bring the matter before the Court of Justice.

B. Vocabulary

1. autonom, selbstregierend 2. Kompetenz, Zuständigkeit 3. Zuteilung, Zuweisung 4. Konsens, Übereinstimmung 5. Stillstand 6. vollziehen, ausführen, durchführen 7. Zusammenarbeit und Abstimmung 8. Grundsatz der Subsidiarität

C. Language Practice

1. to, 2. to, 3. by, 4. to, 5. by, 6. for

Chapter 6

A. Comprehension

1. direct universal suffrage 2. the state's own national voting procedure 3. every 5 years 4. quaestors 5. 18; 6. They prepare the Parliament's opinion on legislative proposals brought to the Council by the Commission. They make suggestions for acceptance, rejection, or amendment of these proposals. 7. A motion of censure, requiring the entire Commission to resign. 8. the Budgetary Treaties of 1970 and 1975 9. compulsory and non-compulsory expenditure: The EP has authorisation over NCE, and the Council over compulsory expenditure. 10. the cooperation procedure

B. Vocabulary

1. to contemplate or envision 2. vote given in favour of a proposed measure 3. attended by all qualified members 4. public official who investigates complaints by private citizens against a community institution 5. procedure for the acceptance of amendments, requiring the "cooperation" of the Commission, Council, and EP 6. expenditure which is not the inevitable consequence of Community legislation 7. a formally drawn request, often signed by those endorsing it.

Chapter 7

A. Comprehension

1. the Council 2. representatives of governments of the Member States, usually ministers 3. the foreign minister 4. The presidency rotates in alphabetical order. 5. The meetings are held privately, although sometimes televised. 6. unanimity, qualified majority, and simple majority 7. a. changes in number of Commissioners b. changes in number of judges and advocates-general in the Court c. acceptance of a new Member State d. appointment of members to the Court of Auditors e. holding a Council meeting in public f. appointment of the Council Secretary-General 8. France 9. the Committee of Permanent Representatives

B. Vocabulary

1. a consensus or undivided opinion--Einstimmigkeit 2. requisite number of votes in favour of a decision exceeding a simple majority--Qualifizierte Mehrheit 3. 51% of the votes -- Einfache Mehrheit

C. Language Practice

C.1 Fill in: distribution, qualified majority, population, weighted

C.2 Matching: 1. c.; 2. b; 3. d.; 4. a.

C.3 Nouns: 1. presidency 2. competence 3. autonomy 4. implementation 5. accordance (or accord) 6. unanimity

Chapter 8

A. Comprehension

A.1 Fill in: appointed, common accord, term, rotation, renominated/reappointed

A.2 Answers to questions: 1. advocate-general 2. an uneven number, because of the majority voting system and the absence of a casting vote 3. They are held in secret and in French without interpreters. 4. the Court of First Instance 5. the Court of Justice 6. literal, historical, contextual, purposive 7. contextual and purposive 8. a. lack of competence b. infringement of an essential procedural requirement c. infringement of the Treaty d. misuse of powers 9. 17 months 10. a. The institution must have acted unlawfully. b. The person bringing the action has to have suffered damage. c. A direct link in the chain of causality must exist between the wrongful act and the damage caused.

B. Vocabulary

1. Tries to ascertain the words in their natural and ordinary meaning--Wortinterpretation 2. Tries to reveal the intention of the legislator--Historische Interpretation 3. Finds the overall context of the legal provision in which the words appear -- Systematische Interpretation 4. Seeks the objectives stated in the law--Teleologische Interpretation. 5. the right to have a case heard in a court

C. Language Practice

1. e.; 2. d.; 3. b.; 4. g.; 5. a.; 6. c.; 7. f.

Chapters 9-12

A. Comprehension

1. (What is) the Economic and Social Committee 2. (What is) the European Investment Bank 3. (What is) the Court of Auditors 4. (What is) the Committee of Regions

B. Vocabulary

1. a.; 2. c.; 3. d.; 4. b.; 5. e.

C. Language Practice

1. with 2. of 3. of 4. in 5. with 6. in 7. to

Chapters 13-15

A. Comprehension

A.1 Answers to questions: 1. It has a constitution and a system of laws based thereupon. 2. with the EFTA; 3. free movement of goods, free movement of persons, free movement of capital, free movement of services; 4. The Community may take action only with measures proportionate to the objective and with burdens minimised. 5. Community law supersedes national laws 6. the Treaty establishing the European Economic Community.

A.2 Fill in: within, competence, accordance, principle, sufficiently, achieved

B. Vocabulary

1. It reduces and even abolishes trade barriers between Member States. 2. Workers may move freely in a Member State for reasons of employment. 3. Residents of Member States may provide services in other Member States. 4. Capital movements are freed only to the extent necessary to ensure proper functioning of the common market.

C. Language Practice

C.1 Sentence structure: 1. From where is the President of the Court appointed? 2. Whereby is an absolute ban on importation established? 3. In which territory may workers move freely?
C.2 Matching: 1. b.; 2. a.; 3. e.; 4. c.; 5. d.;
C.3 Nouns: 1. exclusivity, exclusiveness, exclusion; 2. quantity, quantitativeness; 3. vigour, vigorousness; 4. sufficiency; 5. conformation, conformity

Chapters 16-18

A. Comprehension

1. They usually take up diplomatic relations in the form of missions. 2. General Agreement on Tariffs and Trade 3. They are still in effect. 4. STABEX 5. SYSMIN 6. European Development Fund 7. European Investment Bank 8. countries of Africa, the Caribbean, and the Pacific 9. European Free Trade Association 10. Austria, Denmark, Norway, Portugal, Sweden, Switzerland, and the United Kingdom 11. the EC and the EFTA; 12. on 2 May 1992; 13. 40%; 14. Any commodity produced anywhere in the EEA may be sold anywhere in the EEA unless specific requirements stand in the way. (free movement of goods)

B. Vocabulary: 1. b.; 2. c.; 3. e.; 4. a.; 5. d.

C. Language Practice:

1. with; 2. in; 3. under; 4. in, with

Chapters 19-23

A. Comprehension

1. the purpose or objective 2. A regulation is "binding in its entirety" and directly applicable to all Member States. A directive is binding, as far as the result to be achieved, but may only apply to one Member State. The form and methods of implementation are left to the Member States. 3. They are non-binding. 4. opinions of the Court of Justice 5. a decision.

B. Vocabulary: 1. a.; 2. d.; 3. e.; 4. b.; 5. c.

C. Language Practice: 1. residential; 2. initial; 3. stipulatory; 4. favourable; 5. advisory

Chapters 24-26

A. Comprehension

1. the cooperation procedure and the conciliation and veto procedure 2. The EC law has priority over national law. 3. the fundamental rights of the country 4. It explained the meaning of measures having equivalent effect to quantitative restrictions. 5. the Cassis de Dijon principle

B. Vocabulary: 1. d.; 2. c.; 3. b.; 4. e.; 5. a.

C. Language Practice: 1. by; 2. into; 3. by; 4. to; 5. in

Chapters 27-29

A. Comprehension

1. It is more dangerous because the shifting of large amounts of capital may influence financial markets or even national economies. 2. The fact that every Member State has its own currency. 3. The loss of confidence in the US Dollar and the two oil crises of the 1970's. 4. European Monetary System; It was believed that it would help governments

fight inflation and promote trade throughout Europe. 5. The Exchange Rate Mechanism allows for fluctuation of exchange rates. 6. European Monetary Cooperation Fund; the governors of the central banks. 7. It overcame several crises, exchange rates remained more stable in comparison to other monetary systems, inflation rates were reduced, and economic policies gained on stability. 8. It aimed to attain an internal market by proposing measures for the removal of physical, technical and fiscal barriers. 9. elimination of exchange costs, the boosting of trade production of welfare gains, generation of more stability, influence against US $ and Japanese Yen, symbolic identity of unified Europe; 10. 1 January 1993

B. Vocabulary: 1. a.;2. c.;3. b.; 4. d.

C. Language Practice: 1. establishment; 2. fluctuation; 3. generate; 4. symbolic; 5. removal

Chapter 30

A. Comprehension

1. Lower prices and wider selection for the consumer 2. supply and demand 3. An agreement must contribute to the improvement of production or distribution of goods or to the promotion of technical or economic progress. It must benefit the consumer. It must not impose restrictions which are not indispensable to the attainment of the objectives, and must not permit the elimination of competition in respect of a substantial part of the products in question. 4. The condition that an agreement must contribute to economic progress. 5. The Commission issues block exemptions. 6. the abuse of a dominant position 7. the monopoly provision

B. Vocabulary: 1. c.; 2. d.; 3. e.; 4. a.; 5. b.;

C. Language Practice: 1. unfair; 2. incompatible; 3. non-competitive; 4. independent; 5. non-discriminatory; 6. inexplicit

Chapters 31-33

A. Comprehension

1. It now encompasses education, health, and culture as well. 2. It demands equal treatment, in addition to equal pay. 3. Social Security 4. The United Kingdom believed it would diminish the flexibility of the market. 5. public procurement 6. foreign bidders on contracts 7. To enable companies to cooperate within the Community.

B. Vocabulary: 1. a.; 2. e.; 3. d.; 4. b.; 5. c.

C. Language Practice: 1. to; 2. on; 3. to; 4. on; 5. to; 6. on; 7. in, as

Chapters 34-36

A. Comprehension

A.1 Answers to questions: 1. common agricultural policy; Both the producers' and the consumers' interests are considered. 2. An import tax is imposed on imports from outside of the Member States, making them more expensive. 3. the target price- a price agreed upon by the Council, which allows farmers to plan their production and to know which price they can expect on the market. It includes the cost of transport to deficit areas. The intervention/guarantee price- the price for which the government will buy surplus products. It is lower than the target price. The threshold price- the price for imported

cereals. 4. the maximum guaranteed quantity; It regulates overproduction of milk. If overproduction occurs, support payments to farmers are reduced.
A.2 Answers in question form: 1. (What is) the recognition of professional qualifications of a person from another Member State 2. (What is) the issuing of directives for each profession 3. (What is) the Mutual Recognition Directive 4. (What are) courses which improve general knowledge but don't provide actual occupational preparation
B. Vocabulary: 1. a.; 2. c.; 3. d.; 4. b.
C. Language Practice: 1. dealt; 2. forbade; 3. lent; 4. woke.

Chapters 37-38

A. Comprehension
1. 1 January 1993; 2. trans-European network 3. the exchange of information between the national networks and the integration of outlying regions of the Community 4. "television without frontiers" 5. There is a time-limit of 15% of the daily transmission time. Certain medicinal products, tobacco, and alcohol are all under restriction. 6. It states that pornographic, racist, or violent themes may only be shown late in the evening or not at all.
B. Vocabulary: 1. b.; 2. c.; 3. d.; 4. a.; 5. e.
C. Language Practice: 1. efficiency; 2. elimination; 3. acknowledgement; 4. introduction; 5. characteristic, characterisation; 6. recognition; 7. improvement; 8. integration

Chapters 39-40

A. Comprehension
1. by a European tax imposed on coal and steel firms; 2. the increase in budgetary powers of the EP; 3. a. The EP was given exclusive right to adopt the annual budget. b. The "inverted majority rule" is to be used when modifications to the compulsory part of the budget have been proposed. c. the establishment of the Court of Auditors; 4. the Inter-institutional Agreement of 1988; 5. The Audit Board; 6. 30 June 1968; 7. Customs duties between Member States were abolished and a common customs tariff for goods coming from non-EC countries was agreed upon.
B. Vocabulary
1. All items of revenue and expenditure shall be included in the budget of the EC. 2. The budget shall be authorised for one financial year. 3. All revenue and expenditures being entered in the budget must be listed in full without any adjustments against each other. 4. There is no lump sum classification allowed for expenditures entering the budget. They must be specified exactly. 5. All revenue sources must always be available to cover all expenditures and may not be assigned to certain expenditures in advance. 6. The sum of revenue must correspond with the sum of expenditures.
C. Language Practice
1. The land on which the house was built belongs to her. 2. The pet store from which we bought our dog is right across the street. 3. The price on which we agreed was fair.
4. The man to whom you were speaking was Mr. Miller. 5. The door through which we just came is made of cedar. 6. The theatre piece about which you read is playing tonight.

SECTION D

GLOSSARY

abolish frontiers (to)	Grenzen abschaffen
abolition of restrictions	Abschaffung/Beseitigung von Beschränkungen
absolute majority	absolute Mehrheit
abuse of a dominant position	Mißbrauch einer beherrschenden Stellung
academic recognition	akademische Anerkennung
accede (to)	beitreten
access to a profession	Zugang zu einem Beruf
accession	Beitritt
accession treaty	Beitrittsvertrag
accounting unit	Verrechnungseinheit
acquis communautaire	Übernahme des bestehenden EG-Rechts
Act of Accession	Beitrittsakte
acte clair	Grundsatz, daß der EuGH nicht im Vorabentscheidungsverfahren zur Auslegung eines Textes angerufen wird, wenn dem behandelnden Gericht die Bedeutung des auszulegenden Textes klar ist (frz.)
action against inactivity	Klage gegen Untätigkeit (eines Organs)/Untätigkeitsklage
action against Member States	Klage gegen Mitgliedstaaten
action for annulment	Anfechtungsklage
action for damages	Schadenersatzklage
action for failure to act	Untätigkeitsklage
action to have the infringement established	Klage auf Feststellung einer Vertragsverletzung
ad-hoc groups	Ad-hoc-Sitzung
addressee	Adressat
admission	Zulassung, Aufnahme
adopt (to)	annehmen, verabschieden
adoption	Annahme, Harmonisierung
adoption of a single currency	Einführung einer einheitlichen Währung
adoption of common standards	Harmonisierung gemeinschaftlicher Normen
advisory bodies	beratende Organe
advisory circular	beratendes, unverbindliches Rundschreiben
advisory committee	beratender Ausschuß
Advisory Committee on the Opening Up of Public Procurement	Beratender Ausschuß für die Liberalisierung des öffentlichen Auftragswesen
advisory committee procedure	Verfahren des Beratenden Ausschusses
advisory function	beratende Funktion
advocate-general	juristischer Berater eines Richters am EuGH
Advocates-General	Generalanwalt (EuGH)
aggregation	Anhäufung, Ansammlung
agreement	Vereinbarung, Vertrag, Übereinkunft
agreement between undertakings	Vereinbarung zwischen Unternehmen
agreement on joint purchase	Vereinbarung über den gemeinsamen Einkauf
agreement on joint sale	Vereinbarung über den gemeinsamen Verkauf

agricultural advisory committee (Council and Commission)	Beratender Ausschuß für die wichtigsten landwirtschaftlichen Erzeugnisse (Rat und Kommission)
agricultural levy	Agrarabschöpfung
agricultural policy	Agrarpolitik
aid	Hilfe, Subventionen
aid programmes	Hilfsprogramme
align tax rates (to)	Steuersätze angleichen/ harmonisieren
alignment	Angleichung, Harmonisierung
allocation of portfolios	Ressortzuteilung
amend (to)	ändern, abändern, ergänzen
amendment	Ergänzung, Nachtrag, Novelle, Abänderung
ancillary organ	Hilfsorgan, untergeordnetes Organ
anti-competitive agreements	wettbewerbswidrige Vereinbarungen
anti-competitive cartels	wettbewerbsschädliche Kartelle
anti-dumping duty	Antidumping-Abgabe
anti-dumping provisions	Antidumping-Vorschriften
anti-dumping rules	Antidumping-Vorschriften
approximate (to)	angleichen
approximation of law	Annäherung/Angleichung des Rechts
approximation of taxes	Annäherung/Harmonisierung der Steuern
aptitude test	Eignungstest, Eignungsprüfung
arbitrary discrimination	willkürliche Diskriminierung
assent	Zustimmung, Genehmigung
assessment of the environmental impact of Community measures	Beurteilung der Umweltverträglichkeit der Gemeinschaftsmaßnahmen
assistance mechanism	Beistandsmechanismus
association	Vereinigung, Anschluß, Verbindung, Verband
Association agreement	Assoziierungsabkommen
asssociated with (to be)	verbunden sein mit, in Verbindung stehen mit
attainment of economic and monetary union	Verwirklichung der Wirtschafts- und Währungsunion
attribute (to)	zuschreiben, beilegen
attribution of state powers	Zuschreibung von staatlichen Hoheitsrechten
audio-visual policy	Medienpolitik
authentic language	authentische Sprache
autonomy	Autonomie, Selbstständigkeit
award of contract	Zuschlag, Auftragsvergabe
balance of payment	Zahlungsbilanz
balance-of-payments difficulties	Zahlungsbilanzschwierigkeiten
Bank for International Settlements (BIS)	Bank für Internationalen Zahlungsausgleich (BIZ)
bank supervision	Bankenaufsicht
banking and credit	Kredit- und Bankwesen
banking supervision policy	Bankenaufsichtspolitik
barrier	Schranke, Hindernis, Beschränkung
Benelux Economic Union	Benelux Wirtschaftsunion
bilateral trade agreements	bilaterale Handelsabkommen

block exemption	Gruppenfreistellung
Block Exemption Regulation (1983/84)	Gruppenfreistellungsverordnung (1983/84)
bodies	Organe, Institutionen
bonded warehouse	Zollager
border check	Grenzkontrolle
breach	Bruch, Verletzung, Übertretung
breach (to)	brechen, verletzen, übertreten
breach of treaty obligations	Verletzung von Vertragsbestimmungen, Vertragsbruch
Brussels Convention on Jurisdiction and the Enforcement of Judgements in Civil and Commercial Matters	Brüsseler Übereinkommen über die gerichtliche Zuständigkeit und die Vollstreckung gerichtlicher Entscheidungen in Zivil- und Handelssachen
budget	Haushalt
budget deficit	Haushaltsdefizit
budgetary power	Haushaltsbefugnis
Budgetary Treaty 1970	Haushaltsvertrag 1970
bypass (to)	abweichen von
Cabinet	Beamtenkabinett
cabotage	Kabotage
CAP (Common Agricultural Policy)	GAP (Gemeinsame Agrarpolitik)
capital and payments	Kapital- und Zahlungsverkehr
capital market	Kapitalmarkt
capital movement	Kapitalverkehr
capital outflow	Kapitalabfluß
cartel	Kartell
Cassis de Dijon principle	Cassis de Dijon Prinzip
Cassis de Dijon ruling	Cassis de Dijon-Entscheidung
CEN (Comité Europeen de Normalisation/European Committee for Standardization)	Europäisches Komitee für Normung
CENELEC (European Committee for Electrotechnical Standardization)	Europäisches Komitee für elektrotechnische Normung
central bank	Zentralbank
Central Bank Governors	Zentralbankpräsidenten
CFI (Court of First Instance)	Gerichtshof Erster Instanz
CFP (Common Fisheries Policy)	Gemeinsame Fischereipolitik
Chamber (ECJ)	Kammer (EuGH)
Chef de Cabinet	Kabinettchef
choose by lot (to)	auslosen
citizenship of the Union	Unionsbürgerschaft
CMLR (Common Market Law Reports)	Sammlung der Rechtssprechung des EuGH
code of behaviour	Verhaltensregel
code of rules treaty	Normenvertrag, Gesetzesvertrag
cohesion	Zusammenhalt, Kohäsion
Cohesion Fund	Kohäsionsfonds
collective bargaining	Tarifverhandlungen

Comité des Représentants Permanents (COREPER)	Ausschuß der Ständigen Vertreter
Comité Europeen de Normalisation (CEN)	Europäisches Kommitee für Normung
Commission Decision	Entscheidung der Kommission
Commission Recommendation	Empfehlung der Kommission
Commission Regulation	Verordnung der Kommission
Commission's Department	Dienststelle der Kommission
Commission's Notice on Agreements of Minor Importance (1986)	Bekanntmachung über Vereinbarungen von geringer Bedeutung (1986)
Commissioner	Kommissionsmitglied
commitment appropriation	Verpflichtungsermächtigung
Committe for Agriculture	Landwirtschaftsausschuß
committe of inquiry	Untersuchungsausschuß
Committe on Budgets	Haushaltsausschuß
Committee for Scientific and Technical Research(Council and Commission)	Ausschuß für wissenschaftliche und technische Forschung (Rat und Kommission)
Committee of government representatives	Ausschuß von Regierungsvertretern
Committee of Governors of the Central Banks	Ausschuß der Zentralbankpräsidenten
Committee of Permanent Representatives	Ausschuß der Ständigen Vertreter
Committee of the Regions	Ausschuß der Regionen
Commmunity competence	Gemeinschaftszuständigkeit
common accord	gegenseitiges Einvernehmen
Common Agricultural Policy (CAP)	Gemeinsame Agrarpolitik
Common Commercial Policy	gemeinsame Handelspolitik
Common Customs Tariff	Gemeinsamer Zolltarif
Common Defence Policy	gemeinsame Verteidigungspolitik
common domain	gemeinsames Aufgabengebiet
Common Fisheries Policy (CFP)	Gemeinsame Fischereipolitik
Common Foreign and Security Policy	Gemeinsame Außen- und Sicherheitspolitik
Common Market	Gemeinsamer Markt
Common Market Law Reports (CMLR)	Sammlung der Rechtsprechung des EuGH
Common Market Reports	Englische Übersetzung von Urteilen des EuGH
common objectives	gemeinsame Ziele
common position	gemeinsamer Standpunkt
common standards	gemeinschaftliche Normen
common units of account	Verrechnungseinheiten
communication	Mitteilung, Verständigung
Community borrowing	Gemeinschaftsanleihen
Community Charter of the Fundamental Social Rights of Workers, 1989	Sozialcharta von 1989
Community citizen	Gemeinschaftsbürger
Community Civil Service	Beamtenschaft der Gemeinschaften
Community co-insurance	Mitversicherung auf Gemeinschaftsebene
Community Funds	Gemeinschaftsfonds

Community funds	Gemeinschaftsmittel
Community interest	Gemeinschaftsinteresse
Community law	Gemeinschaftsrecht
Community lending operation	Gemeinschaftsdarlehen
Community loan	Gemeinschaftsanleihe
Community order	Gemeinschaftsanordnung
Community policies	Politiken der Gemeinschaft
Community spending	Gemeinschaftsausgaben
Community system of legal protection	Rechtsschutzsystem der EG
Community-wide market	Binnenmarkt
compartmentalization	Abschottung
compatible	(aufeinander) abgestimmt, im Einklang
competence	Zuständigkeit, Kompetenz
competition	Wettbewerb, Konkurrenz
competition law	Wettbewerbsrecht
Competition Policy	Wettbewerbspolitik
competitiveness	Wettbewerbsfähigkeit
complainant	Beschwerdeführer, Antragsteller, Kläger
complaint	Beschwerde
complementary legislation	ergänzende Rechtsvorschriften
completion of the internal market	Vollendung des Binnenmarktes
completion of the Single Market	Vollendung des Binnenmarktes
compulsory consultation	obligatorische Anhörung
compulsory expenditure	zwingende Ausgaben
compulsory items	zwingende Ausgaben
concerted action	abgestimmtes Verhalten
concerted practice	abgestimmtes Verhalten
concerted practices	abgestimmte Verhaltensweisen
concession contract	Konzessionsvertrag
conciliation and veto procedure	Verfahren der Mitentscheidung
Conciliation Committee	Vermittlungsausschuß
conciliation procedure	Konzertierungsverfahren, Schlichtungsverfahren
concurrent competence	konkurrierende/parallele Zuständigkeit
confederation	Konföderation, Staatenbund
Confederation of European industry (Unice)	Verband der Industrien der Europäischen Gemeinschaft (Unice)
Conference of Foreign Ministers	Außenministerkonferenz
Conference of Parliaments („Assises“)	Konferenz der Parlamente („Assises“)
Conference on Security and Cooperation in Europe (CSCE)	Konferenz für Sicherheit und Zusammenarbeit in Europa (KSZE)
conjunctural policy	Konjunkturpolitik
consensus	Konsens
constitutional documents	Verfassung
consultation procedure	Beratungsverfahren
Consultative Committee	Beratender Ausschuß
Consultative Committee on Cartels and Monopolies	beratender Ausschuß für Kartelle und Monopole

consumer credit	Konsumentenkredit
consumer protection	Verbraucherschutz, Konsumentenschutz
consumer protection policy	Konsumentenschutzpolitik
Consumers' Consultative Committee	Beratender Verbraucherausschuß
Contact Committee	Kontaktausschuß
contextual interpretation	systematische Auslegung
contractual liability	vertragliche Haftung
control on capital movement	Kapitalverkehrskontrolle
convention	Konvention, Abkommen, Übereinkunft
Convention of Lomé 1975	Lomé-Abkommen 1975
convergence criteria	Konvergenzkriterien
convergence of the member states' economies	Konvergenz der Volkswirtschaften der Mitgliedsstaaten
conversion loan	Umstellungsdarlehen
cooperation agreement	Abkommen zur Zusammenarbeit, Kooperationsabkommen
cooperation procedure	Verfahren der Zusammenarbeit
Coordination Committee	Koordinierungsausschuß
coordination directive	Koordinierungsrichtlinie
coordination of economic policies	Koordinierung der Wirtschaftspolitik
COREPER (Comité des Représentants Permanents)	Ausschuß der Ständigen Vertreter
Council act	vom Rat erlassener Rechtsakt
Council Decision	Entscheidung des Rates
Council Directive	Richtlinie des Rates
Council of Economic and Finance Ministers (ECOFIN)	Rat der Wirtschafts- und Finanzminister
Council of Europe	Europarat
Council of Ministers	Ministerrat
Council of Ministers of Foreign Affairs	Rat der Außenminister
Council of the EMI	Rat des EWI
Council Presidency	Ratsvorsitz
Council Regulation	Verordnung des Rates
countervailing duty	Gegenmaßnahme tarifärer Natur
countervailing measure	Gegenmaßnahme
country of destination	Bestimmungsland
country of origin	Ursprungsland
Court of Auditors	Rechnungshof
Court of First Instance (CFI)	Gerichtshof Erster Instanz
Court of Justice (ECJ)	Europäischer Gerichtshof (EuGH)
creation of an area without internal frontiers	Schaffung eines Raumes ohne Binnengrenzen
cross-border	grenzüberschreitend
CSCE (Conference on Security and Cooperation in Europe)	Konferenz für Sicherheit und Zusammenarbeit in Europa (KSZE)
currency exchange	Währungsumtausch
currency fluctuation	Wechselkursschwankung
customs	Zoll, Zollabgaben

customs barriers	Zollgrenzen
customs tariff	Zoll, Zolltarif
customs union	Zollunion
Dassonville formula	Dassonville Formel
dawn raids	nicht angekündigte Inspektionen „im Morgengrauen“
De Minimis rule (agreements of minor importance)	De-minimis-Regel (Vereinbarungen von geringer Bedeutung)
decision	Entscheidung
decision by associations of undertakings	Beschluß von Unternehmensvereinigungen
decision granting a discharge in respect of implementation of the Community budget	Beschluß über die Entlastung der Führung des Haushaltsplans
decision-making process	Prozeß zur Entscheidungsfindung
declaratory	erklärend, erläuternd
delegated legislation	übertragene Gesetzgebung
delegation of state powers	Übertragung von staatlichen Hoheitsrechten
deliberate (to)	beraten, überlegen
deliberation	Beratung
deliver an opinion (to)	Stellungnahme abgeben
Delors-Report (1989)	"Delors-Bericht" (1989)
derogation	Beschränkung, Teilaufhebung, Abänderung, Minderung, Abweichung
revaluation	Aufwertung
development aid	Entwicklungshilfe
development cooperation	Entwicklungszusammenarbeit
direct applicability	unmittelbare Geltung
direct effect	unmittelbare Anwendbarkeit
direct election	Direktwahl
direct elections (to the EP)	direkte Wahlen (zum Europaparlament)
direct universal suffrage	allgemeine und direkte Wahl
directive	Richtlinie
directive on banking	Bankenrichtlinie
Director-General	Generaldirektor (Kommission)
Directorates-General	Generaldirektion
disclosure	Offenlegung, Bekanntgabe, Enthüllung
discrimination	Diskriminierung, Benachteiligung
discriminatory agreement	Diskriminierungsvereinbarung
discriminatory tax	diskriminierende/benachteiligende Steuer
discriminatory tax practice	Steuerdiskriminierung
disguised restriction	verschleierte Beschränkung
dismantle (to)	abbauen, demontieren
dismantling	Abbau
disproportionate	unverhältnismäßig, unangemessen
disputed passage	strittiger Text
distortion	Verzerrung
distortion of competition	Wettbewerbsverzerrung

doctrine of acte clair	Grundsatz, daß der EuGH nicht im Vorabentscheidungsverfahren zur Auslegung eines Textes angerufen wird, wenn dem behandelnden Gericht die Bedeutung des auszulegenden Textes klar ist (frz.).
domestic monetary policy	interne Geldpolitik
dominant position	beherrschende Stellung
doorstep selling	Haustürverkauf
double taxation	Doppelbesteuerung
draft budget	Haushaltsentwurf
draft convention	Vertragsentwurf
dual mandate	Doppelmandat
dumping	Dumping
duty to implement	Pflicht zur Vollziehung, Durchführung
EAEC (European Atomic Energy Community [Euratom]) Treaty	Vertrag über die Europäische Atomgemeinschaft (Euratom)
EAGGF (European Agricultural Guidance and Guarantee Fund)	EAGFL (Europäischer Ausrichtungs- und Garantiefonds für die Landwirtschaft)
EAGGF, Guarantee Section	EAGFL, Abteilung Garantie
EAGGF, Guidance Section	EAGFL, Abteilung Ausrichtung
EBRD (European Bank for Reconstruction and Development)	Europäische Bank für Wiederaufbau und Entwicklung
EC (European Community)	EG (Europäische Gemeinschaft)
EC standards	gemeinschaftliche Normen
ECB (European Central Bank)	EZB (Europäische Zentralbank)
ECJ ((European) Court of Justice)	Europäischer Gerichtshof (EuGH)
ECOFIN (Council of Economic and Finance Ministers)	Rat der Wirtschafts- und Finanzminister
Economic and Financial Committee	Wirtschafts- und Finanzausschuß
economic and monetary policy	Wirtschafts- und Währungspolitik
Economic and Monetary Union (EMU)	Wirtschafts- und Währungsunion
economic and social cohesion	wirtschaftlicher und sozialer Zusammenhalt
Economic and Social Committee	Wirtschafts- und Sozialausschuß
economic cohesion	wirtschaftlicher Zusammenhalt
economic convergence	wirtschaftliche Konvergenz
economic integration	wirtschaftliche Integration
Economic Policy Committee (Council and Commission)	Ausschuß für Wirtschaftspolitik (Rat und Kommission)
economic union	Wirtschaftsunion
ECSC (European Coal and Steel Community)	Europäische Gemeinschaft für Kohle und Stahl (EGKS)
ECSC (European Coal and Steel Community) Treaty	Vertrag über die EGKS (Europäische Gemeinschaft für Kohle und Stahl)
ECU (European Currency Unit)	ECU (Europäische Währungseinheit)
ECU clearing system	ECU-Verrechnungssystem
EDC (European Defence Community)	Europäische Verteidigungsgemeinschaft
EDF (European Development Fund)	EEF (Europäischer Entwicklungsfonds)

education	allgemeine und berufliche Bildung, Schul- und Ausbildung
EEA (European Economic Area)	EWR (Europäischer Wirtschaftsraum)
EEA Consultative Committee	Beratender EWR-Ausschuß
EEA Council	EWR-Rat
EEA Joint Committee	Gemeinsamer EWR-Ausschuß
EEA Joint Parliamentary Committee	Gemeinsamer Parlamentarischer EWR-Ausschuß
EEC (European Economic Community) Treaty	Vertrag über die Europäische Wirtschaftsgemeinschaft
EEIG (European Economic Interest Grouping)	EWIV (Europäische Wirtschaftliche Interessenvereinigung)
EFTA (European Free Trade Association)	EFTA (Europäische Freihandelszone)
EFTA Consultative Committee	Ständiger Ausschuß der EFTA-Mitgliedstaaten
EFTA Council	EFTA-Rat
EFTA Court	EFTA-Gerichtshof
EFTA Surveillance Authority	EFTA-Überwachungsbehörde
EIB (European Investment Bank)	EIB (Europäische Investitionsbank)
EIF (European Investment Fund)	EIF (Europäischer Investitionsfonds)
EJC (European Court of Justice)	EuGH (Europäischer Gerichtshof)
electoral system	Wahlsystem
eligibility for employment	Eignung, Befähigung zur Anstellung
eliminate (to)	abschaffen, ausschalten, eliminieren
elimination of customs duties	Abschaffung der Zölle
elimination of measures having equivalent effect	Abschaffung der Maßnahmen gleicher Wirkung
elimination of quantative restrictions	Abschaffung der mengenmäßigen Beschränkungen
EMCF (European Monetary Cooperation Fund)	EFWZ (Europäischer Fonds für währungspolitische Zusammenarbeit)
EMF (European Monetary Fund)	EWF (Europäischer Währungsfonds)
EMI (European Monetary Institute)	Europäisches Währungsinstitut (EWI)
EMS (European Monetary System)	EWS (Europäisches Währungssystem)
EMU (Economic and Monetary Union)	Wirtschafts- und Währungsunion
endorse (to)	billigen, gutheißen, sich anschließen
enforcement	Anwendung,Durchsetzung, Vollstreckung
enforcement of Community law	Anwendung des Gemeinschaftsrechts
enlargement of the communities	Erweiterung der Gemeinschaften
entry in the internal market	Einreise in den Binnenmarkt
equality	Gleichheit, Gleichberechtigung
equality of treatment	Gleichbehandlung
ERASMUS programme	ERASMUS-Programm
ERM (exchange rate mechanism)	Wechselkursmechanismus
ERTA (European Road Transport Agreement)	Europäisches Straßentransportabkommen
ESA (European Space Agency)	Europäische Raumfahrtbehörde
ESCAPE project	ESCAPE-Projekt

ESCB (European System of Central Banks)	EZBS (Europäisches Zentralbankensystem)
ESCB Council	EZBS-Rat
ESPRIT programme	ESPRIT-Programm
EU (European Union)	EU (Europäische Union)
EUA (European Unit of Account)	Europäische Verrechnungseinheit
EURATOM (European Atomic Energy Community)	EURATOM (Europäische Atomgemeinschaft)
EUREKA project	EUREKA-Projekt
European Agricultural Guidance and Guarantee Fund (EAGGF)	Europäischer Ausrichtungs- und Garantiefonds für die Landwirtschaft (EAGFL)
European Atomic Energy Community (EAEC)	Europäische Atomgemeinschaft (Euratom)
European Bank for Reconstruction and Development (EBRD)	Europäische Bank für Wiederaufbau und Entwicklung
European Central Bank (ECB)	Europäische Zentralbank (EZB)
European Coal and Steel Community (ECSC)	Europäische Gemeinschaft für Kohle und Stahl (EGKS)
European Commission (the)	(die) Europäische Kommission, (die) EG-Kommission
European Commission on Human Rights	Europäische Menschenrechtskommission
European Committee for Electrotechnical Standardization (CENELEC)	Europäisches Komitee für elektrotechnische Normung
European Committee for Standardization (CEN)	Europäisches Komitee für Normung
European Community (EC)	Europäische Gemeinschaft (EG)
European Community budget	Haushalt der Europäischen Gemeinschaften
European Community Statistical Office (EUROSTAT)	EUROSTAT
European Company Statute	Statut für die Europäische Aktiengesellschaft
European Convention on Human Rights 1950	Europäische Menschenrechtskonvention (EMRK) 1950
European Correspondents Group (EPC)	Europäische Korrespondentengruppe (EPZ)
European Council	Europäischer Rat
European Court of Auditors	Europäischer Rechnungshof
European Court of Justice (EJC)	Europäischer Gerichtshof (EuGH)
European Court Reports	Sammlung der EuGH-Entscheidungen
European Currency Unit (ECU)	Europäische Währungseinheit (ECU)
European Defence Community (EDC)	Europäische Verteidigungsgemeinschaft
European Defence Treaty 1952	Vertrag zur Errichtung der Europäischen Verteidigungsgemeinschaft 1952
European Development Fund (EDF)	Europäischer Entwicklungsfonds (EEF)
European Economic Area (EEA)	Europäischer Wirtschaftsraum (EWR)
European Economic Community (EEC)	Europäische Wirtschaftsgemeinschaft (EWG)
European Economic Interest Grouping (EEIG)	Europäische Wirtschaftliche Interessenvereinigung (EWIV)

European Environment Agency	Europäische Umweltagentur
European Free Trade Association (EFTA)	Europäische Freihandelszone (EFTA)
European Investment Bank (EIB)	Europäische Investitionsbank (EIB)
European Investment Fund (EIF)	Europäischer Investitionsfonds (EIF)
European Monetary Cooperation Fund (EMCF)	Europäischer Fonds für währungspolitische Zusamenarbeit (EFWZ)
European Monetary Fund (EMF)	Europäischer Währungsfonds (EWF)
European Monetary Institut (EMI)	Europäisches Währungsinstitut (EWI)
European Monetary System (EMS)	Europäisches Währungssytem (EWS)
European Parliament	Europäisches Parlament
European Patent Convention	Europäisches Patentabkommen
European Policy Cooperation (EPC)	Europäische Politische Zusammenarbeit (EPZ)
European Regional Development Fund (ERDF)	Europäischer Fonds für die regionale Entwicklung (EFRE)
European Regional Fund (ERF)	Europäischer Regionalfonds (ERF)
European Road Transport Agreement (ERTA)	Europäisches Straßentransportabkommen
European Social Fund	Europäischer Sozialfonds
European Space Agency (ESA)	Europäische Raumfahrtbehörde
European standards	europäische technische Normen
European System of Central Banks (ESCB)	Europäisches Zentralbankensystem (EZBS)
European Union (EU)	Europäische Union (EU)
European Unity	Europäische Einheit
Euroscepticism	Euroskeptizismus
EUROSTAT (EC Statistical Office)	EUROSTAT
excessive deficit	übermäßiges Defizit
exchange authorization	devisenrechtliche Genehmigung
exchange control	Devisenkontrolle
exchange of information	Informationsaustausch
exchange of submissions	Austausch von Schriftsätzen
exchange policy	Devisenpolitik
exchange rate	Wechselkurs
exchange rate mechanism (ERM)	Wechselkursmechanismus
exchange restriction	devisenrechtliche Beschränkung
exchange-rate policy	Wechselkurspolitik
exchange-rate support	Wechselkursstützung
excise duties	Verbrauchssteuern
excise duty	Verbrauchsabgabe
exclusive Community competence	ausschließliche Zuständigkeit der Gemeinschaft
exclusive distribution agreement	Alleinvertriebsvereinbarung
exemption	Ausnahme
expenditure	Ausgaben, Aufwand
explicit duty	ausdrückliche Pflicht
external relations	Außen(handels-)beziehungen
federalism	Föderalismus
federation	Zusammenschluß, Vereinigung

field of competence	Zuständigkeits-, Tätigkeitsbereich
financial and budgetary provisions	Finanz- und Haushaltsbestimmungen
financial common market	Finanzraum
financial market	Finanzmarkt
Financial Provisions Treaty 1975	Finanzvorschriftenänderungsvertrag 1975
Financial Regulation	Finanzverordnung
financial resources	Finanzmittel
fine	Geldbuße, Geldstrafe
First Advocate-General (ECJ)	Erster Generalanwalt (EuGH)
fiscal barriers	steuerliche Schranken
fix (to)	festlegen, festsetzen
fixed exchange rate	festgelegter Wechselkurs
fluctuation	Schwankung, Fluktuation
foreign policy	Außenpolitik
founding treaties	Gründungsverträge
framework treaty	Rahmenvertrag
franchise agreement	Franchise-Vereinbarung
free flow of capital	freier Kapitalverkehr
free insurance market	freier Versicherungsmarkt
free movement of capital	freier Kapitalverkehr
free movement of goods	freier Warenverkehr
free movement of labour/workers	Freizügigkeit der Arbeitnehmer
free movement of persons	freier Personenverkehr
free movement of services	freier Dienstleistungsverkehr
free movement of students	Freizügigkeit der Studenten
free trade area	Freihandelszone
freedom of association	Vereinigungsfreiheit
freedom of competition	Wettbewerbsfreiheit
freedom of establishment	Niederlassungsfreiheit
freedom of investment	Investitionsfreiheit
freedom of movement	Bewegungsfreiheit
freedom of movement for capital	Freizügigkeit für Kapital
freedom of movement for goods	Freizügigkeit für Waren
freedom of movement for persons	Freizügigkeit für Personen
freedom of movement for services	Freizügigkeit für Dienstleistungen
freedom of movement for workers	Freizügigkeit der Arbeitnehmer
freedom of movement of capital	freier Kapitalverkehr
freedom of religion	Religions- und Bekenntnisfreiheit
freedom to engage in business and to choose and practise a profession	Wirtschafts- und Berufsfreiheit
freedom to move capital	freier Kapitalverkehr
freedom to provide services	Dienstleistungsfreiheit, freier Dienstleistungsverkehr
frontier	Grenze
frontier control	Grenzkontrolle
frontier-free market	Binnenmarkt
fundamental freedoms	Grundfreiheiten
fundamental rights	Grundrechte

GATT (General Agreement on Tariffs and Trade)	GATT (Allgemeines Zoll- und Handelsabkommen)
General Agreement on Tariffs and Trade (GATT)	Allgemeines Zoll- und Handelsabkommen (GATT)
General Council of the ECB	Erweiterter Rat der EZB
general principles of law	allgemeine Rechtsgrundsätze
general right of privacy	allgemeines Persönlichkeitsrecht
General Secretariat of the Council	Generalsekretariat des Rates
give precedence to (to)	Vorrang einräumen
Governing Council of the ECB	EZB-Rat
grant for research	Forschungsbeihilfe
gross domestic product	Bruttoinlandsprodukt (BIP)
gross saving	Bruttoersparnis
group of undertakings	Konzern
growing centralism	wachsender Zentralismus
guarantee price	garantierter Mindestpreis
harmonization	Anpassung, Harmonisierung
harmonization of legislation	Harmonisierung der Rechtsvorschriften
harmonization of standards	Anpassung von Normen
Havana Charter	Havanna Charter
health protection	Gesundheitsschutz
Helsinki Final Act	Schlußakte von Helsinki
hierarchy of the Community Acts	Rangordnung der Rechtsakte der Gemeinschaft
High Authority Decision (ECSC)	Entscheidung der Hohen Behörde (EGKS)
historical interpretation	Auslegung aus der Entstehungsgeschicthte
home affairs	innere Angelegenheiten
horizontal agreement	horizontale Vereinbarung
IMF (International Monetary Fund)	(IWF) Internationaler Währungsfonds
impartial authority	unabhängiges Gremium
impartiality	Unparteilichkeit, Unvoreingenommenheit
implementation	Vollziehung, Durchführung, Umsetzung, Anwendung
implementation of secondary legislation	Anwendung des abgeleiteten Gemeinschaftsrechts
implicit duty	mitinbegriffene Pflicht
implied powers	Zuständigkeiten kraft Sachzusammenhang
import quota	Importquote
imported inflation	importierte Inflation
incentive measures	stimulierende Maßnahmen
incorporation	Aufnahme, Einverleibung, Umsetzung
incorporation of community law	Aufnahme/Einverleibung/Inkorporation/Eingliederung des Gemeinschaftsrechts
indirect discrimination	indirekte Diskriminierung, indirekte Benachteiligung
individual exemption	Einzelfreistellung
industrial policy	Industriepolitik
infringement of an essential procedural requirement	Verletzung einer wesentlichen Formvorschrift

infringement of Community law	Verletzung des Gemeinschaftsrechts
infringement of the Treaties or of any rules of law relating to their application	Verletzung der Verträge oder einer bei ihrer Durchführung anzuwendenden Rechtsnorm
infringement proceeding	Vertragsverletzungsverfahren
injunction	einstweilige Anordnung
institution	Organ, Institution
institutional integration	institiutionelle Integration
integration	Integration
interdependence	Abhängigkeit
interest groups	Interessensgruppen
interest subsidy	Zinszuschuß
interest-rate cut	Senkung des Zinssatzes
intergovernmental conference	Regierungskonferenz
intergovernmental organization	zwischenstaatliche Organisation
interinstitutional cooperation	interinstitutionelle Zusammenarbeit
internal cohesion	innere Geschlossenheit
internal market	Binnenmarkt
International Monetary Fund (IMF)	Internationaler Währungsfonds (IWF)
international organizations	Internationale Organisationen
international standards	internationale Normen
interpretation of Community law	Auslegung/Interpretation des Gemeinschaftsrechts
intervention board for agricultural products	Einfuhr- und Vorratsstelle für landwirtschaftliche Erzeugnisse
intervention mechanism	Interventionsmechanismus
intervention price	Interventionspreis, garantierter Mindestpreis
intra-Community barrier	innergemeinschaftliche Schranke
introduction of a citizenship of the Union	Einführung einer Unionsbürgerschaft
introduction of a single currency	Einführung einer einheitlichen Währung
investment loan	Investitionsdarlehen
irrevocable fixing of exchange rates	unwiderrufliche Festlegung der Wechselkurse
JOE (Journal Officiel des Communautés Européennes)	Amtsblatt der Europäischen Gemeinschaften
join (to)	sich anschließen, beitreten
joint boycott	gemeinsamer Boykott
joint competence	gemeinsame Zuständigkeit
joint decision-making power	Mitentscheidungsrecht
Joint Research Center	Gemeinsame Forschungsstelle
judge-rapporteur	Berichterstatter
judicial control	gerichtliche Kontrolle
jurisconsult	Jurist, Rechtsgelehrter
know-how agreement	Know-how-Vereinbarung
lack of competence	Unzuständigkeit
Language Service	Sprachdienst
law coordination	Rechtsangleichung
law of international institutions	Recht der internationalen Organisationen

League of Nations	Völkerbund
legal barrier	gesetzliches Hindernis
legal entity	juristische Person
legal integration	rechtliche Integration
legal personality	Rechtspersönlichkeit
Legal Service	Juristischer Dienst
legislation	Gesetzgebung
legislative powers	Gesetzgebungsbefugnisse
legislative process	Rechtsetzungsverfahren
legislative programme	Gesetzgebungsprogramm
legislative proposals	Gesetzgebungsvorschläge
legitimate interest	berechtigtes Interesse
letter of formal complaint	formelle Beschwerde (-note)
levy	Abschöpfung, Umlage, Steuer, Abgabe
levy (to)	einheben
liberalization	Liberalisierung, Befreiung
liberalization of services	freier Dienstleistungsverkehr
literal interpretation	wörtliche Auslegung
locus standi	das Recht, bei Gericht gehört zu werden; Prozeßführungsrecht
Lomé Conventions	Lomé-Abkommen
Luxembourg Compromise	Luxemburger Kompromiß
Maastricht Treaty	Vertrag von Maastricht
majority voting	Mehrheitsentscheidung
management committee	Verwaltungsausschuß
market dominance	marktbeherrschende Stellung
market segmentation	Marktaufteilung
market share	Marktanteil
matter of mutual interest	Angelegenheit von gemeinsamem Interesse
maximum guaranteed quantity (MGQ)	garantierte Höchstquoten
Member of Parliament	Parlamentsmitglied, Abgeordneter zum Europaparlament
memorandum	Memorandum
MEQR (measures having equivalent effect to quantitative restrictions)	Maßnahmen gleicher Wirkung (wie mengenmäßige Beschränkungen)
merger	Verschmelzung, Fusion
Merger Treaty 1965	Fusionierungsvertrag 1965
mirror legislation	
misuse of powers	Ermessensmißbrauch
Monetary Committee	Währungsausschuß
Monetary Committee with advisory status	Beratender Währungsausschuß
monetary integration	Währungsintegration
Monetary Policy	Geldpolitik
monetary reserve	Währungsreserve
monetary union	Währungsunion
money laundering	Geldwäsche
most-favoured-nation treatment	Meistbegünstigungsklausel

motion of censure	Mißtrauensvotum
movement of payments	Zahlungsverkehr
municipal law	Recht eines Mitgliedstaates
mutual recognition	gegenseitige Anerkennung
mutual recognition directive	Richtlinie über die gegenseitige Anerkennung
mutual recognition of diplomas, certificates and other evidence of formal qualifications	gegenseitige Anerkennung der Diplome, Prüfungszeugnisse und sonstiger Befähigungsnachweise
national audit body	einzelstaatliches Rechnungsprüfungsorgan
national central bank	nationale Zentralbank
national fiscal policy	Haushaltspolitik der einzelnen Staaten
national sovereignity	nationale Eigenständigkeit
NATO (North Atlantic Treaty Organization)	NATO (Nordatlantisches Verteidigungsbündnis)
NEC(non-compulsory expenditure)	nicht zwingende Ausgaben
needs-related examination	Bedürfnisprüfung, Bedarfsprüfung
negative clearance	Negativattest
non-compulsory expenditure (NEC)	nicht zwingende Ausgaben
non-compulsory items	nicht zwingende Ausgaben
non-contractual liability	außervertragliche Haftung
non-obligatory expenditure	nichtobligatorische Ausgaben
non-tariff trade barriers	nicht-tarifäre Handelsbe-schränkungen/Handelshemmnisse
North Atlantic Treaty Organization (NATO)	Nordatlantisches Verteidigungsbündnis (NATO)
objection	Einwand
objective ruling	objektive Stellungnahme
obligatory expenditure	obligatorische Ausgaben
observation	Bemerkung, Wahrnehmung
observatory status	Beobachterstatus
OECD (Organization for Economic Cooperation and Development)	OECD (Organisation für wirtschaftliche Zusammenarbeit und Entwicklung)
Official Journal of the E.C.	Amtsblatt der EG
ombudsman	Bürgerbeauftragter
operating budget	Funktionshaushalt
opinion	Stellungnahme, Urteil, Gutachten
optional consultation	fakultative Anhörung
Organization for Economic Cooperation and Development (OECD)	Organisation für wirtschaftliche Zusammenarbeit und Entwicklung (OECD)
outermost regions	Gebiete in äußerster Randlage
parallel currency	Parallelwährung
parallel import	Parallelimport, Paralleleinfuhr
parliamentary committee	Parlamentsausschuß, parlamentarischer Ausschuß
parliamentary democracies	parlamentarische Demokratien
patent licensing agreement	Patentlizenzvereinbarung
payment appropriation	Zahlungsermächtigung
period of transition	Übergangszeit, Übergabgsperiode

Permanent Representation	Ständige Vertretung
Permanent Representatives Committee	Ausschuß der Ständigen Vertreter
personal consumption	persönlicher Verbrauch
physical barriers	materielle Schranken
plea of illegality	inzidente Normenkontrolle (Art. 184 EWGV)
plenary jurisdiction	Plenargerichtsbarkeit
plenary session	Plenartagung, Vollsitzung
police cooperation	polizeiliche Zusammenarbeit
policies and forms of cooperation	Politiken und Formen der Zusammenarbeit
Political Committee (EPC)	Politisches Komitee (EPZ)
political cooperation	politische Kooperation, politische Zusammenarbeit
Political Cooperation Secretariat (EPC)	Sekretariat der Politischen Zusammenarbeit (EPZ)
Political Directors (EPC)	Politische Direktoren (EPZ)
political groups (in the EP)	politische Gruppen (im Europaparlament)
political integration	politische Integration
power of assent	Zustimmungsrecht
preferential tariff	Vorzugszoll
preliminary decision	vorläufige Entscheidung
preliminary draft budget	Vorentwurf eines Haushaltsplans
preliminary ruling	Vorabentscheidung (EuGH)
preparatory enquiry stage	Stufe des vorbereitenden Ermittlungsverfahrens
prerogative	Vorrecht, Privileg
President of Chambers (ECJ)	Kammerpräsident (EuGH)
President of the Commission	Kommissionspräsident
President of the Court	Präsident des Europäischen Gerichtshofs
President of the Court of Auditors	Präsident des Rechnungshofes
preventive measures	vorbeugende Maßnahmen
price maintenance	Preisbindung
price stability	Preisstabilität
primary Community legislation	primäres Gemeinschaftsrecht
primary source of Community law	primäre Quelle des Gemeinschaftsrechts
principle of equality	Gleichheitsgrundsatz
principle of legal certainty	Grundsatz der Rechtssicherheit
principle of legality in administration	Grundsatz der Gesetzmäßigkeit der Verwaltung
principle of plenary jurisdiction	Grundsatz der Plenargerichts-barkeit
principle of proportionality	Verhältnismäßigkeitsgrundsatz
principle of specific attribution of powers	Prinzip der begrenzten Einzelermächtigung
principle of subsidiarity	Subsidiaritätsprinzip
principle that legitimate expectations must be protected	Grundsatz des Vertrauensschutzes
privacy of correspondence	Briefgeheimnis
private consumption	privater Verbrauch
procedural requirement	Verfahrensvorschrift
procurement policy	Auftragswesen
procurement procedures	Ausschreibung(-sverfahren)

product liability	Produkthaftung
proportionality	Verhältnismäßigkeit, Proportionalität
proposal	Vorschlag, Entwurf
protective measure	Schutzmaßnahme
Protocol	Zusatzprotokoll
prudential supervision	Aufsicht
public disclosure	Veröffentlichung
public health	Gesundheitswesen
public procurement	öffentliches Auftragswesen
public procurement contract	öffentlicher Lieferauftrag
public purchasing and construction	öffentliches Auftragswesen
public service contracts	öffentliche Versorgungsverträge
public supplies	öffentliche Versorgung
public supply contract	öffentlicher Lieferauftrag
public undertakings	öffentliche Unternehmen
public utilities	öffentliche Versorgungsbetriebe
public works	öffentliche Anlagen
public works contracts	öffentliche (Bau)Aufträge
public-sector construction contract	öfentlicher Bauauftrag
purposive interpretation	teleologische Auslegung
quaestor	Quästor
qualified majority	qualifizierte Mehrheit
quantitative restriction	mengenmäßige Beschränkung
Question Time	Fragestunde
quotas	Quoten
R & D (Research & Development)	Forschung und Entwicklung
rapporteur	Berichterstatter
reading (in the EP)	Lesung (im Europaparlament)
reasoned decision	begründete Entscheidung
reasoned opinion	mit Gründen versehene Stellungnahme, begründete Stellungnahme
reasoned submissions	begründete Eingaben
reception of Community law	Aufnahme, Annahme des Gemeinschaftsrechts
reciprocity	Reziprozität, Gegenseitigkeit
recognition of foreign qualifications	Anerkennung von fremden Befähigungsnachweisen
recognize (to)	anerkennen
recommendation	Empfehlung
redress	Wiedergutmachung, Entschädigung
regional imbalance	regionales Ungleichgewicht
regional policy	Regionalpolitik
Registrar (ECJ)	Kanzlei (EuGH)
regulation	Verordnung
regulatory committee	Regelungsausschuß
reject (to)	ablehnen, verwerfen, zurückweisen
report	Bericht
reporting commitment	Berichtspflicht
request for information	Auskunftsverlangen

Research and Development Agreement	Forschungs- und Entwicklungsvereinbarung
research and information technologies	Forschungs- und Informations-technologien
reservation	Vorbehalt
restricted procedure	beschränkte Ausschreibung
restriction	Beschränkung, Hemmnis, Behinderung
restrictive practice	wettbewerbsbeschränkende Geschäftspraktik
Restrictive Trade Practices Law	Kartellrecht
retaliatory measure	Vergeltungsmaßnahme
devaluation	Abwertung
revenue	Einnahmen, Einkünfte
review	Nachprüfung
right of association	Koalitionsrecht
right of entry	Einreiserecht
right of establishment	Niederlassungsrecht
right of initiative	Initiativrecht
right of ownership	Eigentumsrecht
right of residence	Wohnrecht, Aufenthaltsrecht
right to a fair hearing	Grundsatz des rechtlichen Gehörs
right to petition the European Parliament	Petitionsrecht beim Europäischen Parlament
right to provide services	Recht zur Erbringung von Dienstleistungen
RP (Rule of Procedure of the Community Court)	Verfahrensregeln des Gemeinschaftsgerichts
Rule of Procedure of the Community Court (RP)	Verfahrensregeln des Gemeinschaftsgerichts
rules of procedure	Geschäftsordnung
rules on competition	Wettbewerbsregeln
safeguard clause	Schutzklausel
sales promotion	Verkaufsförderung
SAVE programme	SAVE-Programm
Schengen Agreement	Schengener Abkommen
Schuman Plan	Schuman Plan
Scientific and Technical Committee	Ausschuß für wissenschaftliche und technische Belange/Angelegenheiten
scission	Spaltung
SEA (Single European Act)	Einheitliche Europäische Akte (EEA)
secondary Community legislation	sekundäres Gemeinschaftsrecht
secondary source of Community law	sekundäre Quelle des Gemeinschaftsrechts
secondary sources	sekundäre Rechtsquellen
secret arrangement	geheime Absprache
Secretariat-General	Generalsekretariat
Secretary General	Generalsekretär
sectoral directive	sektorielle Richtlinie
security policy	Sicherheitspolitik
selective distribution system	selektiver Vertrieb
selective harmonization	Angleichung des Rechts in ausgewählten Gebieten
self-executing treaty	unmittelbar anwendbarer Vertrag

separation of powers	Gewaltenteilung
simple majority	einfache Mehrheit
simplified amendment procedure	vereinfachtes Änderungsverfahren
single currency	einheitliche Währung
Single European Act (SEA) 1986	Einheitliche Europäische Akte (EEA) 1986
Single European Economic Area	Einheitlicher Europäischer Wirtschaftsraum
Single Market	Binnenmarkt
small- and medium-sized enterprises	Klein- und Mittelbetriebe
Social Charter	Sozialcharter
social policy	Sozialpolitik
social security	Sozialversicherung
Solemn Declaration on European Union	Feierliche Erklärung zur Europäischen Union
solidarity	Solidarität
source of revenue	Einnahmequelle
sources of Community law	Rechtsquellen des Gemeinschaftsrechts
specialization agreement	Spezialisierungsvereinbarung
specialized Council meeting	Fachministertagung
specialized section	Fachgruppe
spending	Ausgaben
Spinelli draft	Spinelli-Entwurf
staff case	Beamtensache
Staff Regulation	Dienstvorschriften
standard	Norm, Standard
standardisation	Vereinheitlichung
standing committee	ständiger Ausschuß
state aid	staatlicher Zuschuß/ Unterstützung
state of affair	Standpunkt
state subsidy	staatliche Beihilfe
Statistical Office	Statistisches Amt
structural adjustment	Strukturanpassung
structural funds	Strukturfonds
structural instruments	strukturelle Instrumente
sub-committee	Unterausschuß
subsidiarity	Subsidiarität
subsidiary power to act	subsidiäre Handlungsermächtigung
subsidies	Förderungen, Zuschüsse, Subventionen, Beihilfen
subsidized exports	geförderte/gestützte/ subventionierte Exporte
substantial resources	umfangreiche Finanzmittel
substantiated (to be)	begründet sein
substantiation	Begründung
summit	Gipfelkonferenz
summit meeting	Gipfeltreffen
supervisory authority	Aufsichtsbehörde
supplementary budget	Nachtragshaushalt
supply contract	Zuliefervertrag
supranational organization	übernationale Organisation

supremacy	Vorrang, Überlegenheit
supremacy of Community law	Vorrang des Gemeinschaftsrechts
surplus	Überschuß
surrender of sovereignity	Übertragung von Hoheitsrechten
target price	Richtpreis
tariff quota	Zollkontingent
tariff trade barrier	Zollschranke
tax privilege	Steuervorteil
tax rate	Steuersatz
taxation	Steuerwesen
technical barriers	technische Schranken, technische Handelshemmnisse
technical standard	Industrienorm
teleological interpretation	teleologische Auslegung
temporary derogation	zeitlich begrenzte Ausnahmeregelung
tendering and award procedures	Ausschreibungs- und Vergabeverfahren
term of office	Amtszeit
threshold price	Schwellenpreis, Einschleusungspreis
threshold value	Schwellenbetrag
tie-in sale	Kopplungsgeschäft
time-limit	Frist
total restraint of trade	Wettbewerbsverbot
trade	Handel
trade agreement	Handelsabkommen
trade association	Handelsverband
trade barrier	Handelsschranke, Handelsbeschränkung
trade law	Handelsrecht
Trans-European Network (TEN)	Transeuropäisches Netz
transformation	Umwandlung
transitional agreement	Übergangsregelung
transitional period	Übergangszeit
transitory provision	Übergangsbestimmung
transmission	Übertragung, Überlassung
transport policy	Verkehrspolitik
Treaties of Rome	Römische/Römer Verträge
Treaty of Paris	Vertrag von Paris
Treaty on European Union	Vertrag über die Europäische Union
treaty-making power	Kompetenz zum Abschluß von Verträgen
turnover tax	Quellensteuer, Umsatzsteuer
type testing and certification	Prüf- und Zertifizierungsverfahren
UN Economic Commission for Europe	UNO-Wirtschaftskommission für Europa
unanimity	Einstimmigkeit
unanimous	einstimmig
undertaking	Unternehmen
unification	Vereinigung
unified economic area	einheitlicher Wirtschaftsraum
unilateral measure	einseitige Maßnahme
units of account	Verrechnungseinheiten

unity	Einheit, Einigkeit, Eintracht
valuation rule	Bewertunsregel
value-added tax (VAT)	Mehrwertsteuer (MWSt)
vertical agreement	vertikale Vereinbarung
Vice-President	Vizepräsident
Vienna Convention applicable to world organizations (1986)	Wiener Übereinkommen/ Konvention über das Recht zwischen den internationalen Organisationen (1986)
Vienna Convention on Treaties (1969)	Wiener Vertragsrechtskonvention (WVK) (1969)
vocational training	Berufsausbildung
void	nichtig, ungültig, unwirksam
voluntary self-restriction	freiwillige Eigenbeschränkung
weighted voting	Stimmengewichtung
Western European Union (WEU)	Westeuropäische Union (WEU)
White Paper	Weißbuch
World Bank	Weltbank
written opinion	schriftliche Stellungnahme
written procedure	schriftliches Verfahren
Yaounde Convention	Abkommen von Jaunde

Abänderung	derogation
Abbau	dismantling
abbauen	to dismantle
Abgabe	levy, charge, duty
Abgeordneter zum Europaparlament	Member of the European Parliament (MEP)
abgestimmte Verhaltensweisen	concerted practices
abgestimmtes Verhalten	concerted action, concerted practice
Abhängigkeit	interdependence
Abkommen	convention, treaty
Abkommen von Jaunde	Yaounde Convention
Abkommen zur Zusammenarbeit	cooperation agreements
ablehnen	to reject
abschaffen	to eliminate
Abschaffung der Maßnahmen gleicher Wirkung	elimination of measures having equivalent effect
Abschaffung der mengenmäßigen Beschränkungen	elimination of quantitative restrictions
Abschaffung der Zölle	elimination of customs duties
Abschaffung von Beschränkungen	abolition of restrictions
Abschöpfung	levy
Abschottung	compartmentalization
absolute Mehrheit	absolute majority
Abstimmung der Außen- und Sicherheitspolitik	harmonization of foreign and security policies
abweichen von	to bypass, to deviate, to derogate
Abweichung	derogation
Abwertung	devaluation
Ad-hoc-Sitzung	ad-hoc groups
Adressat	addressee
Agrarabschöpfung	agricultural levy
Agrarpolitik	agricultural policy
akademische Anerkennung	academic recognition
Alleinbezugsvereinbarung	exclusive purchase agreement
Alleinvertriebsvereinbarung	exclusive distribution agreement
allgemeine Rechtsgrundsätze	general principles of law
allgemeine und direkte Wahl	direct universal suffrage
allgemeines Persönlichkeitsrecht	general right of privacy
Allgemeines Zoll- und Handelsabkommen (GATT)	General Agreement on Tariffs and Trade (GATT)
Amtsblatt der EG	Official Journal of the E.C.
Amtszeit	term of office
ändern	to amend
anerkennen	to recognize
Anerkennung von fremden Befähigungsnachweisen	recognition of foreign qualifications
Anfechtungsklage	action for annulment
Angelegenheit von gemeinsamem Interesse	matter of mutual interest

angleichen	to approximate, to align, to adopt to harmonize
Angleichung	alignment, approximation, harmonization, adoption
Angleichung des (Bildungs-)niveaus	harmonization of the level (of education)
Angleichung des Rechts	approximation of law
Angleichung des Rechts in ausgewählten Gebieten	selective harmonization
Anhäufung	aggregation
Anlegerschutz	protection of investors
Anmeldung	filing, notification
Annäherung der Steuern	approximation of taxes
Annäherung des Rechts	approximation of law
Annahme	adoption
Annahme des Gemeinschaftsrechts	reception of Community law
annehmen	to adopt
Anpassung	harmonization
Anpassung von Normen	harmonization of standards
Ansammlung	aggregation
Antidumping-Abgabe	anti-dumping duty
Antidumping-Vorschriften	anti-dumping rules, anti-dumping provisions
Antragsteller	complainant, applicant
Anwendung	application, implementation, enforcement
Anwendung des abgeleiteten Gemeinschaftsrechts	implementation of secondary Community legislation
Anwendung des Gemeinschaftsrechts	enforcement of Community law
Assoziierungsabkommen	association agreement
Aufenthaltsrecht	right of residence
Aufnahme	incorporation, admission
Aufnahme des Gemeinschaftsrechts	incorporation of Community law
Aufsicht	supervision
Aufsichtsbehörde	supervisory authority
Auftragsvergabe	award of contract
Auftragswesen	procurement policy
Aufwand	expenditure
Aufwertung	revaluation
Ausbildung	education
Ausbildungssysteme	education systems
ausdrückliche Pflicht	explicit duty
Ausgaben	spending, expenditure
Auskunftsverlangen	request for information
Auslegung des Gemeinschaftsrechts	interpretation of Community law
auslosen	to choose by lot
Ausnahme	exemption
ausschalten	to eliminate
ausschließliche Zuständigkeit der Gemeinschaft	exclusive Community competence

Ausschreibung	invitation to tender, invitation to bid
Ausschreibungsverfahren	procurement procedures, tendering and award procedures
Ausschuß der Regionen	Committee of the Regions
Ausschuß der Ständigen Vertreter	Comité des Représentants Permanents (COREPER)/ Committee of Permanent Representatives/ Permanent Representatives Committee
Ausschuß der Zentralbankpräsidenten	Committee of Governors of the Central Banks
Ausschuß für Wirtschaftspolitik (Rat und Kommission)	Economic Policy Committee (Council and Commission)
Ausschuß für wissenschaftliche und technische Belange/Angelegenheiten	Scientific and Technical Committee
Ausschuß für wissenschaftliche und technische Forschung (Rat und Kommission)	Committee for Scientific and Technical Research(Council and Commission)
Ausschuß von Regierungsvertretern	Committee of government representatives
Austausch von Schriftsätzen	exchange of submissions
Außen(handels-)beziehungen	external relations
Außengrenzen	external frontiers
Außenhandelsinstrumentarien	external trade instruments
Außenministerkonferenz	Conference of Foreign Ministers
Außenpolitik	foreign policy
außervertragliche Haftung	non-contractual liability
authentische Sprache	authentic language
Autonomie	autonomy
Bank für Internationalen Zahlungsausgleich (BIZ)	Bank for International Settlements (BIS)
Bankenaufsicht	bank supervision
Bankenaufsichtsbehörden	banking supervision authorities
Bankenaufsichtspolitik	banking supervision policy
Bankenliquidität	bank liquidity
Bankenrichtlinie	directive on banking
Barrieren	barriers
Beamtenkabinett	Cabinet
Beamtensache	staff case
Beamtenschaft der Gemeinschaften	Community Civil Service
Bedarfsprüfung	needs-related examination
Befähigungsnachweise	qualifications
Befreiung	liberalization, exemption
begründet sein	to be substantiated
begründete Eingaben	reasoned submissions
begründete Stellungnahme	reasoned opinion
Begründung	substantiation, reasoning
beherrschende Stellung	dominant position
Behinderung	restriction
Beihilfe	subsidy

Beistandsmechanismus	assistance mechanism
beitreten	to accede, to join
Beitritt	accession
Beitrittsakte	Act of Accession
Beitrittsvertrag	accession treaty
Bekanntgabe	disclosure
Bekanntmachung über Vereinbarungen von geringer Bedeutung (1986)	Commission's Notice on Agreements of Minor Importance (1986)
benachteiligende Steuer	discriminatory tax
Benachteiligung	discrimination
Benelux Wirtschaftsunion	Benelux Economic Union
Beobachterstatus	observer status, observatory status
beraten	to deliberate; to advise
beratende Funktion	advisory function
beratende Organe	advisory bodies
Beratender Ausschuß	Consultative Committee, Advisory Committee
Beratender Ausschuß für die Liberalisierung des öffentlichen Auftragswesen	Advisory Committee on the Opening Up of Public Procurement
Beratender Ausschuß für die wichtigsten landwirtschaftlichen Erzeugnisse (Rat und Kommission)	agricultural advisory committee (Council and Commission)
beratender Ausschuß für Kartelle und Monopole	Consultative Committee on Cartels and Monopolies
Beratender EWR-Ausschuß	EEA Consultative Committee
Beratender Verbraucherausschuß	Consumers' Consultative Committee
Beratender Währungsausschuß	Monetary Committee with advisory status
beratendes, unverbindliches Rundschreiben	advisory circular
Beratung	deliberation
Beratungsverfahren	consultation procedure
berechtigtes Interesse	legitimate interest, justified interest
Bericht	report
Berichterstatter	judge-rapporteur, rapporteur
Berichtspflicht	reporting commitment
Berufsausbildung	vocational training
Beschäftigungsbedingungen	working conditions
Beschluß über die Entlastung der Führung des Haushaltsplans	decision granting a discharge in respect of implementation of the Community budget
Beschluß von Unternehmensvereinigungen	decision by associations of undertakings
beschränkte Ausschreibung	restricted procedure
Beschränkung	barrier, restriction, derogation
Beschwerde	complaint
Beschwerdeführer	complainant
Beseitigung von Beschränkungen	abolition of restrictions
Bestimmungsland	country of destination

Beurteilung der Umweltverträglichkeit der Gemeinschaftsmaßnahmen	assessment of the environmental impact of Community measures
Bewegungsfreiheit	freedom of movement
Bewertunsregel	valuation rule
bilaterale Handelsabkommen	bilateral trade agreements
Bildung	education
Bildungsprogramme	education programmes
Bildungswesen	education
billigen	to endorse
Binnenmarkt	Single Market, internal market, frontier-free market, Community-wide market
brechen	to breach
Briefgeheimnis	privacy of correspondence
Bruch	breach
Brüsseler Übereinkommen über die gerichtliche Zuständigkeit und die Vollstreckung gerichtlicher Entscheidungen in Zivil- und Handelssachen	Brussels Convention on Jurisdiction and the Enforcement of Judgements in Civil and Commercial Matters
Bruttoersparnis	gross saving
Bruttoinlandsprodukt (BIP)	gross domestic product (GDP)
Bürgerbeauftragter	ombudsman
Cassis de Dijon Prinzip	Cassis de Dijon principle
Cassis de Dijon-Entscheidung	Cassis de Dijon ruling
Chancengleichheit	equal opportunities
Dassonville Formel	Dassonville formula
De-minimis-Regel (Vereinbarungen von geringer Bedeutung)	De Minimis rule (agreements of minor importance)
Delors-Bericht (1989)	Delors-Report (1989)
Demokratiedefizit	democratic deficit
demontieren	to dismantle
Devisenkontrolle	exchange control
Devisenpolitik	exchange policy
devisenrechtliche Beschränkung	exchange restriction
devisenrechtliche Genehmigung	exchange authorization
Dienstleistungsfreiheit	freedom/right to provide services
Dienststelle der Kommission	Commission's Department
Dienstvorschriften	Staff Regulations
Dienstzettel (schriftlicher Arbeitsnachweis)	form of employment contract
direkte Wahlen (zum Europaparlament)	direct elections (to the EP)
Direktzahlungen	direct payments
diskriminierende Steuer	discriminatory tax
Diskriminierung	discrimination
Diskriminierungsvereinbarung	agreement with discriminative character, discrimination agreement, discriminatory agreement
Doppelbesteuerung	double taxation

Doppelbesteuerungsabkommen	double taxation agreement
Doppelmandat	dual mandate
Dumping	dumping
Durchsetzung	enforcement
EAGFL (Europäischer Ausrichtungs- und Garantiefonds für die Landwirtschaft)	EAGGF (European Agricultural Guidance and Guarantee Fund)
EAGFL, Abteilung Ausrichtung	EAGGF,Guidance Section
EAGFL, Abteilung Garantie	EAGGF,Guarantee Section
ECU (Europäische Währungseinheit)	ECU (European Currency Unit)
ECU-Verrechnungssystem	ECU clearing system
EEF (Europäischer Entwicklungsfonds)	EDF (European Development Fund)
EFTA (Europäische Freihandelszone)	EFTA (European Free Trade Association)
EFTA-Gerichtshof	EFTA Court
EFTA-Rat	EFTA Council
EFTA-Überwachungsbehörde	EFTA Surveillance Authority
EFWZ (Europäischer Fonds für währungspolitische Zusammenarbeit)	EMCF (European Monetary Cooperation Fund)
EG (Europäische Gemeinschaft)	EC (European Community)
EG-Kommission	European Commission
EIB (Europäische Investitionsbank)	EIB (European Investment Bank)
EIF (Europäischer Investitionsfonds)	EIF (European Investment Fund)
Eigenständigkeit	independence, autonomy
Eigentumsrecht	right of ownership
Eignung zur Anstellung	eligibility for employment
Eignungsprüfung	aptitude test
Eignungstest	aptitude test
einfache Mehrheit	simple majority
Einfuhr- und Vorratsstelle für landwirtschaftliche Erzeugnisse	intervention board for agricultural products
Einführung einer einheitlichen Währung	introduction/adoption of a single currency
Eingliederung des Gemeinschaftsrechts	incorporation of Community law
einheben	to levy
Einheit	unity; unit; union
Einheitliche Europäische Akte (EEA) 1986	Single European Act (SEA) 1986
einheitliche Steuersätze	uniform tax rates
einheitliche Währung	single currency
Einheitlicher Europäischer Wirtschaftsraum	Single European Economic Area
einheitlicher Wirtschaftsraum	unified/single economic area
Einigkeit	unity
Einkünfte	revenue
Einnahmen	revenue
Einnahmequelle	source of revenue
Einreise in den Binnenmarkt	entry in the internal market
Einreiserecht	right of entry

Einschleusungspreis	threshold price
einseitige Maßnahme	unilateral measure
einstimmig	unanimous
Einstimmigkeit	unanimity
Einstimmigkeitsprinzip	principle of unanimity
einstweilige Anordnung	injunction
Einverleibung des Gemeinschaftsrechts	incorporation of Community law
Einwand	objection
Einzelfreistellung	individual exemption
einzelstaatliches Rechnungsprüfungsorgan	national audit body
Empfehlung	recommendation
Empfehlung der Kommission	Commission Recommendation
Energiepolitik	energy policy
Entschädigung	redress
Entscheidung	decision
Entscheidung der Hohen Behörde (EGKS)	High Authority Decision (ECSC)
Entscheidung der Kommission	Commission Decision
Entscheidung des Rates	Council Decision
Entwicklungshilfe	development aid
Entwicklungszusammenarbeit	development cooperation
Entwurf	draft, proposal
Entwurf	draft
ERASMUS-Programm	ERASMUS programme
ergänzen	to amend, to add, to complete
ergänzende Rechtsvorschriften	complementary legislation
Ergänzung	amendment, addition, completion
erklärend	declaratory
erläuternd	declaratory
Ermessen	discretion
Ermessensmißbrauch	misuse of powers/discretion
Erster Generalanwalt (EuGH)	First Advocate-General (ECJ)
Erweiterter Rat der EZB	General Council of the ECB
Erweiterung der Gemeinschaften	enlargement of the communities
ESCAPE-Projekt	ESCAPE project
ESPRIT-Programm	ESPRIT programme
EU (Europäische Union)	EU (European Union)
EuGH (Europäischer Gerichtshof)	EJC (European Court of Justice)
EURATOM (Europäische Atomgemeinschaft)	EURATOM (European Atomic Energy Community)
Eurokraten	Eurocrats
Europäische Atomgemeinschaft (Euratom)	European Atomic Energy Community
Europäische Bank für Wiederaufbau und Entwicklung	European Bank for Reconstruction and Development (EBRD)
Europäische Einheit	European Unity
Europäische Freihandelszone (EFTA)	European Free Trade Association (EFTA)

Europäische Gemeinschaft (EG)	European Community (EC)
Europäische Gemeinschaft für Kohle und Stahl (EGKS)	European Coal and Steel Community (ECSC)
Europäische Investitionsbank (EIB)	European Investment Bank (EIB)
Europäische Kommission	European Commission
Europäische Korrespondentengruppe (Organ der EPZ)	European Correspondents Group (institution of EPC)
Europäische Menschenrechtskonvention (EMRK) 1950	European Convention on Human Rights 1950
Europäische Politische Zusammenarbeit (EPZ)	European Policy Cooperation (EPC)
Europäische Polizeistelle (EUROPOL)	EUROPOL
Europäische Raumfahrtbehörde	European Space Agency (ESA)
europäische technische Normen	European standards
Europäische Umweltagentur	European Environment Agency
Europäische Union (EU)	European Union (EU)
Europäische Verrechnungseinheit	European Unit of Account (EUA)
Europäische Verteidigungsgemeinschaft	European Defence Community (EDC)
Europäische Währungseinheit (ECU)	European Currency Unit (ECU)
Europäische Wirtschaftliche Interessenvereinigung (EWIV)	European Economic Interest Grouping (EEIG)
Europäische Wirtschaftsgemeinschaft (EWG)	European Economic Community (EEC)
Europäische Zentralbank (EZB)	European Central Bank (ECB)
Europäischer Ausrichtungs- und Garantiefonds für die Landwirtschaft (EAGFL)	European Agricultural Guidance and Guarantee Fund (EAGGF)
Europäischer Entwicklungsfonds (EEF)	European Development Fund (EDF)
Europäischer Fonds für Regionale Entwicklung (EFRE)	European Regional Development Fund (ERDF)
Europäischer Fonds für währungspolitische Zusamenarbeit (EFWZ)	European Monetary Cooperation Fund (EMCF)
Europäischer Gerichtshof (EuGH)	(European) Court of Justice (ECJ)
Europäischer Investitionsfonds (EIF)	European Investment Fund (EIF)
Europäischer Rat	European Council
Europäischer Rechnungshof	European Court of Auditors
Europäischer Regionalfonds (ERF)	European Regional Fund (ERF)
Europäischer Sozialfonds (ESF)	European Social Fund (ESF)
Europäischer Währungsfonds (EWF)	European Monetary Fund (EMF)
Europäischer Wirtschaftsraum (EWR)	European Economic Area (EEA)
Europäisches Komitee für elektrotechnische Normung	European Committee for Electrotechnical Standardization (CENELEC)
Europäisches Komitee für Normung	European Committee for Standardization/Comitè Europeen de Normalisation (CEN)

Europäisches Parlament	European Parliament
Europäisches Straßentransportabkommen	European Road Transport Agreement (ERTA)
Europäisches Währungsinstitut (EWI)	European Monetary Institut (EMI)
Europäisches Währungssytem (EWS)	European Monetary System (EMS)
Europäisches Zentralbankensystem (EZBS)	European System of Central Banks (ESCB)
Europarat	Council of Europe
Euroskeptizismus	Euroscepticism
EWF (Europäischer Währungsfonds)	EMF (European Monetary Fund)
EWIV (Europäische Wirtschaftliche Interessenvereinigung)	EEIG (European Economic Interest Grouping)
EWR (Europäischer Wirtschaftsraum)	EEA (European Economic Area)
EWR-Rat	EEA Council
EWS (Europäisches Währungssystem)	EMS (European Monetary System)
EZB (Europäische Zentralbank)	ECB (European Central Bank)
EZB-Rat	Governing Council of the ECB
EZBS (Europäisches Zentralbankensystem)	ESCB (European System of Central Banks)
EZBS-Rat	ESCB Council
Fachgruppe	specialized section
Fachministertagung	specialized Council meeting
fakultative Anhörung	optional consultation
festgelegter Wechselkurs	fixed exchange rate
festlegen	to fix
festsetzen	to fix
Finanz- und Haushaltsbestimmungen	financial and budgetary provisions
Finanzmarkt	financial market
Finanzmittel	financial resources/means
Finanzraum	financial common market
Finanzverordnung	Financial Regulation
Finanzvorschriftenänderungsvertrag 1975	Financial Provisions Treaty 1975
flankierende Maßnahmen	supporting measures
Fluktuation	fluctuation
Föderalismus	federalism
Förderung	subsidy
formelle Beschwerde(-note)	letter of formal complaint
Formvorschrift	procedural requirement
Forschung und Entwicklung	R & D (Research & Development)
Forschungs- und Entwicklungsvereinbarung	research and development agreement
Forschungs- und Informationstechnologien	research and information technologies
Forschungsbeihilfe	grant for research
Fragestunde	Question Time
Franchise-Vereinbarung	franchise agreement
Freiberufler	self-employed person

freier Dienstleistungsverkehr	freedom to provide services
freier Kapitalverkehr	free movement of capital
freier Personenverkehr	free movement of persons
freier Versicherungsmarkt	free insurance market
freier Warenverkehr	free movement of goods
Freihandelsabkommen	free trade agreement
Freihandelszone	free trade area
freiwillige Eigenbeschränkung	voluntary self-restriction
Freizügigkeit der Arbeitnehmer	freedom of movement for workers
Freizügigkeit der Studenten	free movement of students
Freizügigkeit für Dienstleistungen	free movement of services
Freizügigkeit für Kapital	free movement of capital
Freizügigkeit für Personen	free movement of persons
Freizügigkeit für Waren	free movement of goods
Frist	time-limit
Funktionshaushalt	operating budget
Fusion	merger
Fusionierungsvertrag 1965	Merger Treaty 1965
GAP (Gemeinsame Agrarpolitik)	CAP (Common Agricultural Policy)
garantierte Höchstquoten	maximum guaranteed quantity (MGQ)
garantierte Preise	guaranteed prices
garantierter Mindestpreis	interventione price, guarantee price
GATT (Allgemeines Zoll- und Handelsabkommen)	GATT (General Agreement on Tariffs and Trade)
Gebiete in äußerster Randlage	outermost regions
geförderte Exporte	subsidized exports
Gegenmaßnahme	countervailing measure
Gegenmaßnahme tarifärer Natur	countervailing duty
gegenseitige Anerkennung	mutual recognition
gegenseitige Anerkennung der Diplome, Prüfungszeugnisse und sonstiger Befähigungsnachweise	mutual recognition of diplomas, certificates and other evidence of formal qualifications
gegenseitiges Einvernehmen	common accord
Gegenseitigkeit	reciprocity
geheime Absprache	collusive agreement, secret arrangement
Geldbuße	fine
Geldpolitik	Monetary Policy
Geldstrafe	fine
Geldwäsche	money laundering
Gemeinsame Agrarpolitik	Common Agricultural Policy (CAP)
Gemeinsame Aktionen	joint activities, concerted practices, common measures
Gemeinsame Außen- und Sicherheitspolitik	common foreign and security policy
Gemeinsame Fischereipolitik	Common Fisheries Policy (CFP)
Gemeinsame Forschungsstelle	Joint Research Center
gemeinsame Handelspolitik	Common Commercial Policy

gemeinsame Verteidigungspolitik	Common Defence Policy
Gemeinsame Wirtschaftspolitik	Common Economic Policy
gemeinsame Ziele	common objectives
gemeinsame Zuständigkeit	joint competence
gemeinsamer Außenzolltarif	common external tariff
gemeinsamer Boykott	joint boycott
Gemeinsamer EWR-Ausschuß	EEA Joint Committee
Gemeinsamer Markt	Common Market
Gemeinsamer Parlamentarischer EWR-Ausschuß	EEA Joint Parliamentary Committee
gemeinsamer Standpunkt	common position
Gemeinsamer Zolltarif (GZT)	Common Customs Tariff (CCT)
gemeinsames Aufgabengebiet	common domain
Gemeinschaftliche Normen	common standards, EC standards
Gemeinschaftsanleihe	Community loan, Community borrowing
Gemeinschaftsanordnung	Community order
Gemeinschaftsausgaben	Community spending
Gemeinschaftsbürger	Community citizen
Gemeinschaftsdarlehen	Community lending operation
Gemeinschaftsfonds	Community Funds
Gemeinschaftsinteresse	Community interest
Gemeinschaftsmittel	Community funds
Gemeinschaftsrecht	Community law
Gemeinschaftszuständigkeit	Commmunity competence
Genehmigung	assent
Generalanwalt (EuGH)	Advocates-General
Generaldirektion	Directorates-General
Generaldirektor (Kommission)	Director-General
Generalsekretär	Secretary General
Generalsekretariat	General Sectretariat, Secretariat-General
Generalsekretariat des Rates	General Secretariat of the Council
gerichtliche Kontrolle	judicial control
Gerichtshof Erster Instanz	Court of First Instance (CFI)
Geschäftsordnung	rules of procedure
Gesetzesvertrag	code of rules treaty
Gesetzgebung	legislation
Gesetzgebungsbefugnisse	legislative powers
Gesetzgebungsprogramm	legislative programme
Gesetzgebungsverfahren	legislative process
Gesetzgebungsvorschläge	legislative proposals
gesetzliches Hindernis	legal barrier
gestützte Exporte	subsidized exports
Gesundheitsschutz	health protection
Gesundheitswesen	public health
Gewaltenteilung	separation of powers
Gipfelkonferenz	summit
Gipfeltreffen	summit meeting
Gleichbehandlung	equality of treatment

Gleichbehandlung (am Arbeitsplatz)	equal treatment (at work)
Gleichberechtigung	equality
Gleichheit	equality
Gleichheitsgrundsatz	principle of equality
Grenze	frontier
Grenzen abschaffen	to abolish frontiers
Grenzkontrolle	frontier control, border check
grenzüberschreitend	cross-border
Grundfreiheiten	fundamental freedoms
Grundrechte	fundamental rights
Grundsatz der Gesetzmäßigkeit der Verwaltung	principle of legality in administration
Grundsatz der Plenargerichtsbarkeit	principle of plenary jurisdiction
Grundsatz der Rechtssicherheit	principle of legal certainty
Grundsatz der Subsidiarität	subsidiarity principle
Grundsatz der Transparenz	transparency principle
Grundsatz des rechtlichen Gehörs	right to a fair hearing
Grundsatz des Vertrauensschutzes	principle that legitimate expectations must be protected
Grundsatz, daß der EuGH nicht im Vorabentscheidungsverfahren zur Auslegung eines Textes angerufen wird, wenn dem behandelnden Gericht die Bedeutung des auszulegenden Textes klar ist (frz.).	doctrine of acte clair
Gründungsverträge	establishing treaties, founding treaties
Grundverkehr	transfer of land
Gruppenfreistellung	block exemption
Gruppenfreistellungsverordnung (1983/84)	Block Exemption Regulation (1983/84)
Gutachten	opinion
gutheißen	to endorse
Handel	trade
Handelsabkommen	trade agreement
Handelsbeschränkung	trade barrier
Handelspolitik	commercial policy, trade policy
Handelsrecht	trade law
Handelsschranke	trade barrier
Handelsverband	trade association
Harmonisierung	harmonization, alignment, approximation, adoption
Harmonisierung der Rechtsvorschriften	harmonization of legislation
Harmonisierung der Steuern	approximation/harmonization of taxes
Harmonisierung gemeinschaftlicher Normen	adoption of common standards
Haushalt	budget

Haushalt der Europäischen Gemeinschaften	European Community budget
Haushaltsausschuß	Committee on Budgets
Haushaltsbefugnis	budgetary power
Haushaltsdefizit	budget deficit
Haushaltsentwurf	draft budget
Haushaltspolitik der einzelnen Staaten	national fiscal policy
Haushaltsvertrag 1970	Budgetary Treaty 1970
Haustürgeschäft	doorstep selling
Haustürverkauf	doorstep selling
Havanna Charter	Havana Charter
Hemmnis	restriction
Hilfe	aid
Hilfsorgan	ancillary organ
Hilfsprogramme	aid programmes
Hindernis	barrier
historische Auslegung	historical interpretation
horizontale Vereinbarung	horizontal agreement
importierte Inflation	imported inflation
Importquote	import quota
indirekte Benachteiligung	indirect discrimination
indirekte Diskriminierung	indirect discrimination
Industrienorm	technical standard
Industriepolitik	industrial policy
Informationsaustausch	exchange of information
Initiativrecht	right of initiative
innere Angelegenheiten	home affairs
innere Geschlossenheit	internal cohesion
innergemeinschaftliche Schranke	intra-Community barrier
institiutionelle Integration	institutional integration
Institution	institution, body
Integration	integration
Interessensgruppen	interest groups
interinstitutionelle Zusammenarbeit	interinstitutional cooperation
internationale Normen	international standards
Internationale Organisationen	international organizations
Internationaler Währungsfonds (IWF)	International Monetary Fund (IMF)
interne Geldpolitik	domestic monetary policy
Interpretation des Gemeinschaftsrechts	interpretation of Community law
Interventionsmechanismus	intervention mechanism
Interventionspreis	intervention price
Investitionsdarlehen	investment loan
Investitionsfreiheit	freedom of investment
inzidente Normenkontrolle (Art. 184 EWGV)	plea of illegality
IWF (Internationaler Währungsfonds)	IMF (International Monetary Fund)
Jurist	lawyer, jurisconsult
juristische Person	legal entity

juristischer Berater eines Richters am EuGH	advocate-general
Juristischer Dienst	Legal Service
Kabinettchef	Chef de Cabinet
Kabotage	cabotage
Kammer (EuGH)	Chamber (ECJ)
Kammerpräsident (EuGH)	President of Chambers (ECJ)
Kanzlei (EuGH)	Registrar (ECJ)
Kapital- und Zahlungsverkehr	capital and payments
Kapitalabfluß	capital outflow
Kapitalmarkt	capital market
Kapitalverkehr	capital movement
Kapitalverkehrskontrolle	control on capital movement
Kartell	cartel
Kartellrecht	Restrictive Trade Practices Law
Klage auf Feststellung einer Vertragsverletzung	action to have the infringement established
Klage gegen Mitgliedstaaten	action against Member States
Klage gegen Untätigkeit (eines Organs)	action against inactivity
Kläger	complainant
Klein- und Mittelbetriebe	small- and medium-sized enterprises
Know-how-Vereinbarung	know-how agreement
Koalitionsrecht	right of association
Kohäsion	cohesion
Kohäsionsfonds	Cohesion Fund
Kommissionsmitglied	Commissioner
Kommissionspräsident	President of the Commission
Kommunalrecht	municipal law
Kompetenz	competence
Kompetenz zum Abschluß von Verträgen	treaty-making power
Konferenz der Außenminister	Conference of Foreign Ministers
Konferenz der Parlamente („Assises“)	Conference of Parliaments („Assises“)
Konferenz für Sicherheit und Zusammenarbeit in Europa (KSZE)	Conference on Security and Co-operation in Europe (CSCE)
Konföderation	confederation
Konjunkturpolitik	economic policy
Konkurrenz	competition
konkurrierende Zuständigkeit	concurrent competence
Konsens	consensus
Konsumentenkredit	consumer credit
Konsumentenschutz	consumer protection
Konsumentenschutzpolitik	consumer protection policy
Kontaktausschuß	Contact Committee
Konvention	convention
Konvergenz der Volkswirtschaften der Mitgliedsstaaten	convergence of the member states' economies
Konvergenzkriterien	convergence criteria

Konzern	group (of undertakings)
Konzertierungsverfahren	conciliation procedure
Konzessionsvertrag	concession contract
Kooperationsabkommen	cooperation agreement
Koordinierung der Wirtschaftspolitik	coordination of economic policies
Koordinierungsausschuß	Coordination Committee
Koordinierungsrichtlinie	coordination directive
Kopplungsgeschäft	tie-in sale, linked transaction, package deal
Kredit- und Bankwesen	banking and credit
Landwirtschaftsausschuß	Committe for Agriculture
Lesung (im Europaparlament)	reading (in the EP)
Liberalisierung	liberalization
Lomé-Abkommen 1975	Lomé Convention, Convention of Lomé 1975
Luxemburger Kompromiß	Luxembourg Compromise
Marktabschottung	market isolation
Marktanteil	market share
Marktaufteilung	market sharing, territory allocation, market segmentation
marktbeherrschende Stellung	market dominance
Marktordnungen	market regulations
Maßnahmen gleicher Wirkung wie mengenmäßige Beschränkungen	MEQR (measures having equivalent effect to quantitative restrictions)
materielle Schranken	physical barriers
Medienpolitik	audio-visual policy
Mehrheitsentscheidung	majority voting
Mehrwertsteuer (MWSt)	value-added tax (VAT)
Meistbegünstigungsklausel	most-favoured-nation treatment
Memorandum	memorandum
mengenmäßige Beschränkung	quantitative restriction
Mindestangleichung von Rechtsvorschriften	minimum harmonization of statutory regulations
Mindestnormen	minimum standards
Ministerrat	Council of Ministers
Mißbrauch einer beherrschenden Stellung	abuse of a dominant position
Mißtrauensvotum	motion of censure
Mitentscheidungsrecht	joint decision-making power
mitinbegriffene Pflicht	implicit duty
Mitteilung	communication
Mitversicherung auf Gemeinschaftsebene	Community co-insurance
Nachprüfung	review
Nachtrag	amendment
Nachtragshaushalt	supplementary budget
nationale Eigenständigkeit	national sovereignity
nationale Zentralbank	national central bank
NATO (Nordatlantisches Verteidigungsbündnis)	NATO (North Atlantic Treaty Organization)

Negativattest	negative clearance
nicht zwingende Ausgaben (im Budget)	non-compulsory items/expenditure (NEC)
nicht-tarifäre Handelsbeschränkung	non-tariff trade barrier
nicht-tarifäre Handelshemmnisse	non-tariff trade barriers
nichtangekündigte Inspektionen "im Morgengrauen"	dawn raids
nichtig	void
nichtobligatorische Ausgaben	non-obligatory expenditure
Niederlassungsfreiheit	freedom of establishment
Niederlassungsrecht	right of establishment
Nordatlantisches Verteidigungsbündnis (NATO)	North Atlantic Treaty Organization (NATO)
Norm	standard
Normenvertrag	code of rules treaty
Novelle	amendment
objektive Stellungnahme	objective ruling
obligatorische Anhörung	compulsory consultation
obligatorische Ausgaben	obligatory expenditure
OECD (Organisation für wirtschaftliche Zusammenarbeit und Entwicklung)	OECD (Organization for Economic Cooperation and Development)
öfentlicher Bauauftrag	public-sector construction contract
Offenlegung	disclosure
öffentliche Anlagen	public works
öffentliche Bauaufträge	public works contracts
öffentliche Ordnung	public order
öffentliche Sicherheit	public security
öffentliche Unternehmen	public undertakings
öffentliche Versorgung	public supplies
öffentliche Versorgungsbetriebe	public utilities
öffentliche Versorgungsverträge	public service contracts
öffentlicher Lieferauftrag	public supply/procurement contract
öffentliches Auftragswesen	public procurement and construction, public purchasing and construction, public procurement
Öffnung	openness, liberalization
Organ	institution, body
Organisation für wirtschaftliche Zusammenarbeit und Entwicklung (OECD)	Organization for Economic Cooperation and Development (OECD)
parallele Zuständigkeit	concurrent competence
Paralleleinfuhr	parallel import
Parallelimport	parallel import
Parallelwährung	parallel currency
parlamentarische Demokratien	parliamentary democracies
parlamentarischer Ausschuß	parliamentary committee
Parlamentsausschuß	parliamentary committee
Parlamentsmitglied	Member of Parliament
Patentlizenzvereinbarung	patent licensing agreement

persönlicher Verbrauch	personal consumption
Persönlichkeitsrecht	right of privacy
Petitionsrecht beim Europäischen Parlament	right to petition the European Parliament
Pflicht zur Durchführung	duty to implement
Pflicht zur Vollziehung	duty to implement
Plenargerichtsbarkeit	plenary jurisdiction
Plenartagung	plenary session
Politiken der Gemeinschaft	Community policies
Politiken und Formen der Zusammenarbeit	policies and forms of cooperation
Politische Direktoren (EPZ)	Political Directors (EPC)
politische Gruppen (im Europaparlament)	political groups (in the EP)
politische Integration	political integration
politische Kooperation	political cooperation
Politische Union	political union
politische Zusammenarbeit	political cooperation
Politisches Komitee (EPZ)	Political Committee (EPC)
polizeiliche Zusammenarbeit	police cooperation
Präsident des Europäischen Gerichtshofs	President of the Court
Präsident des Rechnungshofes	President of the Court of Auditors
Preisbindung	price fixing, price maintenance
Preisstabilität	price stability
Preisstützungen	price subsidies
primäre Quelle des Gemeinschaftsrechts	primary source of Community law
primäres Gemeinschaftsrecht	primary Community legislation
Prinzip der begrenzten Einzelermächtigung	principle of specific attribution of powers
privater Verbrauch	private consumption
Privileg	prerogative
Produkthaftung	product liability
Produktionsaufteilung	allocation of production
Produktionsobergrenzen	maximum production limits
Proportionalität	proportionality
Prozeß zur Entscheidungsfindung	decision-making process
Prozeßführungsrecht	locus standi
Prüf- und Zertifizierungsverfahren	type testing and certification
qualifizierte Mehrheit	qualified majority
Quästor	quaestor
Quellensteuer	turnover tax
Quoten	quotas
Rahmenvertrag	framework treaty
Rangordnung der Rechtsakte der Gemeinschaft	hierarchy of the Community Acts
Rat	Council

Rat der Außenminister	Council of Ministers of Foreign Affairs
Rat der Wirtschafts- und Finanzminister	Council of Economic and Finance Ministers (ECOFIN)
Rat des EWI	Council of the EMI
Ratsvorsitz	Council Presidency
Rechnungseinheit	accounting unit
Rechnungshof	Court of Auditors
Recht der internationalen Organisationen	law of international institutions
Recht, bei Gericht gehört zu werden	locus standi
rechtliche Integration	legal integration
Rechtsangleichung	coordination/harmonization of laws
Rechtsetzungsverfahren	legislative process
Rechtsgrundsatz	principle of law
Rechtspersönlichkeit	legal personality
Rechtsquellen des Gemeinschaftsrechts	sources of Community law
Rechtsschutzsystem der EG	Community system of legal protection
Regelungsausschuß	regulatory committee
Regierungskonferenz	intergovernmental conference
regionale Vereinigungen	regional associations
regionales Ungleichgewicht	regional imbalance
Regionalismus	regionalism
Regionalpolitik	regional policy
Religions- und Bekenntnisfreiheit	freedom of religion
Reziprozität	reciprocity
Richtlinie	directive
Richtlinie des Rates	Council Directive
Richtlinie über die gegenseitige Anerkennung	mutual recognition directive
Richtpreis	target price
Römer Verträge	Treaties of Rome
Römische Verträge	Treaties of Rome
Sammlung der Rechtsprechung des EuGH	Common Market Law Reports (CMLR)
SAVE-Programm	SAVE programme
Schadenersatzklage	action for damages
Schaffung eines Raumes ohne Binnengrenzen	creation of an area without internal frontiers
Schengener Abkommen	Schengen Accord, Schengen Agreement
Schengener Abkommen (von 1985)	Schengen Agreement (of 1985)
Schlagbaum	turnpike, tollbar
Schlichtungsverfahren	conciliation procedure
Schlußakte von Helsinki	Helsinki Final Act
Schranke	barrier
schriftliche Stellungnahme	written opinion
schriftliches Verfahren	written procedure
Schuman Plan	Schuman Plan
Schutz der nationalen Identität	protection of national identity

Schutzklausel	safeguard clause
Schutzmaßnahme	protective measure
Schwankung	fluctuation
Schwellenbetrag	threshold value
Schwellenpreis	threshold price
Sekretariat der Politischen Zusammenarbeit (EPZ)	Political Cooperation Secretariat (EPC)
sektorielle Richtlinie	sectoral directive
sekundäre Quelle des Gemeinschaftsrechts	secondary source of Community law
sekundäre Rechtsquellen	secondary sources
sekundäres Gemeinschaftsrecht	secondary Community legislation
Selbstständigkeit	autonomy
selektiver Vertrieb	selective distribution system
Senkung des Zinssatzes	interest-rate cut
sich anschließen	to join; to endorse
Sicherheitspolitik	security policy
Solidarität	solidarity
Sozialcharter	Social Charter
Sozialpolitik	social policy
Sozialversicherung	social security
Spaltung	scission
Spezialisierungsvereinbarung	specialisation agreement
Spinelli-Entwurf	Spinelli draft
Sprachdienst	Language Service
Staatenbund	confederation
staatliche Beihilfe	state subsidy
staatliche Unterstützung	state aid
staatlicher Zuschuß	state aid
Standard	standard
Ständige Vertretung	Permanent Representation
ständiger Ausschuß	standing committee
Ständiger Ausschuß der EFTA-Mitgliedstaaten	EFTA Consultative Committee
Standpunkt	state of affair
Statistisches Amt	Statistical Office
Statut für die Europäische Aktiengesellschaft	European Company Statute
Stellungnahme	opinion
Stellungnahme abgeben	to deliver an opinion
Steuerdiskriminierung	discriminatory tax practice
steuerliche Schranken	fiscal barriers
Steuersatz	tax rate
Steuersätze angleichen	to align tax rates
Steuersätze harmonisieren	to align tax rates
Steuerschranken	fiscal barriers
Steuervorteil	tax privilege
Steuerwesen	taxation

Stimmengewichtung	weighted voting
stimulierende Maßnahmen	incentive measures
strittiger Text	disputed passage
Strukturanpassung	structural adjustment
strukturelle Instrumente	structural instruments
Strukturfonds	structural funds
Stufe des vorbereitenden Ermittlungsverfahrens	preparatory enquiry stage
Stützungsmaßnahmen	price support mechanism
subsidiäre Handlungsermächtigung	subsidiary power to act
Subsidiarität	subsidiarity
Subsidiaritätsprinzip	principle of subsidiarity
Subvention	subsidy
Subventionen	subsidies, aid
subventionierte Exporte	subsidized exports
supranationale Organisation	supra-national organization
systematische Auslegung	contextual interpretation
Tarifverhandlungen	collective bargaining
Tätigkeitsbereich	field of competence
technische Handelshemmnisse	technical barriers
technische Schranken	technical barriers
Teilaufhebung	derogation
teleologische Auslegung	teleological interpretation, purposive interpretation
Transeuropäisches Netz	Trans-European Network (TEN)
Überarbeitung	revision
Übereinkunft	convention
Übereinkunft	agreement
Übergangsbestimmung	transitory provision
Übergangsfristen	transitional periods
Übergangsperiode	period of transition, transitional period
Übergangsregelung	transitional agreement
Übergangszeit	period of transition, transitional period
Überlegenheit	supremacy
übermäßiges Defizit	excessive deficit
Übernahme des bestehenden EG-Rechts	acquis communautaire
übernationale Organisation	supranational organization
Überschuß	surplus
übertragene Gesetzgebung	delegated legislation
Übertragung	transmission
Übertragung von Hoheitsrechten	delegation of state powers, surrender of sovereignty
Übertretung	breach
umfangreiche Finanzmittel	substantial resources
Umlage	levy
Umsatzsteuer	turnover tax
Umsetzung	implementation
Umstellungsdarlehen	conversion loan

Umwandlung	transformation
unabhängiges Gremium	impartial authority
unangemessen	disproportionate
ungültig	void
Unionsbürgerschaft	citizenship of the Union
unmittelbar anwendbarer Vertrag	self-executing treaty
unmittelbare Anwendbarkeit	direct effect
unmittelbare Geltung	direct applicability
UNO-Wirtschaftskommission für Europa	UN Economic Commission for Europe
Unparteilichkeit	impartiality
Untätigkeitsklage	action for failure to act
Untätigkeitsklage (gegen ein Organ)	action against inactivity, action for failure to act
Unterausschuß	sub-committee
untergeordnetes Organ	ancillary organ
Unterlassungsanordnung	cease and desist order
Unternehmen	undertaking
Untersuchungsausschuß	committe of inquiry
unverhältnismäßig	disproportionate
Unvoreingenommenheit	impartiality
unwiderrufliche Festlegung der Wechselkurse	irrevocable fixing of exchange rates
unwirksam	void
Unzuständigkeit	lack of competence
Ursprungsland	country of origin
Urteil	opinion, decision, judgement
verabschieden	to adopt
Verband	association
Verband der Industrien der Europäischen Gemeinschaft (Unice)	Confederation of European industry (Unice)
Verbindung	association
Verbraucherschutz	consumer protection
Verbrauchsabgabe	excise duty
Verbrauchssteuern	excise duties
verbunden sein mit	to be associated with
Vereinbarung	agreement
Vereinbarung über den gemeinsamen Einkauf	agreement on joint purchase
Vereinbarung über den gemeinsamen Verkauf	agreement on joint sale
Vereinbarung zwischen Unternehmen	agreement between undertakings
vereinfachtes Änderungsverfahren	simplified amendment procedure
Vereinheitlichung	harmonization, standardization, alignment
Vereinigung	unification; association; federation
Vereinigungsfreiheit	freedom of association
Verfahren der Mitentscheidung	conciliation and veto procedure
Verfahren der Zusammenarbeit	cooperation procedure

Verfahren des Beratenden Ausschusses	advisory committee procedure
Verfahrensregeln des Gemeinschaftsgerichts	Rule of Procedure of the Community Court (RP)
Verfassung	constitutional documents
Vergabeverfahren	procurement procedures
Vergeltungsmaßnahme	retaliatory measure
Verhaltensregel	code of behaviour
Verhältnismäßigkeit	proportionality
Verhältnismäßigkeitsgrundsatz	principle of proportionality
Verkaufsförderung	sales promotion
Verkehrspolitik	transport policy
verletzen	to breach
Verletzung	infringement, breach
Verletzung der Verträge oder einer bei ihrer Durchführung anzuwendenden Rechtsnorm	infringement of the Treaties or of any rules of law relating to their application
Verletzung des Gemeinschaftsrechts	infringement of Community law
Verletzung von Vertragsbestimmungen	breach of treaty obligations
Verletzung wesentlicher Formvorschriften	infringement of essential procedural requirements
Vermittlungsausschuß	Conciliation Committee
Veröffentlichung	public disclosure
Verordnung	regulation
Verordnung der Kommission	Commission Regulation
Verordnung des Rates	Council Regulation
Verpflichtungsermächtigung	commitment appropriation
Verrechnungseinheiten	(common) units of account, accounting units
Verschärfung des Wettbewerbs	increase in competition
verschleierte Beschränkung	disguised restriction
Verschmelzung	merger
Verständigung	communication, notification
Vertiefung der politischen Zusammenarbeit	intensification of political cooperation
vertikale Vereinbarung	vertical agreement
Vertrag über die Europäische Atomgemeinschaft (Euratom)	EAEC (European Atomic Energy Community [Euratom]) Treaty
Vertrag über die Europäische Gemeinschaft für Kohle und Stahl (EGKS)	ECSC Treaty (European Coal and Steel Community)
Vertrag über die Europäische Union	Treaty on European Union
Vertrag über die Europäische Wirtschaftsgemeinschaft	EEC Treaty (European Economic Community)
Vertrag von Maastricht	Maastricht Treaty
Vertrag von Paris	Treaty of Paris
Vertrag zur Errichtung der Europäischen Verteidigungsgemeinschaft 1952	European Defence Treaty 1952
vertragliche Haftung	contractual liability

Vertragsbruch	breach of treaty obligations
Vertragsentwurf	draft convention
Vertragsverletzungsverfahren	infringement proceeding
Vertriebswege	distribution channels
Verwaltungsausschuß	management committee
verwerfen	to reject
Verwirklichung der Wirtschafts- und Währungsunion	attainment of economic and monetary union
Verzerrung	distortion
Vizepräsident	Vice-President
Völkerbund	League of Nations
Volksabstimmung	referendum, plebiscite
Vollendung des Binnenmarktes	completion of the internal market/Single Market
Vollsitzung	plenary session
Vollstreckung	enforcement
vom Rat erlassener Rechtsakt	Council act
Vorabentscheidung (EuGH)	preliminary ruling
Vorbehalt	reservation
vorbeugende Maßnahmen	preventive measures
Vorentwurf eines Haushaltsplans	preliminary draft budget
vorläufige Entscheidung	preliminary decision
Vorrang	supremacy
Vorrang des Gemeinschaftsrechts	supremacy of Community law
Vorrang einräumen	to give precedence to
Vorrecht	prerogative
Vorschlag	proposal
Vorzugszölle	preferential tariffs
wachsender Zentralismus	growing centralism
Wahlsystem	electoral system
Wahrnehmung	observation
Währung	currency
Währungsausschuß	Monetary Committee
Währungsintegration	monetary integration
Währungsreserve	monetary reserve
Währungsumtausch	currency exchange
Währungsunion	monetary union
Warenaustausch	exchange of goods
Warenkontrollen	merchandise inspections
Warenverkehr	movement of goods
Wechselkurs	exchange rate
Wechselkursmechanismus	exchange rate mechanism (ERM)
Wechselkurspolitik	exchange-rate policy
Wechselkursschwankung	currency fluctuation
Wechselkursstützung	exchange-rate support
Weißbuch	White Paper
Weltbank	World Bank
Westeuropäische Union (WEU)	Western European Union (WEU)

Wettbewerb	competition
wettbewerbsbeschränkende Geschäftspraktik	restrictive practice
Wettbewerbsfähigkeit	competitiveness
Wettbewerbsfreiheit	freedom of competition
Wettbewerbspolitik	Competition Policy
Wettbewerbsrecht	competition law
Wettbewerbsregeln	rules on competition
wettbewerbsschädliche Kartelle	anti-competitive cartels
Wettbewerbsverbot	total restraint of trade, prohibition to compete
Wettbewerbsverzerrung	distortion of competition
wettbewerbswidrige Vereinbarungen	anti-competitive agreements
Wiedergutmachung	redress
Wiener Übereinkommen/ Konvention über das Recht zwischen den internationalen Organisationen (1986)	Vienna Convention applicable to world organizations (1986)
Wiener Vertragsrechtskonvention (WVK) (1969)	Vienna Convention on Treaties (1969)
willkürliche Diskriminierung	arbitrary discrimination
wirtschaftliche Integration	economic integration
wirtschaftliche Konvergenz	economic convergence
wirtschaftlicher und sozialer Zusammenhalt	econnomic and social cohesion
wirtschaftlicher Zusammenhalt	economic cohesion
Wirtschafts- und Berufsfreiheit	freedom to engage in business and to choose and practise a profession
Wirtschafts- und Finanzausschuß	Economic and Financial Committee (M)
Wirtschafts- und Sozialausschuß	Economic and Social Committee
Wirtschafts- und Währungspolitik	economic and monetary policy
Wirtschafts- und Währungsunion (WWU)	Economic and Monetary Union (EMU)
Wirtschaftsunion	economic union
Wohnrecht	right of residence
wörtliche Auslegung	literal interpretation
WWU (Wirtschafts- und Währungsunion)	EMU (Economic and Monetary Union)
Zahlungsbilanz	balance of payment
Zahlungsbilanzschwierigkeiten	balance-of-payments difficulties
Zahlungsermächtigung	payment appropriation
Zahlungsverkehr	movement of payments
zeitlich begrenzte Ausnahmeregelung	temporary derogation
Zentralbank	central bank
Zentralbankpräsidenten	Central Bank Governors
Zersplitterung (der Märkte)	segmentation (of the markets)
Zinszuschuß	interest subsidy
Zoll	customs duty, customs tariff
Zollabgaben	customs duties
Zollager	bonded warehouse

Zollgrenzen	customs barriers
Zollkontingent	tariff quota
Zollschranke	tariff trade barrier
Zolltarif	customs tariff
Zollunion	customs union
Zugang zu einem Beruf	access to a profession
Zugangsbeschränkungen	restrictions (on the access)
Zulassung	admission
Zuliefervertrag	supply contract, subcontract
zurückweisen	to reject
Zusammenhalt	cohesion
Zusammenschluß	merger, fusion; federation
Zusatz	addition
Zusatzprotokoll	Protocol
Zuschlag	award of contract
zuschreiben	to attribute
Zuschreibung von staatlichen Hoheitsrechten	attribution of state powers
Zuschuß	subsidy
Zuständigkeit	competence
Zuständigkeitsbereich	field of competence
Zustimmung	assent
Zustimmungsrecht	power of assent
zwingende Ausgaben	compulsory items/expenditure
zwischenstaatliche Organisation	intergovernmental organization

BIBLIOGRAPHY - LITERATURVERZEICHNIS -

Aicher J., Fischer P., Hafner G., Europarecht - Texte und Fälle, Universitätsverlag, Wien, 1989

Brochures of the European File series, Commission of the European Communities, Brussels

Cuthbert M., E.C. Law, Nutshells, Sweet and Maxwell, London, 1994

Europäischer Unionsvertrag, 2. Auflage, Beck Texte im dtv, München, 1993

Fehr H., Umsatzsteuerharmonisierung in der EG, Teile A und B, Transfer Verlag, Regensburg, 1992

Fischer P. & Köck H.F., Europarecht einschließlich des Rechtes supranationaler Organisationen, Prugg Verlag, Eisenstadt, 1986

Foster N., EC Legislation, Fourth Edition, Blackstone's, London, 1993

Jackson J.M., World Trade and the Law of the GATT, Indianapolis, Ind., Bobbs-Merrill, 1969

Lasok D. & Bridge J.W., Law and Institutions of the European Communities, Fifth Edition, Butterworths, London, 1991

Neisser H., Das Politische System der EG, Holzhausen Verlag, Wien, 1993

Pfister W., Europäisches Gesellschaftsrecht, Peter Lang Verlag, Frankfurt am Main, 1993

Rudden B., Basic Community Cases, Clarendon Press, Oxford, 1987

Strasser R., EG-Hochschuldiplomrichtlinie, Manz Verlag, Wien, 1993

Treaty on European Union, Office for Official Publications of the European Communities, 1992

Vertrag über die Europäische Union, Office for Official Publications of the European Communities, 1992

Walder S., The Budgetary Procedure of the European Economic Community, Edited by Hummer W., Böhlau Verlag, Wien - Köln - Weimar, 1992

Weatherill S. & Beaumont P., EC Law, Penguin Books, London, 1993

Weiss F., Public Procurement in European Community Law, European Community Law Series 4, The Athlone Press Ltd, London 1993

A

B

C

D

E

F

G

H

I

O

P

Q

R

U

V

W

Y

Z